A World of Culture, Oil and Golf

David Allard

D1025865

www.TotalPublishingAndMedia.com

Copyright © 2016, David Allard

All rights reserved.

No part of this book may be reproduced, stored in a retrieval system, or transmitted by any means, electronic, mechanical, photocopying, recording, or otherwise, without written permission from the author.

ISBN 978-1-63302-036-8

Dedication

This book is dedicated to Deborah, my lovely wife
and Graham, my son, for all that we have done.

May people working in challenging and
remote places of the world find peace.

Thanks

Thanks to Bill Allard for artistic inspiration,
Peter Biadasz for publishing persistence
and Joshua Lease for heavily editing this book.

www.DuckSpots.net
www.totalpublishingandmedia.com
www.AegisEditing.com

Places in the world the author visited or lived.

Table of Contents

Disclaimer

This is a work of creative nonfiction. The author has tried to recreate events, locales and conversations from his journals, memories and experiences to the best of his recollection. He has changed the names of individuals as well as changed or avoided the inclusion of identifying characteristics and details such as physical properties and places of residence. The opinions expressed in this book are solely the author's and do not represent the opinions of the publisher or any of the people or entities mentioned in the book. Although the author and publisher have made every effort to ensure the information in this book was correct at press time, the author and publisher do not assume and hereby disclaim any liability to any party for any loss, damage, or disruption caused by errors or omissions, whether such errors or omissions result from negligence, accident, or any other cause.

Introduction

While growing up, I traveled a fair bit across North America, but the sights and sounds over those years paled in comparison to what I would see in the business world. I selected geology as a career and was lucky to find myself in such a dynamic industry that allowed for amazing international cultural experiences and business opportunities. The point of this book is to share stories and information with the reader about places I have seen, observations of different cultures and customs and business notes of interest, including the international oil business.

The international oil business is an expensive, risky, and fascinating business, which involves many years of effort to find and develop new reserves. I think there are a lot of people out there who are interested and want to understand more about this business and our world.

As always, humor is included, and I mention golf where I can. I hope you enjoy reading about these places as much as I did experiencing them. May this book inspire you to travel your own path in life; a life filled with awe and wonder.

Chapter 1
A Mountain Village in Turkey

September, 1988

In the morning I leave for Turkey. My flight leaves from Houston, with stops in Amsterdam and Munich before finally landing in Ankara, the capital of Turkey. It is a series of long flights and car rides that will take two days.

As a young man I thought of being a touring rocker because I love music and traveling, I love the earth sciences as well. I selected geology as a major and got a job in San Francisco during the early eighties oil boom. A year later I switched companies and began working in Midland, Texas, which, after several years, led to a transfer to Houston to work in International exploration. It turns out traveling business class and going places for oil exploration for more than one night is a better way to see exotic places of this world than being a traveling musician!

I will be out of the country for three weeks. How long I will *really* be gone doesn't hit me until I am on the plane. It is all happening so fast. This Turkey trip is the first time I will be away from my wife for a long time; we were just married a year ago.

We moved from West Texas to Houston to take jobs—me doing international exploration for my company and my wife to a different major oil company. I had only been working in the Houston group a few days when the group secretary says, "Here are your tickets. You need to visit the international medical center before you go to get shots."

I did not yet know I was on an adventure!

The search for oil and gas is exciting. The risk and reward, the science and the business dealings have kept me interested enough to stay in this business. Being part of an industry that provides energy for civilizations is satisfying—in spite of some of the negative views some people are prone to apply to the oil business. The opportunity to add

1

international travel to my business experience is very exciting. It is, after all, a world filled with a variety of cultures.

I am not sure I will be able to sleep on the nine-hour overnight flight to Amsterdam. I will arrive early the following morning.

A limo picks me up in Houston—total surprise! The flight is so long the company puts us in first class. In those days, the airline sent a limousine—which turned out to be a *Rolls*!

I'm pretty excited. Okay, anxious. I find out flying at 600 miles an hour in the dark of night literally *flies* by—in about four hours.

I have eight hours to kill in Amsterdam before my connecting flight to Munich. I am *not* going to spend it cooped up in the airport; this is *Europe*! I take a train into town to hang out and take in the culture and scenery.

I am immediately struck by the grand architecture. The downtown train station is massive, and it makes me think of WWII films with European scenes. It is a sunny day, and people are hanging around outside as I walk toward the canal district of this old vibrant city. I feel right at home among these friendly Dutch people—many of whom speak fluent English. Apparently they have to take several years of English to graduate high school, which I am sure gives them an edge in international business.

Right now one US dollar equals 2.05 guilders, which is a favorable exchange rate that helps as I see the museums, visit quaint coffee shops, ride street cars, and frequent narrow streets packed with little shops. I make a mental note to myself that I would like to visit here with more than a few hours to spare. All too soon I am back on the train headed back to the airport.

A Brief Stop in Ankara

I fly a quick hop from Amsterdam to Munich. From there we fly about two hours to Ankara, Turkey. Just as I'm getting settled in—I'm the only person in that section of the plane—we land.

The venture office driver, picks me up at the airport—I'm glad, as it's getting late. Hamed tells me Ankara is home to about three million people, the second largest city in Turkey after Istanbul.

I get dropped off at the hotel, and the first thing I do when I arrive in my room is look out at the view from my fourteenth floor window. A huge mosque dominates in the near distance as the lights of the city stretch away on rolling arid hills all around me. It is beautiful and yet very different from the U.S. At this point in my life, I have had very little exposure to the Muslim world—that is soon to change.

Early the next morning I hear my first call to prayer bellow from the mosque. In the daylight I can see Ankara is a very busy city with lots of construction and significant pollution due to cars. I'm told in winter, it gets even worse due to the coal burned for heat in many apartment buildings.

I walk to the venture office, located just up the hill from my hotel and past the many large embassies. We actually use the fourth and upper floors of a converted apartment building, which is served by a small, four-person capacity elevator—claustrophobic. Upstairs are two engineers and the geologist office; downstairs are a few accountants, a lawyer, and the Turkey area manager, Mick Taylor. This is not "home." Tomorrow I fly east to Diyarbakir then go by car five hours up the mountain to the drilling well location.

Diyarbakir

Flying from Ankara to Diyarbakir on Turkish Air I get a scare. After boarding the plane from the rear and finding a seat, they call my name and tell me to come forward. Trouble with my papers? I have that sinking feeling you get when you see the flashing red and blue lights in your rear view mirror.

I am told to point out my bags from those laying on the tarmac for loading, which I do. They then let me take my seat next to a GE guy who has been working in Turkey on power generation for three years.

"They ask foreigners to do that," he explains, "If your bags have a bomb in them you would not get on the plane or would not point out your bag—theoretically." Comforting.

The rest of the flight is uneventful, and as I wait for my bags, I talk to the only other obvious non-Turk, who I thought may be the mud logging company guy flying in to work with me. He's not—he's an

Italian magazine journalist visiting the region to investigate the Kurdish refugees who are coming into Turkey from Iraq. The Kurds got stuck in the middle when the land was divided up after World War I and are trying to hold their culture together living among parts of Iran, Iraq, Syria, and Turkey. I walk out of the airport to a sea of people waiting and spot a guy holding a sign with just my company name–he speaks no English. I get in the Toyota Land Cruiser with him and think—what if I am being kidnapped!

A Turkish military airbase surrounds Diyarbakir airport, and there is a military base on the edge of town. You are not allowed to take pictures of airports or anything military. If you do, the Turkish authorities would be unhappy and do things like taking your camera, question you, and who knows what else; so I keep my camera securely packed away.

Driving east from Diyarbakir with the driver, Amet, we pass many farming communities with mud houses that grow tobacco and cotton to sell at market. We also drive by two cigarette factories. I see lots of cattle and sheep, tended typically by young boys. During the first hour of about a five hour drive, Amet looks over at me and says "music?" I say yes and notice only one cassette tape in the car. He says: "Michael Jackson?" It is going to be a long ride.

We stop in Siirt to pick up a guy, Emir, who's riding up to the rig with us and works as a radio operator. I buy dinner for the three of us in Siirt, as it was the last town before driving into the hills to the rig. We have tomato/onion salad, grilled green peppers, three colas, and shish-ka-bob meat served with thick pita bread. Total, 4,000 Turkish lire, a mere $2.50 US.

After dinner, we drive up the winding roads to the rig. It's a fantastic location high in the hills with a beautiful view of the mountains ranging from 4,000 to 8,000 feet. This part of Turkey is an arid landscape with reddish, tan rock and soil and some scrubby oak trees on the lower area of the hills. Reminds me of Big Bend on the Texas/Mexico border.

There are two small villages near the rig, which I hope to visit if I have a break or time to scout the area. The Turkish army's elite Jandarma protect the location from terrorist attacks. The army has an out of sight base camp near the location. The geologist I was there to replace is Rick. He told me they killed a couple of Kurdish rebels when they moved into the area initially. I told him about the five hour Michael Jackson car ride and he said, "That would be a good story for your journal." I obviously took note of that statement; no pun intended!

Around the location at strategic points I see cement huts where teams of two soldiers are posted at all times. I learn that at night they communicate by whistling to each other around the lighted perimeter. No one is permitted pass the security gate to the well location after 8:00 p.m. I'm not sure whether I feel reassured or worried by the military presence here to keep us safe.

The rig is large, and the location has trailers for the workers, which total about forty men. Expatriates and Turkish workers each have a mess hall, and the area is surrounded by the usual assortment of containers of supplies, trucks, and other gear. We have phone lines and some TV reception, so I may get to see some of the Olympics. This is home for the next couple weeks.

It's Sunday night at the well site. We have been drilling without sample returns for the entire weekend—"drilling blind." Instead of circulating the drilling mud, which carries up rock samples of drilled formation and any gas or oil shows, the mud is going into the formation and not coming back. This could be a dangerous situation if not monitored closely. We have a gas detection hose in the pipe above the BOP (blow out preventers) to sniff for gas until the problem is corrected. We have drilled over 600 feet of carbonate—probably very fractured, but no shows of gas.

Since we are drilling blind, there is not much to do. Mike, another company geologist is at the well, so I am free to take a walk. Emir, the radio operator I rode up with offers to go with me to visit the village of Ozpinar, over the hills not far from the well. We set out walking about 9:00 a.m. even though he works 7:00 p.m. to 7:00 a.m. Emir tells me more about the soldiers, including their four whistle codes such as, "I am here and I am awake," or, "I am approaching and I am friendly, don't shoot!" Good thing he knows them, as he once had to walk up to the well in the dark from Ozpinar where he had to be at work. Emir

5

can speak Arabic, Turkish, Kurdish, English, and bits of Yugoslavic, French, and German. I hesitate to think about what a bright guy Emir is and yet how small his pay check may be. As we get to the edge of town, a lady comes out of her garden and gives us a large bunch of grapes. I say, "Tushe curadedem!" (Turkish for "Thank you"). The town is a small accumulation of one to two story tan stucco-like buildings. After stopping to eat, we go to the center of town, walk by the teahouse and to the mosque. Inside the mosque, we take off our shoes and look around the first floor. There is a big open space covered with carpets for the men—women use the balcony area.

We go back and sit in the teahouse, which is dimly lit. Some older men and a few young men, all smoking, sit drinking tea. The young boy that runs the place serves us. I give some grapes to the blind man next to me and we talk of many things with Emir as interpreter. They are curious about the success of the well, how much money we make, and where we are from.

Outside, I give cookies to some children. Some are shy and need a little coaxing. I see women pounding wheat with large wooden hammers, women and children carrying water, mules loaded with green tree branches to be stored for winter firewood, boys playing soccer, hay piled high for winter feed for the goats, and a few cows as well as mules. It's an agrarian peaceful scene you rarely see back in the US.

Emir picks some pistachios right from a tree for us, and as we are leaving town, a man named Ali invites us to his home. Ali works at the rig as a security guard, not a soldier, but gains his main income from his garden.

We sit on rugs and pillows in his main room—living room by day, bedroom by night—and meet his mother and his children. We talk, look at photos, and eat some melon. We do not meet his wife. Ali asks if I would take a picture of him and his mother and mail it to him, which I agree to do. They apparently do not have a camera.

On the way to visit Ali's garden, we passed more people walking with mules loaded with firewood. Apparently they cut only the green branches so they will have wood next year. Each family has certain trees near the town, and I learn it is illegal to cut down trees without permission.

Here they are growing wheat, corn, melons, beans, and tomatoes in small terraces. Little streams of water irrigate each terrace—very ingenious. Each village gardener has a portion of this "green belt" valley area—an oasis in this region. We go on to Ali's garden where we eat apples, grapes, and rest under the shade of the grape vines.

Even though we refused to have lunch at Ali's home due to the need to get back to the rig, I see Ali's mother walking up with a big pack on her back. She begins serving us lunch, unpacking many items from newspapers—boiled eggs and three large, wheat pita-like breads that are still warm, cheese, bread crackers, salt, and sugar to go in our hot tea. They serve tea in small glasses with a small silver spoon.

Only the men eat. The custom is for women to eat later. As we prepare to leave, Ali and his mother load a large bag with grapes and figs.

On the way, we pass by many women and girls near the spring tending a herd of sheep in their colorful dress. We bid goodbye to Ali and hike back up the hills to the rig. Such generous people, these Kurds; I will never forget them.

History Lessons

We are drilling ahead, with no returns. While Mike is on duty, I take a run to the top of the mountains behind the rig. The rocky, treeless slopes make for slow going. Just over the top I can see a small village and garden spots in the valley below. On the way down, I come across an old hand-built pool made of stones near a spring. I'm eager to learn more about this area and its fascinating history.

We decide to take a core of this limestone before we drill through it completely without any samples. While they tripped (pulled the pipe) out of the hole, Mike and I travel back to Siirt with the rig security man. I learn Siirt is about four thousand years old—older than Istanbul! The Euphrates River goes south near here down into the Arabian Peninsula where human civilization was first noted in Mesopotamia. It's hard to believe the US and Western culture are so young compared to this cradle of civilization.

Near Siirt is a town called Aydinlar, which we also visit. The name means "those who have knowledge," but the old name of this town is Tillo. Many famous religious leaders are buried here with mosques built around their tombs. The most elaborate tomb/mosque belonged to the leader of the Sheikh sect of Islam. People visit this town to see the tomb and small museum of a pioneer in astrology. He was also a philosopher and religious leader who lived from 1657-1711, during, which time he invented a calendar that *is still accurate*—which we get to see. The Ottoman Empire had a great influence on this area of Turkey, yet the empire did not start until much later, about 1400 A.D. Many castles were built in Turkey during this time, one of which we visit in the hills around Siirt. This castle was rather large with many towers. Today it sits barren on the hill with some walls partially crumbled. It must be five hundred years old or more. We take the steep, winding road back down and drive on.

We drive into the town of Sirvon where we meet the leader of the Jandarma for that area, a second lieutenant. They serve us tea. We go to see a place where carpets are made by hand. Two to four girls sit at a large loom on, which the carpet is rolled up as it is made. These are high quality carpets, with high knot density per square inch and the work is government supported. We stop by the government office and meet the Mayor of Sirvon. He talks mainly to Jehan in Turkish. At both places we are given is a big splash of a fragrant aftershave/cologne liquid to apply as a refresher.

I am up on the rig floor at 5:30 a.m. to observe the start of cutting the core. A special drill bit is on the end of the drill pipe with the cutting face in the shape of a donut and a hole in the middle where a tube of rock is taken up into the pipe as we drill deeper. The core is out of the hole at 2:00 p.m. and at 11:00 p.m. we are done with the interpretation, so I write reports, and go to sleep at midnight.

A few days later at 4:15 a.m. local time, I'm driving with Amet and Jehan back to Diyarbakir to take core boxes to load on a plane back to Ankara (and on the USA) and to pick up the drilling manager. We arrive in town early enough to eat breakfast and see a few sights, including the Grand Mosque, which dates back to about 600 A.D. We also drive through an old market area by the Great Wall—no, not the one in China. The Great Wall of Turkey is the second largest in the world and is about five kilometers long. No one know for sure how old it is—somewhere between 1,500 and 2,000 years old.

Outside the city, I see a bridge the Romans built between 30 BC and 400 AD. I am treated to an amazing view back at the huge wall on the hill protecting Diyarbakir.

It's a hot drive back to the rig, and we pick up a tool pusher named Jimmy from Mississippi. He has been in Turkey for three years. He tells me there are people living in caves even today and more about the Roman bridge and the oldest castle in all of Turkey, which is southeast of Batman on the way to Midyat.

I use running as a way to stay in shape but it is also a fantastic way to cover a lot of ground and see the surrounding area. On one of my runs, I find the ruins of an old village up in the hills Jehan told me about. When the Hittites inhabited this village is not clear; likely late in their age of existence. Hittites spanned from around 1500 B.C. to 1180 BC when the civilization splintered at the end of the Bronze Age and the arrival of the Sea Peoples. One of the mudloggers (people who monitor the drill cutting and samples coming out the well) mentioned that he found some old coins in the area. Mike identified the markings on the coins as Hittite-age.

I come across a number of stone outlines that were probably houses, with some type of roof that's now long gone. There were at least six to eight buildings and some possible water wells. I was surprised to find one place littered with pottery fragments.

Moving down into the more open valley, I see fences or outlines made of rock, which possibly contained animals and crops some 3,500 years ago. I hitch a ride on the road, as I have been gone two hours. The electric logging engineer picks me up on his way up to start our logging run in the well bore. We were busy the rest of the day and night. My time dreaming about finding lost worlds is gone due to the focus required to monitor the electric logging job, a key data gathering step in drilling a well.

Back to the Big City

A few days later it is Wednesday and time to drive with Amet to Diyarbakir and fly to Ankara. I think of this as the first baby steps in reducing my distance from home (7,000-8,000 miles).

Back in Ankara I can immediately smell the difference in air quality, the pollution after the clear air in the mountains near the rig is really noticeable. It's not just the air: the taxi drivers honking like crazy at anything in the way, the street vendors hawking their wares, the prayers broadcasting from the mosques—it is a huge contrast, and I am surprised by how quickly I had gotten use to the quiet of the well site.

Ankara is rather westernized. It is actually uncommon to see women wearing the face cover so prevalent in most Arabic countries. Ataturk, the leader who revolutionized Turkey in the 1920s outlawed these, as he wished to separate Turkey from other Muslim countries. Machine gun toting guards line embassy row and surround government buildings and banks.

I am working a lot, however I take a couple hours in Ankara to see the Museum of Ancient Civilizations. They have items dated to 7500 BC and up to 300 AD—a fantastic display walking up through the pre-pottery ages. Many empires came and went in this crossroads country. Not only did people move up from Mesopotamia to the Arabian Peninsula four to five thousand years ago, but there were civilizations in Turkey long before that.

I did some shopping in the crowded downtown native shopping area where prices were cheap and small specialized shops lined the narrow streets.

The next day, after taking care of business at the office, I go out with the venture office manager, Ken, to a 10:30 meeting of the Ankara Hash House Harriers. Running a hash is a tradition begun in the late 1930s by British officers in Kuala Lumpur. Now it is an opportunity for international expatriates and others to get together, "run a hash" and drink some beer. Since I like both running and good beer, this seems like a great idea to me.

We drive to the outskirts of town and run a hash around the hills of an Ankaran reservoir. The majority of the participants are British or Australian, fittingly, but some Turks are here also. The idea is to begin along a trail marked with corn flour and follow the running group. The leader spots trail markers and yells "On, on." Quite often, you go down a trail to find it ends with a T. Then they yell "false trail" and you go back to the checkpoint to look for the right trail.

We run all over the hills, stopping for a beer about half way. It's about an hour and a half, mostly spent looking for the trail—what a lot of fun with fun people.

My last night in Ankara I accompany an Australian guy named Mel to their embassy for their happy hour. He gave me a ride back from the hash, and since the communications man is Australian, I invite him too. When we get to the top floor, we join in on a lively party. They have a nice balcony and bar room. I enjoy drinking some Melbourne ale and talking to Aussies, Brits, Canadians (their embassy is two doors down) and Turks.

Home Again!

Flying out of Ankara and back to Munich, I notice all the houses and apartment buildings have a dark reddish roof color. It is an interesting view with them all squeezed together, sprawled across the rolling barren hills. I will fly northwest over Istanbul, Bulgaria, Yugoslavia, the massive northeast towering Alps and drop down into Munich. "Oops, slight change due to air traffic. We will swing out over the Black Sea, Romania, Hungary, and Austria; then cross the Eastern Bavarian Alps, on to Munich," I hear while eating caviar.

My time in Munich is overcast and drizzling, but it doesn't dampen my spirits. I make it to the Hofbrauhaus, where I run into a group of Americans who live in Germany and work for the US military. We drank a "mass" of good German beers with many toasts—a mass is 34 ounces of beer. It is traditional in the old beer halls in Bavaria. I have just missed Oktoberfest, which runs the last two weeks of September and ends in early October—this helps make up for it.

I take a run in the morning to help work off some of the beer mass—and to do some sightseeing. Munich was founded in 1120 AD and was the capital of Bavaria. Bavaria joined with Germany as a country in the 1800s, and the architecture is incredible. I'm standing on the plaza to hear the 11:00 a.m. bells ring and notice the colored (Glockenspiel) figures in one section of the tower begin to move. Other figures come out around the clock on a moving track, including two knights on horses who have a mock duel.

St. Peters is the oldest church in town, so I climb the tower to the top, where there is a spooky observation deck. What a view! If not for the heavy cloud cover on the horizon, I could see the Bavarian Alps. I go inside the church and see amazing ornate displays along the sides (different sections of different ages) and a grand altar with massive gold figures and designs.

I go down the street to another huge cathedral—Frauenkirchi—but I could not enter. It is closed to tourist in respect for the last King of Bavaria, King Strauss who just died a few days ago. They are having a noon mass in his honor and only the most important people are in attendance, with police and TV cameras barricading the rest of us out.

I cut my jog through old buildings, specialty shops, and stoic monuments short because I'm getting cold. I catch a cab back to the hotel, where I check out and head for the airport. We hit some bad turbulence on the flight from Amsterdam to Houston, but I still get to enjoy a six-course meal as we fly just south of Iceland and over Canada. Other than missing my wife, I think my first international well-site trip has gone well; this job allowed me to see remote sites in Turkey.

I have not seen a golf course in three weeks, so I look forward to visiting some rolling greens in Texas.

Chapter 2
Deep in the Guatemalan Jungle

April, 1989

Since the trip to Turkey a few months ago, I worked in the Houston office doing log analysis for international exploration projects and got to know my new co-workers. I also found time for golf on days off. In fact, I have begun to play golf regularly here in Houston—for the first time since I was thirteen.

Living in southern Mississippi as a kid, we enjoyed my parents "foreign assignment"—moving in 1965 from western Massachusetts to Picayune. I learned to play golf and loved it. In those last two years there I played a lot with pals from the neighborhood. I thought working on my golf game year-round in Texas would let me become a great player, or at least approach scratch handicap. I know now that will not likely happen, no matter how much I practice. Pro golfers are a very rare combination of raw talent, dedication, and experience.

Lucky for me I really enjoy being a geologist, and the growth in the oil and gas business during my lifetime has created a tremendous opportunity to grow and travel, not to mention help pay for a few rounds of golf.

A trip to Guatemala interrupts my home life. I take comfort in the adventurous nature of this new assignment. This project is to explore onshore in the jungles of northern Guatemala. It's exciting to know I will be working on carbonate reservoirs, which I learned a lot about working in west Texas. Also of interest to both my wife and me are the 16th century Spanish buildings in the cities and the ancient Maya ruins in the jungles. We hope to take some vacation time to visit Guatemala together after my first hitch.

Flight Time

Continental flies direct from Houston to Guatemala City with an easy two and a half hour flight. I sit next to a young man from El Salvador coming back to visit his parents and enjoy speaking with him about his culture.

As the plane flies into Guatemala City, I am able to see the mountains and the city nestled in amongst them—we bank around, seemingly to give us a better view of green rises and the haze in the middle distance. Apparently April supports a green explosion of the landscape. From the air it looks like a lot of cities, geography excluded, yet I am expecting lots of differences on the ground.

Hugo Garcia picks me up at the airport—he's the geologist working in the venture office and is originally from Peru. It is a short ride from the airport, yet long enough to know Hugo is a likeable guy. He takes me to the Hotel El Dorado, which is very nice. After a quick walk around the area, I meet Hugo for dinner. We head to Palo Alto where we run into Roger and Bernard, company engineers from Houston.

In the morning, I meet some co-workers in the venture office and get oriented. I also learn our well #1 in the area, may not start drilling for a few more days meaning I might have some time to kill in town.

In the morning, I go for a nice four mile run and then walk to the office. After taking care of a few things, we are all off to celebrate an office employee's impending marriage. It's a fine day to escape the office and head to Lake Amatitlan for a picnic—about an hour south of the city. The lake is large and surrounded by volcanic mountains. We fill the time with Frisbee, water balloons, swimming, and special Brazilian rum drinks. This is some great down time before heading out to the rig.

I am up early to meet Jim and Bernard to go to a market at Chichicastenango. This is where the Maya Indians from the area gather to sell their goods on Thursday and Sunday. Although a bike race slows us down as we leave town, soon we are in rolling hills spotted with small farming houses and cultivated fields in all available spaces—even on steep hills, in lush areas of trees and in small towns. It's incredibly scenic and a sharp contrast from Turkey's arid climate.

There is a guide the moment we step out of the car. We go to the church where we observe the Sunday Maya custom; where witchdoctors light candles and give offerings of flowers to the Maya gods. They do this in the old Santo Tonas Church where regular Catholic masses are also held. Outside, incense is burning on the steps where Indians sit in their finest colored Sunday outfits.

There are privately run booths along the streets in all directions from the church. Hand-made textiles dominate—clothes, blankets, bags and so forth. We see masks, jade, and things to eat. Our guide takes us to a special room in one man's home. He has a large array of antique Maya pieces—and other junk. We bargain for things to buy there as well as in the market.

I spot a real Spanish sword from the 1540-1600s—when the Spanish took over Guatemalan Maya areas. I get a little history lesson: the Spanish completed domination of the region in the 1700s after beginning in 1524 with their conquest of Iximche. Iximche became the first Spanish capitol of Guatemala—it was later moved to Antigua. Antigua was the capital from 1543 to 1773 when earthquakes destroyed the city; the capital was then moved to Guatemala City. Guatemala gained independence in 1821. So far Guatemala City has not had its predecessors' bad luck as a capitol location.

On the drive back we pull off the main road to go five kilometers on a dirt road to the ruins at Iximche, a post-Maya civilization. A Mesoamerican group, the Kaqchikel flourished there from 1400-1524, when it was taken over by the Spanish. The ruins are still Maya style with temple buildings, plazas, and game areas covered in short grass. There are murals and evidence of human sacrifice. We get back to the hotel around dinnertime, have a shot in the steam room and a dip in the pool. Yeah this is a tough work day, but long hours deep in the jungle are soon to come.

The Jungle

The fun is over. I am in a downpour deep in the jungle of northern Guatemala near Machaquila, the thick triple canopy jungle all around us. I can't see very far in any direction, except across the well pad clearing, where I will be two weeks.

I flew in a couple of days go by Twin Otter, a small workhorse airplane that can take off and land in nothing flat. They got us an hour north over the mountains into the jungle to a dirt landing strip. You are more cargo than passenger in these guys. A few kilometers via pickup to the river and we all jump in some long boats to head down river for half an hour. No major predators to report, just turtles, ducks, and local peasants. My company built the only road out here, and it is ten kilometers to the well from the river, quite the adventure just getting here.

The well we are drilling is in a clearing, carved out of the jungle for 100-200 meters in all directions with a barbed wire fence surrounding the well and a guard hut at the entrance. The guards are necessary because guerrilla military groups are known to pass through the area on their way to harass government troops further east—Oh, wonderful. They have visited the camp prior to my arrival, however we are not a target; apparently they only wanted some food.

We have about sixty people at this well location. We are self-sufficient with a mess hall, water pumped from a nearby well, and all the equipment needed for drilling and communications. We even have regular phone lines, a satellite telephone and telex lines as backups for emergencies or special use. Very special at twenty dollars a minute.

My real introduction to the joys of the jungle comes right after we have dinner the day I arrive. A quick walk with the drilling supervisor in the dark was enough to be attacked by every kind of bug imaginable, including some weird beetles and something really brightly colored, none of, which I wanted crawling on me. I am told I will get used to it. I doubt it.

A few days later I am in a truck with one of our security men Eduardo, who speaks only Spanish, to take some people down to the river for the boat back. We give some campesinos (peasants) a ride, and at one point Eduardo pulls off the road to show me the village of San Juan—thatched huts in "the land of the eternal spring."

The next day after breakfast we go by boat to another landing so we can drive to El Tigre -no they have never seen a tiger there. I spend most of my time at the rig site, in the mudlog shack, watching the well operations. I get to look around the area when we are shut down.

On the road to El Tigre, thousands of brown and white mariposa (butterflies) crowd along the roads (apparently only in the spring) so thick they seem like they are intent on taking over.

We arrive and find the tiny shop making boxes for us to ship samples. I notice the workers around here are pretty handy carpenters. They can cut boards straight from logs with a chainsaw and make desks, bookshelves, and so forth. They do more with a machete than I thought practical. El Tigre is basically our landing strip with a few huts and some guards.

It's now really hot and nearing noon, but we are stuck waiting until the boats come back. I decide to get a Coke from the little shack store and I grab a few of the great local cigars—a cost of about two cents each. There are a couple of ninas and ninos (children) hanging around looking at me. They are eager to pose for photos.

While taking my pictures, I hear school children singing inside a large hut. Though it's Saturday, they are practicing for a Labor Day (May 1st) event—which they take very seriously here in Guatemala.

I learn some trivia to add to my anthropology file: the Mayan people have actually grown smaller in average height through the ages; especially since being ruled by the Spanish. This is documented in a study, which cited two reasons: First, Mayans are problem drinkers, many are encouraged to drink as children. Second, corn tortillas, beans, and very little meat dominate their diet.

Drilling

It looks like we will start drilling again in the wee hours of the morning at first, but when I get up just after five a.m. to send in a geology report, we still had not started. The startup was delayed for another day, which means I am able to get in a good run in the morning. Good thing because by afternoon, it was 95-100 degrees with soaking humidity. The highlight of my day is a call with my wife via phone hookup to a microwave tower on top of the mountains at Chinaja.

We finally start drilling at 2:45 in the morning, days off from our original estimate. As we get started and I am with the team, it strikes me exactly how international in scope we really are. These people have been all over the world, and they have seen it all. They were evacuated from Argentina when the British jumped into the battle for the Falkland Islands, escaped the fall of the Shah in 1979 offshore from Iran, and taught Chinese geologists to curse with a Texas accent. The malaria stories from Africa remind me it is time to take my weekly dose of Chloroquine, an anti-malaria drug originally thought too toxic for human consumption.

Now that we are drilling, the work is demanding. We are drilling so fast the upper part of the well is the hardest to keep up. The samples I need to look at and write reports about come very quickly, even a few hours' sleep puts me way behind and requires working nearly to midnight to catch up. I looked at over six hundred feet of samples today, stopping only to eat.

Making it even more fun is the rainy season has started, which lasts from May to October. It has rained four of the past five days and probably will today. The rain doesn't abate the heat much, just makes everything wet, and makes the ground a hopeless mud pit. Oh, and guerillas were sighted crossing the road between Machaquila and the river—just to add one more concern to the mix.

I see a high wire act: A spider monkey climbed up the Geronimo line. The height didn't seem to bother this little fellow one bit. The Geroimo line is what we use in case you need to get down fast from the top of the rig—which stands about 140 feet tall. If the rig blows out, the line allows you to escape from the top by riding down the line on a pulley.

Coup d'état

One more night and I can get up and go, assuming Jim shows up to relieve me. Hugo told me this morning that there is a rumor of a coup d'état here in Guatemala. The military have moved in to secure all government buildings in case it is more than a rumor.

By late morning we know it is more than a rumor. The air force and some leftist factions have made a run at the government. By the time we learn of it, it is over. The government reportedly quelled the uprising and remains in power.

Jim is supposed to be on vacation in Guatemala this week visiting various places before heading back to Guatemala City where he will get transported here to take over for me.

"Have you seen Jim?" I ask Hugo.

"No," he replies.

I ask him, "Were there any road blocks related to the coup today?"

"Yes, Guatemala City was closed to any incoming traffic this morning. But," he hurried to add encouragingly, "the government has control now and it is probably open."

I hope Jim shows up here tomorrow. If he doesn't show, I can't go.

The next day passes—raining again, as it has since May 1. There is lots to do and not much time to worry about Jim. I am up all night looking for the depth to set casing, yet in the back of my mind I am worried about how long I could be stuck here when what I really want to do is go home.

I am busy trying to push through being exhausted from my all-nighter when everyone starts talking and pointing—trucks have shown up. I get excited, and sure enough Jim is among those coming in. We have just enough time to talk about a few things—well actually I was still looking for the casing seat and a bit lost in the geology section and Jim was not happy about taking over in the mess we were in. Soon some guys and I are piling into the trucks and headed back to the river.

My exhausted thousand yard stare takes in a five foot iguana on the banks of the river, but other than that, I note very little of the trip. I'm just too strung out.

The flight back to Guatemala City is uneventful, and I am crazy glad to see my old friend the El Dorado Hotel. I have dinner with the company guys, including Alex, who is the drilling supervisor—a Canadian who works the well on the same schedule as me—and Ruben from Argentina.

Morning dawns cloudy and with no evidence of the recent attempt to take over the government. The tanks are all gone, as are the troops. What coup? Everyone seems to act as though this is nothing unusual—for them, maybe it isn't.

I'm glad to catch an early flight to Houston. I can't wait to see my wife and maybe get in some golf. I have survived my first stint in Guatemala—a coup and the bugs. Things are looking up.

Back to the Jungle

After about two weeks at home, I find myself flying back to Guatemala City. Seeing my wife was great, as were the six rounds of golf I got in while home. Landing I find all the good hotels are full due to a convention. The venture office people have a reservation for me downtown at the Ritz. It's not bad—clean with a big TV. Located in the deep city away from the clean tourist areas, it has authentic culture complete with niños peeing on the curb.

A morning jog shows me more of my surroundings. There are small mobile shops filled with clothes and junk with native Guatemalans, instead of tourists frequenting them. After checking in at the office and giving Miguel the authentic Texas cowboy hat he wanted, I manage to show up back at the airport in time to head north.

As we are boarding the boat to head up river, a boat full of about thirty soldiers pulls up in another boat. I wonder if that means the guerillas are active in our area—I'm afraid of the answer.

We are drilling, so it's a daily chore keeping up with the necessary reports. I just got back and I am already counting the days until I can leave—thirteen to go...

Friday begins the Memorial Day weekend and I am here watching the rig drill. What to do for fun? Well, this time I brought my nine iron to practice my swing. It's still the rainy season and it rains every day, so it's very muddy. The entire site is the dirt left from clearing the jungle. The mud sticks to golf balls and running shoes really well. The tape player remains in the mud log trailer for some tunes and evening bullshit sessions with the boys. Tonight's topic: income tax—people who tried to avoid it and what happened.

Sending drilling reports to the venture office at 6:00 am and 3:00 p.m. means I keep odd hours. I have been staying up till 11:00 p.m. to get my reports done and then I am up by 5:00 am to send the morning reports out.

I wake up and look at my watch, it is 5:00 am. I throw on my clothes, walk across the location to look at the latest rocks and realize I am looking at the alarm setting on my watch. It is actually 4:00 am, but there's no point in going back to bed now. I will knock out my report and hit the sack after I get things squared away.

When they are drilling I am busy, but when they are not I try to get in some mud golf and a run every day. It has now rained six of the last eight days, and we are in the first month of the rainy season. Guess I just have to get used to it.

Today is crew change day for some of us. It's interesting to see how people act when they are about to leave. I have the best schedule: two weeks on, two weeks off. Some people work three and three. The rig crew people work twenty-eight days on and twenty-eight days off. I can't imagine being here twenty-eight days straight.

Old Bill, the company drilling supervisor comes in with the new hitch, and his first words are, "Where the hell are we?" We drilled into a thick carbonate zone this morning at 5:30 a.m. We have some fair oil shows that allowed me to correlate to other wells to know "where the hell we are" (a marker bed), keeps me busy all day.

The bugs are now my friends—almost. Large brown and gold moths that don't fly when you touch them seems strange, and an unusual grasshopper got into the Mudlogging unit where I work a lot. It had a bright green back, jet-black legs, a yellow belly, and purple head. Crazy bugs.

I love watching the locals make things out of lumber cut straight from the jungle; tables, benches, boxes, you name it. The most desired wood is mahogany, which is tan and a reddish brown color in this part of the world. Another area special is a drink that is served cold and looks similar to iced tea but darker and has a different aftertaste. It is called Elixir. They say it has special medicinal powers, specifically it helps sexual performance. The natives point out that the cut vine used to make the stuff shows a cross shape on the end just in case I want to cut my own and brew up a batch for my wife.

Speaking of my wife, I am able to get a hold of her—for a change, it was pretty easy to get through. We miss each other so much. Two weeks is a long time.

21

Yesterday I snuck out the front gate to a location where I could get some photos looking back at the well and of the jungle—what luck. While I was standing there with my camera, four campesinos rode in on horses hauling large sacks of something. A great photo opportunity. They had come from gathering achiote, a small red pepper looking thing used as a spice or food decoration. The saddles on the horses were handmade with raw leather wrapped around sticks.

Two planes land on our dirt strip to pick up the departing hitch. There are two because the Guatemala company President, Bobby brought about ten officials from the Guatemalan government to the well for a visit. Most were from the Ministry of Culture, some from the Ministry of Energy and mines. Nice people. I talk to one woman, the Vice President of Culture, who is an archeologist. She said the El Ceibal ruins, near where we will drill the second well, flourished from 800 BC to about 800 AD. They do not know why the civilization perished or moved. They are just beginning to understand the ancient drawings and writing history (hieroglyphics) of the early Mayans.

For a brief time before it was abandoned, El Ceibal became a very important regional capital along a river trade route. At its height, they think it was perhaps home for six to eight thousand people. I wonder if I will get to see it when we drill the second well.

Early Return

I spend what feels like far too little time at home with my wife this time. I get a phone call Wednesday while I'm getting ready to play golf. I hear, "You need to leave for Guatemala on Sunday instead of Tuesday so Jim can get back to Houston and sit in as supervisor." Here I am a few days early—it seems like weeks early—and Jim is headed back.

The flight in was different and earlier than expected. We were on a two-engine, six-seater Aero Commander with a sputtering left prop the mechanics had to check out before we took off. I got to ride as co-pilot, which thanks to the nice pilot meant I also got some flying lessons during our trip—hope the engine behaves.

We left early because Schlumberger's people had to come out on my flight. The drillers got stuck during coring and these guys are going to try a "back off" using an explosive charge on a wire-line to blow a charge down hole. They fish out the stuck portion and manage to pull it loose just as I get in. Now we have a core out for me to describe before the sun goes down.

Now that I am back, the kitchen crew is telling me Willy—what I named this old yellow lab mix we adopted as the rig mascot—is dead. I don't believe them. He's a tough old hound. I go and look around and find him and give him a present, a flea collar. He has a few more scars—they say there isn't a dog in the area that doesn't have scars from chasing wild pigs—but the marks on his head and rear don't look too serious. We have got to look after our mascot.

Guerrilla Visit

Mid-morning I hear loud talking outside. The kitchen entrance is just outside my door so I poke my head outside and see two guerrillas (rebels) talking to a couple guys including Paco a government oil company engineer, and Eduardo, our company security.

The two guerrillas have green uniforms, are carrying assault rifles with large banana clips holding maybe a hundred rounds, and have big knives. One has a German Lugar pistol, a compass, and a machete. They have rubber boots, and they are young—one is twenty-five, maybe, and the other is all of seventeen.

I'm not at all sure what to expect from these two armed men. Others have said the guerrillas don't trouble us, but the voices I hear, speaking Spanish of course are loud—perhaps not hostile.

It takes only moments for me to see that what I have been told is correct. They are not here to make trouble, they just want some food. They are actually very friendly. Paco gets his camera and comes out to take their pictures.

No problem. We all shake hands, and they leave.

"I saw about twenty guerrillas waiting on the edge of the jungle," Eduardo tells me. They get arms from Nicaragua and Cuba through Mexico. It is hard to understand why the guerrillas continue to fight in

Guatemala. There are roughly a thousand left in action. They say the government is too right wing for them. The government still has financial and political problems, yet many guerillas have given themselves up. The army is actively trying to get the rest of the guerrillas, so there are occasional skirmishes in this region.

The Maya and indigenous people, the poor peasants, seem to support the guerrillas and in response the government—run by the military—has been pretty harsh with them. It keeps some rebels fighting. I just hope they don't start fighting in our neck of the woods.

Get Busy, Then Escape

Sometimes my main concerns seem to be getting reports off when we are drilling. It is sort of a nagging feeling knowing I have to keep up. When it's time to run logs, it's different. Drilling stops and pulls the drill string out of the hole, while the geologist (me in this case) works with the electric logging company to run the program of various tools to evaluate the potential oil productive reservoir rocks.

I get short periods of rest when they are rigging up the next tool, but then I am monitoring the tool during the runs in the hole for quality control or looking for oil clues. The excitement of the hunt and employing the high technology tools is all very exciting, to be clear. It is all about the hunt, not the long hours.

With getting things set up, writing reports, and changing programs depending on what we find, I am keeping late hours. Then maybe there's a tool failure—try again. Hurry up and wait.

Hanging over it all requires being as time effective as possible because it costs tens of thousands of dollars a day ($36,000 a day here) to keep the drilling rig and other equipment and people set up. No pressure, right?

From Friday at 5:30 am through the next four days, we run nine different logging runs, and I am beat. I sleep a couple hours here, three hours there a day. The wireline logging crew wakes me up when they are ready for me, so I rest when possible—which isn't often.

The days grind by, then seem to blur. The pressure has us all on edge, and then we are finally done. It is noon on Monday, and I am too tense to rest—too wired to go to sleep. Strangely, I don't feel as bad as I thought I would. In fact my reports might actually make sense. The worst of it may be that I haven't showered since Friday in the constant Guatemalan heat and humidity, which could explain why no one wants to be around me right now.

After my marathon session, I am eager to escape the rig. Eduardo is a spry older guy in his sixties, and he's driving a van full of guys to the plane. So I hop in.

After we see the plane take off at El Tigre, we drive off west to take Dr. Hector to the small clinic the company set up in Las Pazas, then drive the boat up river before arriving at the airstrip. I get to see some of the small towns of the area, consisting of maybe a couple hundred people living in thatched roof huts around a town center.

The doctor delivered, I hop in the cab, and we head for Sayaxche—the biggest town around here at five to ten thousand people. You would never guess it had that many people by looking at it, but Eduardo tells me every little shack has ten people or so living in it. As school lets out, I see thousands of kids crowding the dirt streets—so many kids for such a small area.

Sayaxche has two hotels by the river, a gas station, a church, a number of small stores and a ferry, for crossing the river. We stop to have lunch at The Texan restaurant, a nice little place. They even turn on the lights for us. A few hotels and restaurants have their own small generators—we get the royal treatment.

Eduardo's had assignments in a variety of places since he retired from the military in 1964, most of his time spent working for the company in Thailand, Venezuela, Chile, Colombia, Ecuador, and Nicaragua. He was in Nicaragua when the Sandinistas took over in 1979.

We travel back by a different route to see the ruins of El Ceibal. "This Mayan civilization flourished from 1000 BC to 1000 AD," he tells me. The company had planned to drill a well near El Ceibal, as it is the best of the prospective locations, but it became a political issue with the Guatemalan government—a fight between the Ministry of Culture and the Ministry of Energy. They said "yes" to our construction efforts, then "no," so many times that we finally said, "Enough." The issue had become a public one as well so it was a good decision to halt that drilling project. We are relieved of our commitment well, according to our lawyer. Guatemala plans to restore El Ceibal and hopes it will attract tourism money. But, it's a long way off. Of the many temples, only two are fully restored. Most of the ruins are still covered by dirt and jungle.

The well would put money into the local economy, and if we find oil, it could help the weak Guatemalan economy. The majority of the people don't understand how small of an area a drilling well will effect and how careful we can be. The well would disturb a small portion of the park area—zero if it was dry and we covered up the area and left.

Eduardo and I walk from the visitor area over to the first area, a large mound of dirt, a small hill, really—with some steps uncovered at the base to a temple. In this area I see a couple of Stelae large rectangular stones about six feet tall, with a Maya figure carved on one side standing alone in the grass in front of the temple. Down a little slope is the main restored temple of El Ceibal with large Stelae at the base of the steps in each of the four small rooms. Their purpose is unknown—maybe the king's house or sauna rooms for healing the sick, or witchdoctor headquarters. I notice the width of the steps here are much larger than the steps of the round structure or steps at Tikal.

Northeast of El Ceibal about a hundred kilometers is the grand ruins of Tikal, which cover sixty-five square miles and have some temples about two hundred feet tall. It at one time had a major population, possibly fifty to a hundred thousand people. My wife and I will visit Tikal next month, so El Ceibal is a great warm up for that expedition.

The last few days on the rig are a blessed relief. I hit a couple golf balls between operations work. We celebrate the Fourth of July with some simple fireworks, BBQ chicken, and French fries.

For me the following day is the greater celebration—my relief Brian shows up at 10:30 am, and after I show him around the well, I am more than ready to head out of camp. Back at the office in Guatemala City, Alex, Chip Miller and I decide to visit the central market downtown for some shopping.

The three of us get a cab and find ourselves going down stairs from the street level into the people's central market. It's small and has crowded aisles packed with stuff. One section has food, another has hammocks, trinkets, leather etc. We do some good bargaining. I think we are the only gringos in the whole place.

It's a great way to end this hitch. But right now, all I can think of is getting home to Houston and seeing my wife—and maybe playing a little golf.

Tourista

Rather than spend my two weeks off in Houston, I am in Guatemala, but this time I have my wife with me. We have a great vacation tour planned: Guatemala City, Chichicagastenango, to a hotel on Lake Atitlan, then flying north to stay in the triple canopy jungle near the park to see the great ruins of Tikal, Flores. Then staying with local friends in Antigua a day or two.

We have a great trip. The cultures of these peoples are distinct and colorful. This trip may be the most memorable and impressionable international trip we will ever make.

I get back to the rig to find out the drilling is finished—but with a wild ending. It wasn't technical trouble—it was *guerrillas*. A few days ago, they visited the location. Using a forklift they hauled nearly all the food—hundreds of pounds into the jungle and took some things from people. They also left a list of demands for a large amount of supplies.

A few days later they stopped one of our security people on the road and questioned him about the progress of meeting their demands. When he told them they didn't have management approval, the head guerrilla told him they would burn and destroy everything at the well Sunday morning if they didn't come through with the requested supplies.

On a hot July Sunday, without the company's involvement, five hundred Guatemalan Army soldiers moved in around the rig to ambush the guerrillas. There was no sign of them, and we weren't expecting any. The guerrillas had left the area in a hurry and were hopefully far away, considering they would not want to face a significant force of regular army troops.

When I get in, I only have to clean out the geology files and pack up stuff for shipping. I am expecting an easy day or two—then heading back on the next company plane to Guatemala City, probably Friday. Not only that, this should be my last trip to this area since the well is being plugged as a dry hole and we won't drill another.

I do not know exactly how many millions of dollars were spent on this well or support for the entire project. We did not find the significant oil potential hoped for, and there was the risk of being caught in the middle of fighting between the rebel and regular armies. Oil exploration is risky business but political. Above ground risk is real in many areas of the world accessible by western oil companies.

The workers tear down and burn the thatched roof huts, and I throw a box of data in the fire. It is somehow symbolic I feel—for this area project. I stand in the center of the location tossing items into the fire mound, the smoke smoldering up and dissipating over the jungle. Sweat beads on my neck as I watch the flames and listen to the buzz of bugs in the air (audible since the rig is quiet/torn down) and noise of the few men working; tearing down the operations in this remote, isolated jungle paradise.

Soldiers, including one I talked to who was only fifteen stick around until the last of us are out, their weapons conspicuous as they either watch the forest or look bored. I am sweltering in the heat as I lay down in the bed of the truck listening to music on my Walkman, waiting for the company plane to come in and pick us up. I am looking at the river and the jungle, thinking, "Yo no regresare," *I will not return.*

Sunday morning, looking out of the big bird on the way out of Guatemala—looking down I think, "it's a beautiful country." I spot El Tigre and the river, it disappears as we rise into the clouds.

Khurdish people in Turkey

Hauling water in a Khurdish village

Guatemala army friends

Chapter 3
Desert Life in Chad

October, 1989

I thought it was only a matter of time before I would end up working in Chad, yet here I go. I will probably make four trips (hitches) with two weeks on then two weeks off, as there are two wells left to drill. Each well takes about sixty days. I am sitting in London about to hop over to Amsterdam where I will catch the company charter to Chad in Central Africa. I had been planning on a Saturday flight, but on Thursday I found out we needed to leave Friday, which wiped out the chance to play golf in Houston Saturday morning.

Waiting at Gatwick airport I hear an announcement in five languages not to leave your bag unattended. They have tightened European security due to terrorism. In fact we are flying on a company charter plane between Amsterdam and Chad.

People going to work with us in Chad from Paris flew on commercial airlines until a couple of weeks ago, on a sad September day, when a bomb exploded on the plane out of Chad killing all 170 people on board. Eleven people working for our company died on the flight; one of which was a geologist from my International well site group. It seems it was the Islamic jihadists getting back at the French for how they handled things in the Middle East, yet we may never know. Sometime later news came that the same terrorist group was responsible for the Lockerbie Scotland crash of Pan Am Flight 103 in December, 1989. Both explosions occurred at altitude exceeding 30,000 feet.

The company decided to avoid commercial air in and out of Africa. My wife and I are glad for the charter flight, I am a lucky man. A couple months ago I spoke to my boss about what area to work. I explained to him,

"Considering I have solid experience working carbonate rocks, maybe I should work Guatemala—where carbonates are a target."

He said, "Good point," and immediately switched me to the Guatemala rotation and moved the other geologist to the Chad operations—he is now dead. That could have been me.

Bless my soul for that stroke of luck, and my condolences are with his widow. Now however, I find myself in Chad.

Charter Flight to Chad

I arrive from the USA in Amsterdam in the afternoon and go to the Golden Tulip Hotel near the airport; I catch a train downtown. As I step out of the train station, a few young people are sitting against the building with a guitar and a pipe smoking hash—marijuana is legal in Amsterdam.

I stroll around the canals and old buildings for a while and see the sleazy street where prostitutes sit in windows—weird. It's starting to rain so I catch a cab back to the hotel—55 Guilders (~$100 US). I miss the exchange rate in Guatemala.

I am back at the airport around midnight. It's odd to see Schiphol airport nearly deserted. A company security man meets us, we get our tickets and go to the gate. There's about thirty of us on a 737 with a regular crew. We don't take off until 2:00 a.m., so we have some food and beer to pass the time. The big plane looks empty. We all have our own seat rows to sleep on.

I wake up about 7:00 a.m. and look out to see the massive sand dunes of the Sahara Desert. You can see huge sand ridges even from 30,000 feet.

After a stop on the Island of Palma off the coast of Spain for fuel, we fly into the Chad capitol N'Djamena, in the northern part of the country. The airport is a small funky one. It takes an hour or two for them to check our passports and luggage. Some people from the venture office meet us there to help the process—wonder how long it would take without their help.

While waiting I see a number of lizards on the steps, each over six inches long. One of the big ones munches on a praying mantis while I watch. We load three different Twin Otter planes, two headed south to the drilling operations area and one to the base camp in Sarh, in the central part of Chad.

As we take off one guy points out the army's anti-aircraft guns tracking our charter plane down the runway—not a comforting thought knowing there's some young Chadian soldier with his finger on a trigger. The military is all around the airport including French mirage jets even though the civil war has been over for two years now. When Libya led by Khadafy jumped in to help the rebels in the north, the French helped the government forces push them back. Apparently everyone's still on edge.

While flying to the rig, I see the land is green in southern Chad, which is savannah rather than arid like the north. The four to five month rainy season has just ended. The land is generally flat, but I see a large river and many washed out gullies from the rain.

We land on the red dirt (laterite) airstrip and hop in trucks. Some people stop at the field where the team recently drilled field "appraisal wells" and have started testing zones for oil. The appraisal well has tested large volumes of oil—a thousand barrels a day—from the lowest and first zone they planned to test. The appraisal wells confirm it is a huge field with a larger oil volume than previously estimated. I go on another fifteen kilometers to the wildcat well my company is drilling. The wildcat well is drilling to test a separate structure, a wildcat well that will be a new field discovery if successful.

As we drive down the road, I am surprised to see large trees and tall green grass. They say this grass will all be dead, brown, and gone in a couple of months. The temperature is not too bad right now, maybe 80s or 90s in the heat of the day with some humidity. They say near Lake Chad (the second largest wetland in Africa and lake from which the country gets its name) where we drilled our first two wells, it hits 135 F in the heat of the day and is flat, sandy, and desolate. I am glad I missed out on that place.

We roll into a location which has our typical setup—a little white housing trailers, the rig itself, supplies strewn about on pallets, a tool trailer, trucks, a forklift, and so forth. The local workers (all black) have a tent city set up in one corner. I immediately notice some of the locals have scars arranged on their faces. Later I would learn these are

33

from tribal customs. At the rig I meet Jamie, the geologist I will replace, who has been here three weeks. He has been here since the crash and is ready to leave. We are drilling just below 4000' and very fast when I get there. The plan is to drill to 4900' and set casing. The idea is to set the casing above the potential oil zones then drill out looking for shows of oil, and stop to take whole core thirty foot rock sections for reservoir data collection. Based on the rocks I'm seeing in the drill cuttings samples I want to stop shallower. I call to discuss it with Brian the geologist at Sarh Base and we agree on the strategy.

We agree for the drillers to stop at 4820'. The last five feet drill fast, a "drilling break"; we have stopped, and I go to my trailer. The mud-logger comes to get me before I'm to go back to look at the samples.

In his Welsh accent he says, "We've got oil on the shaker—fucking Texas T.

"Wow, we have discovery" I say, and we scurry about gathering information to relay to headquarters.

This means either the pay sand came in 245 feet high...or this is a new pay sand. There are only twelve wells drilled in this basin. This is the first one to test this structure that is two by three miles of trap area in the subsurface. I'm probably seeing the first oil from what could be a world-class oil field.

The first couple of days are a difficult adjustment due to time zone differences, a difficult work schedule and the excitement of new oil. By the third day on location I finally get a good night's sleep.

Not the Safest Place

The Merisat satellite communications hookup is five miles away at the other rig. All we have at our rig is radio contact with the other rig and Sarh base camp, plus a telex machine for our daily reports. If we are going to fax important log data directly to Houston, we have to travel to the other rig.

Here's the catch: when I leave this location, I'm told I have to pick up a soldier from the camp near ours, who will ride in the back. I have to make the trip at various times of the day and night (Houston is six hours behind). At night, even though I'm going pretty fast I can see a little wildlife. I can also see the other rig burning a thirty foot gas flare from the test zone that lights up the night sky.

In a way having a soldier with me is just incidental, yet in another it makes me wonder why he's necessary. How dangerous is this area we are in, with our fenced compound and camp of soldiers nearby?

Bill, the camp medic, runs with me sometimes, and he tells me about treating the local soldiers when he can. His French is pretty good after two and a half years in Gabon with the Peace Corps. He and I slip out of the barbed wire fence to throw a Frisbee ring with some kids from the nearby village. Bill of course reminds me to take my malaria meds—a few of the guys working for us have gotten it. I remember to take my two kinds of malaria pills as directed and use my bug spray at night. There is a big green bug here they call a blister bug. If he lands on you, you need to flick him off hard and clean. If you slap on top of it, an acid juice is released, which turns into a blister.

The oil company head of security here deals with the military for us. Some people on our team jokingly call him Colonel Half-Track. He tells me the government soldiers are from the north, which is dominantly Arabic speaking and Muslim. They actually defeated the southern rebels. The local workers we employ here in the kitchen and as other common labor: Laundry, carpentry, and rough necks, speak French and they are the southerners who were defeated. The north has been fighting the south for a thousand years and the soldiers guarding us here are desert warriors from the north who won the war. The soldiers living outside our compound in tents get tense when they see us treating the local workers better than them—because they won the war.

This is good information. Note to self: Treat the soldiers well.

The Village

Bill sees me around 4:00 p.m. and asks if I want to take off and see a village near the rig. We pick up Nicholas, a local interpreter. We had to talk the English camp boss into letting the interpreter go with us—

two soldiers accompany us. Since Nicholas will miss pay for the time, we'll slip him some money.

I am surprised to learn that unassuming Nicholas can speak five languages. He is fluent in Arabic, French, and three Chadian languages, including Sari, which the people we are visiting speak. Apparently his Chadian name is "Mani Pa,", which means, "It's like this"

On the way I ask Nicholas about the scars on some men's faces. Understand, I ask Bill in English, and he asks Nicholas in French. It gets complicated. Nicholas says when the Sari men reach fifteen to eighteen, they go through a ceremony to become a man. They cut lines on their faces with a sharp piece of metal—they must not cry. They also learn a secret language that only men learn. Nicholas says he lived for three months without seeing his parents to pass the ritual and learn the secret language. This used to be six months, but due to school it is now shorter. Nicholas tells us he used to be a cotton broker. He would buy cotton from farmers for the factory and keep a profit, sometimes making 300,000 CFA per month. He now works for 90 CFA/hr ($1 US = 300 CFA.) He doesn't trade cotton anymore because when the rebels were really active they tried to stop the farmers from growing cotton to shut down the economy. That would hurt the money and trade flow to the government. Nicholas had a rebel friend who said, "Don't go to the field and buy cotton tomorrow." Nicholas told a buyer friend who would not listen. The next day he and a number of other buyers were killed. The rebels ransacked his house. Nicholas got out of the cotton business.

We turn off the company improved road onto a small road cutting through cotton fields and fields of millet. They sell the cotton in Sarh to buy clothes. We immediately saw bare chested women and young boys with beads and loincloths. A little farther on we see a group of men wearing bush headdresses and carrying spears; they have begun the young men's tribal initiation ceremony.

We arrive in the village and shake hands with each person, saying "Layle,", which means hello in Sari. A woman named Margaret leads us over to her house where we take our seats. The children are all staring at us and we meet older women who were cooking. Soon a big group has gathered around. I estimate there are about ten older women, six men, some young men, and about twenty small children. Initially when we entered the village the children ran away. I learned later it is because, having never seen white people before, the children thought I was a ghost.

One of the sample catchers from our rig, Jocheme, lives in this village; he joins us. They serve us a bowl of stew with ground up lamb meat and we all eat. Bill and I are afraid to eat too much and are glad Jocheme is there to eat most of it so we do not insult anyone.

We get some beer to share—my first taste of Chad's "Gala" beer. Then they bring out a bottle of homemade whiskey. It was distilled with heat from the root of the maniok plant and is powerful stuff. Bill and I take a token sip.

Jocheme tells me it is okay to take pictures. When I pull out my camera, they all jump up for a photo. Bill gets out his camera as well, and the photo fest is on. Some of the women run and change their clothes. One of the soldiers asks us to take his picture and give him a copy so he would always remember this. I stood with him and his M-14.

We take a tour and get to see the chief's house and to meet the chief just as we are leaving. We say goodbye to all our new friends and drive off. This is a proud and happy people, considering how poor they are. Nicholas tells us on the way back it is a status symbol for a Chadian to lay down foreign money at a bar because they must associate with foreigners to get it. I give him an American dollar when we get back, which he had never seen. He tells us he is going to show it to his wife and keep it in his photo album.

I am glad to have this time to see the people of Chad and get a taste of their "southern" culture. Cultural experiences like this are truly one of the benefits of traveling to the far reaches of the world for the oil business.

Schedule Change

Two days after I arrive, I find out from Houston there is a schedule change and I will be here not two weeks but three. I shouldn't cry about being here three weeks. The government drilling engineer got here when the well started and will stay until it's done—including testing, probably three months. I can handle three weeks.

One of the soldiers who went with us the other day told Bill that when they fought against Libya on the Aozou strip, they would go twenty days without eating. Probably a slight exaggeration but not far from true. Libya had planes and bombs. They could charge and pull back time after time. Both sides would chop enemy bodies into little pieces; brutal. I hear there are a lot of brutal things in Africa and being here I get some sense of that. Well, I can handle three weeks here, considering all the comforts we have like food service and air conditioned trailers.

It's not easy when I think that tomorrow is crew change day for some guys. Bill, the medic; Chip the company supervisor that worked with me in Guatemala; and Andy, the mud-logger, are leaving—along with a few others. I will get my chance soon.

I have been very busy at the well since last Thursday and have had very little sleep. As I was finishing up my description of Core #2, they were back on bottom drilling. Starting at 5:00 p.m., Sunday, I began looking for the next place to core. We are drilling in the main potential pay section of this well, so it could happen at any time. We are drilling at a very fast rate so you can hit a drilling break and drill fifteen feet in minutes and miss the top of the next core target zone. The idea is to drill a few feet into it and circulate without drilling until the rock samples come to the surface and then check them for oil. If they have oil, you pull out of the hole, go in with a different bottom hole assembly, core bit and core catching pipe and try to core this good oily sandstone zone. The best way to evaluate a potential oil zone is to get a continuous core of rock through it to see what the rock really looks like.

I finally manage to call my wife, who was wondering what happened to me. After we got caught up, Greg arrived at the well to relieve me so I could head to our base camp at Sarh. I'm surprised to see so many trailers and other equipment in Sarh Base—there are more people working with us here in Chad than I thought.

Security precautions are tighter here in Sarh, and we are advised not to go outside the compound fence. However, from 7:00 p.m. to

9:00 p.m. we go to the compound of the French textile factory next door where they have a little bar. Beer and pool sound heavenly right now, even if I stink at pool.

The trouble comes when I try to go to sleep. I get a call from the rig and then two different calls from Houston to find out what's going on. That's the problem with Houston being six hours behind us.

Roger, the head of security and I get out of the compound today, first to talk to the manager of the textile factory—Roger speaks fluent French—and then to head into town. Now I can see why we live in the compound. Mud brick houses line dusty dirt roads; people mill about all through town.

He says, "If you have an accident, run for that flag down there— that's the police station. They will protect you. Maybe. If you hit a kid on the street, the people will surround the car, roll it over, and set it on fire." I resolve to be *very* careful if I ever have to drive here. We stop at the hotel so Roger can get things set up for some managers visiting next week. I get him to stop by a craft shop, where I look over some local handiwork—wood carvings, slave bracelets, art prints, and the like.

I manage to get some running in on some days. I go with Jimmy, the rig company drilling supervisor. He tells me that most every poisonous snake known on this continent lives here; vipers, cobras, and spitting cobras. I guess I won't run this trail after dark.

Greg is sick back at the rig and hasn't been getting much sleep— working constantly, like I was. Houston managers hear this, and they want me back out there tomorrow. This means I did nine days and nights on the rig and only four in Sarh—and I'll be nine more days on the rig. I drink another Gala beer at the textile mill bar and get ready for the 7:00 am flight out to the rig.

Just Finish the Hitch

Back at the rig the bugs are thick, and I'm picking them off constantly as I watch the drilling rate noting the time it takes to drill each foot. What a Saturday night.

The driller lets me take the drilling controls for a moment, regulating how much of the 125,000 pound drill string and equipment is let down on the bit—WOB or weight on bit. We were drilling with 15,000 WOB. I was trying to keep it there, and it slipped up to 18,000—oops, then 30,000. That's the end of my drilling. The driller takes the big metal handle, eases it back, and gets her on track. "You have to develop a feel for it," he says. I think I'll stick with geology and golf.

Even though I've had enough sleep lately, I start to wear down as the grind catches up. In the third week you begin to tire just being here, working long hours, taking meds, and eating the food. I try not to think about it, but in the last week it's hard not to think about being home soon, seeing my wife, getting regular sleep, good food, sports, fun, and the dogs. The last couple of nights, we have been up on the rig at night while we are coring. The bugs are a nightmare. It rained recently so they are unusually bad. They swarm around the lights bounce off you, and you are constantly picking them off. You sort of get used to it.

Tuesday we have to drill 100-150 feet below the base of core #9 and look for another core point. I stay in the logging unit watching the drill rate and samples for drill breaks and shows but don't find a good core spot until 4:00 a.m. We stopped at 6121' to start core #10. I write up the geology morning reports, send them and get to bed at 6:00 a.m.—I get three hours sleep—this is rig life. When we are just drilling it's not too bad keeping up because you can take breaks. Wire line electrical logging jobs can go on continuously for days.

I've got just three more get ups and one get up and go. I spend the time learning French from some the coring guys—and then some fun British phrases from the mud-loggers from England. "You wanker," "cheers," and the universal "sacked"—for getting fired—are my favorites. So funny that we speak the same language…but don't.

I grind out the rest of the time, and from Sarh base I fly to the capital, N'Djamena where I snag a couple souvenirs. Most noteworthy is the deep green malachite jewelry for my wife. Then it's onto the charter plane to Amsterdam before finally landing at Gatwick in London, whew—back in the first world. Security is really tight leaving Chad, and again I have to point out my bag. I make it—with no incidents, with my Chadian souvenirs to London. Nice people tell me to take the train not a cab. On the way into town I see the famous factory smoke stacks on Pink Floyd's *Animals* album cover. London is huge. Eight million people and the city spreads in every direction as far as you can see. I am lucky—the sun is out, partly cloudy, and probably won't rain. Good, because I don't have a coat.

I get to the Washington Sarova Hotel—very nice. Off a main street on a quiet back street just north of Buckingham Palace and next to Shepherd Market off Piccadilly Street. After checking in I get my camera and take off on a sightseeing tour. I walk across Hyde Park to Buckingham Palace. There are a surprising number of people crowded around the tall iron fence for this time of year. Maggie Thatcher is inside knighting someone and parliament is in session.

Next up is Westminster Abby, which is a fantastic old church with a number of different chapel sections. Ancient royalty are buried here, like Edward III, Elizabeth I, and others—you know, low-numbered royalty.

Then I walk and jog along the river past boats and bridges, Westminster Waterloo, to Black Friar's Pub, where I have a cold lager. I walk around the corner and up the hill to the huge St. Paul's Cathedral. Buried here are King James, Henry III, and military leaders. A magnificent sight inside; a very ornate altar, large wooden wall decorations, and high vaulted ceilings painted with various scenes. I climb the stairs high into the upper dome where I can look down into the church. Then I go still higher so I can see sweeping views of London from the balcony.

Afterward I catch a cab ride further up the river to the Tower of London, which is actually a large, rambling old castle with various displays of weapons, knights, armor, and the Crown Jewels. These old towers held prisoners until their death—like Sir Walter Raleigh. There were hangings and beheadings. The crown jewels are most impressive—massive gold pieces. There were also jeweled scepters with the huge star of Africa diamond and crowns. A lot of the military displays showed how England had empires all over the world such as India and Africa and the weapons of various wars.

Thanksgiving in Chad is Extra Boring

I hate being gone from home for Thanksgiving, but I find myself entering the heat of central Africa just in time to enjoy the holiday— oil business style. I had thought I would be gone earlier, but they want to drill deeper. It's a little depressing knowing I have twenty-three more days here, and it won't be very busy as drilling slows the deeper you go; it will be extra *boring*. I did bring a 9-iron golf club this time, which caused some people to cast a curious eye.

They made an effort at lunch by serving turkey with regular potatoes, white sweet potatoes, and some cranberry. I'm glad my wife and I had our own Thanksgiving dinner before I left Houston. I go for a short jog to smooth out after arriving in Chad. I am keeping a sharp eye out because they killed a six-foot *cobra* snake here a few days ago.

One day I get out of Sarh to visit the nearby village of Helibongo—a cluster of whitewashed buildings amid some mud houses. On the way back, we see the most interesting thing: A huge fire with about twenty-five large (two or three gallon) clay pots being fired in it. Three ladies are working. They pull a pot from the fire with a long stick then finish curing it by rolling it along the ground and throwing cotton seed hulls on it causing it to briefly burst into flames then blacken. Then another woman brushes across it with a branch of green leaves.

International Golf

When Greg finally shows up, I drag him around with me to the local hotel and later for a drive to Helibongo. I enjoy his company and we use my 9-iron to hit the ball around the compound. We get really creative and set up a six-hole course with circles in the dirt.

I have a couple guys with me playing the golf course. A guy Bob, got some orange tape and made outlines of "greens" by nailing it into the ground and putting a small flag in the middle. The longest hole is only eighty-eight yards, but it's much easier to see. We extended it to a nine hole, par twenty-two course.

After lunch I come back to see the radio operator Ron has made a score card with rules, notes, and a handicap system. It even has a course outline on the back. They built a small holder for our one club and three balls.

We tee off our new course. I currently hold the course record, one under par 21. There is a different touch to the course since it is all in either sand or hard packed, baked clay. The idea is to hit to the circle and stop the ball in the circle. Putting would be absurd.

Suddenly the Chari Meadows Golf and Country Club is born.

A few nights later we go out on the pretext of an "Ex-Pat Christmas Party," and after pool at the little bar in the textile factory, we're off to the Hotel in town for cold Galas and official business discussions of the Chari Meadows Golf and Country Club—rules, regulations, and officer elections. We hold an election for Club positions. Ron is Club President and I am head golf pro, "Nick Aldo" (the world wide well site fellows started calling me Aldo after that and the nickname stuck). After a few beers, singing every Christmas carol we can muster sounds like a good idea—we don't sound very good but at least we got the spirit.

One day I have to drive from one field well to another to call Houston. That's where the Merisat satellite hookup is. On the way back we stop at a village the road goes through. We see some women drawing water from a well. The wells here in the village are dug by hand, sixty to a hundred feet deep, sometimes more if necessary. Bill the medic is with me. He asks me to try filling the bucket or to go and pull up the rope. The girls get a big laugh out of that.

As we are messing around, we notice about twenty or thirty kids gathering to look at us. The rig had just moved through there a few days ago. Trucks with white people went by, but we apparently are the first to stop. I turn to look at the kids and make a funny face—they all burst out laughing. One other funny look and they are roaring with laughter. So I take a step toward them, and they run back, scared. Will and I act like we are leaving and they get closer. Whispering, "One, two, three..." we turn around, jump towards them, and they scatter, screaming. The old people laugh. These kids, too, have never seen white people up close, but we finally convince them to let us take some pictures with them. Amazing day.

I'm getting ready to leave and may not be back—so I stop by the first village I visited where I took pictures. I had them developed in the States and show them to the village people we had met before. They are glad to see us and the photos.

We find our soldier escort and say good-bye to the village. We pause on the way out so Bill can trade his cap for a nice woven wide brim hat. The guy says he made it in one day. Another photo session of three boys and their two cows pulling a wagon, then it is back to the rig. Funny to think in two days, we will be on a 737 headed for Amsterdam.

Heading out of Chad is uneventful. They have snow in Amsterdam (for the first time in five years). I talk to an older fellow who has traveled the world in the oil business. There's obviously a lot for me to learn of languages and various customs, yet I don't think I want to travel as much as he has.

Return to Chad

It's only Saturday, but I'm already thinking about Monday's departure. A summer in Houston, and now it's time to go again. I did get to play golf today at the Falls Resort Course and enjoyed working off the stress of the work week.

The fellows and I always talk about the fast bent grass greens. "If you are not careful, you will four putt." I don't win any bets that day, but I don't four putt either. I thought I would never come back to Chad when I left in December of last year, but apparently I need to make at least one more trip before I join the Thailand rotation next month.

The limo comes for me after a good jog with my wife. I'm all packed, and we're out back taking pictures when the phone rings. "The limo should be outside your door," the voice on the other side says. And there he is, knocking on the door.

Time to head back to Africa.

I kiss my wife, grab my stuff, and hop into the car for the 2:30 flight to Amsterdam. I meet Paul at the airport, a fellow geologist, who is going with me to Chad, along with four other guys from my company—which makes the flight fun.

After holing up in our Amsterdam day room and napping till noon, Paul and I set off on a train to town. Our tour includes a diamond shop, a first Heineken at what turns out to be a gay bar, a cigar store, bar number two, and a Van Gogh museum, then we meet up with the other guys downtown. We check out of the hotel, then stumble on to the chartered midnight flight to Chad. I sleep while they refuel in Palma and awake to a sunrise breakfast over the Sahara.

I see lots of familiar faces in Sarh—but the golf course is ruined from the rainy season. "We need you to design a new course," they tell me. "Hope you brought your golf course architect notebooks." Ha ha. I spend some time getting the golf course set up again. Chari Meadows III is an interesting par 32; some doglegs and shots over pipe racks plus water hazards. We have water hazards from the big mud holes left by tracks from the forklift and trucks during the rainy season.

Late Thursday, we spud an exploration well—that is lingo for the start of drilling, the first earth penetration of the well. It's the first well to test an undrilled structure that the team mapped out—with a closure that's about three by five miles in subsurface, which could be a good size field if filled with oil.

After a quick tour of the rig, I fly back to Sarh base. Nothing much is happening. I talk to Paul at the rig twice a day on the radio, work on some other things, eat, workout, and call Houston. I find myself giving the secretary Sofia a ride home most days. She lives here with her husband who runs a small store and tries to do good things as a missionary. I stop to look into their little store: Hardware supplies, stationary, and a few toys. I notice they have some new one-speed bikes, the old style, at $250 US. Apparently it's expensive to import these. I stay for a cup of coffee and get to meet the town doctor and surgeon who comes to visit. Sofia tells me it costs about 1000 CFA ($3 US) for a woman to have a baby here. A third of that is for the birth certificate. With a recent birth certificate, they are allowed to buy soap for the baby.

Apparently there is a new danger here in Chad since the last time I was here. The walk along the walls near the bar where we play pool and drink Gala beer take you under some large trees. There are a few security lights along the way, but something new since last year is the danger from a large group of egrets—birds. They look like white cow birds and they nest in one particular tree at night. If you happen to walk under their tree, it's possible they will use your head for target practice. Some people now wear hats for that very reason, and reportedly Dr. Sedigi ran under the tree clapping his hands to bomb the people behind him with bird shit. How funny.

We spend a lot of time talking about what would happen if we have to evacuate because of a military crisis. This is still a Muslim controlled country, and it would take seventeen hours to fly all the expatriates to Cameroon with two Twin Otters. The radio dispatcher says he would work to get everyone out then he would rather take his chances going underground in Sarh. He has worked here four years, knows locals and speaks fluent French. He fears flying with a group because of SAMs—surface to air missiles. He was in Libya in 1969 when Gaddafi took over. The camp boss was in Somalia not long ago and they had to evacuate. I am glad I'm switching to the Thailand team—a much more stable place.

I get to learn a lot more about Chad. About 2,500 years ago when Pericles was eating on the floor of the Greek Senate, Lake Chad was almost as large as present-day Greece and Yugoslavia combined. It even connected with the Nile. The area was much wetter, and wild animals were abundant. Because of this, some of the richest prehistoric archaeological sites in Africa are found within the Chad boarders, especially in the far north around Tibesti where there are rock art engravings.

Lake Chad has been shrinking since then.

The prehistoric people known to live around the lake are collectively called Sao. They migrated from the Nile valley. In the ninth century, a king was declared and the state of Kanem lasted for a thousand years. Chad was an intersection point for two major African caravan routes. They trade in salt, copper, cotton, gold, and slaves, which brought increasing contact with the Muslim world. By 1200 AD, Islam was the dominant religion.

The kingdom known as Kanem-Bornu expanded, with an economy dominated by slave trade, which peaked in the 1600s. Other lesser Arab kingdoms flourished during the 1800s. The black people in southern Chad had a decentralized government so they were easy prey for the better-organized Arab groups who rounded them up with cavalry. The French conquered southern Chad in the early 1900s and were popular for ending the slave trade. Resistance lasted until 1930 in the north. The northerners lost out in World War II when Italy, which ruled Libya, and the pro-Nazi Vichy government of France signed a treaty giving Libya the Aouzou strip in northern Chad. This is why they fought the Libya-Chad War. The Aouzou strip was thought to contain decent volumes of mine resources—probably copper, gold, and zinc. Chad was a French colony until 1960 when it gained independence.

Good Bye Sarh Base Compound

I am nearly finished with my last big workout the day before I leave. I run and jump rope then strain to lift the makeshift weights of welded metal bars, auto rims, and scrap iron. I lift my eyes to the pale blue sky. The hot midday sun does not quite blot out the buzzards circling over the garbage pit.

I'm on the edge of the portable trailer village. A kitchen helper comes out and dumps some garbage. The huge birds begin swooping down and landing, one after another—black with scruffy gray white chests and a red throat decoration hanging under their heads. There must be thirty on the ground now with twenty or more still circling overhead.

As I hang from the bar, a bright green snake slithers quickly under one of the trailers nearby.

Soon I will get away from this Sarh Base compound. I try not to talk about it in front of guys who have to stay longer, but it's now hard to sleep at night I'm so ready to get up and go. Some guys boast about it in front of anyone, but they've been here four or five weeks, some eight weeks depending on what company they work for. My company is great about taking care of their people and allowing us short tours and good support, compared to most oil field service companies.

The day I leave we fly two hours to Ndjamena—walking across the tarmac feels like an oven. I find out later it had hit 43 Celsius (109 F). Wow!

As we fly across the Mediterranean Sea after dark, I can see orange dots from 35,000 feet where they are burning the gas from wells in Algeria, near the north coast of Africa. The gas has such little value so it is burned in order to get the oil production up since it all comes out of the ground together.

In Amsterdam again, I finally make it to my hotel, we get in about 4:30 am and I have to wait until 6:00 am to get a KLM hotel voucher and catch the downtown train. I take a cruise along the canals and out into the harbor, which is very scenic. I learn that Amsterdam was named for a guy who put a dam on the Amstel River.

I land in Houston, where my wife has cancelled the limo to pick me up. I'm ready to see her. I have the biggest bunch of red and yellow tulips you can imagine. It's great to be home, even as big and hot as Houston is.

Chapter 4
The Many People of China

February, 1990

It's 8:00 a.m. Thursday and I'm sitting in our berth in Hong Kong harbor waiting to ride the ferry to Shekou, China. Hong Kong harbor is shrouded in fog and we just sway back and forth as we wait.

My wife helped me pack and I left Houston Monday afternoon then flew to San Francisco. This leaving for nearly a month at a time is getting old for both of us. When I left Houston it had been rainy and cold, which caused some golf match rainouts. When I return it will be green and warm.

The Hong Kong harbor is littered with a variety of seagoing vessels and all around are tall buildings—with more on the way, and people–there are people everywhere. A large flock of pink flamingos were walking around a pond and up some steps. On the top of the hill was a circular bird zoo with a variety of exotic birds just across an elevated walkway from my hotel. In the area around the Kowloon Hotel where I stayed, I passed shop after shop of cameras, watches, jewelry, and clothes. Large shops dominate on the bigger streets, tiny backstreet shops packing in the cracks, block after block—it's amazing. You can walk to the waterfront and look across the channel to Hong Kong Island. It is crowded along the water's edge with numerous tall buildings, which quickly give way to steep pointed hills behind.

Time to go to work. We finally make a morning bow wave headed from Hong Kong for Shekou, Peoples Republic of China. Our boat hugs the coastline, which for the entire one hour ride was steep green hills with occasional buildings—and all kinds of boats in the water from large ships to small junks.

After docking, I have to clear customs. I fill out a health form and get in line to show passports and visas. There are guards in green uniforms with a large white sign above them with Chinese calligraphy and two large red stars.

In the chaos of arrival I manage to miss Greg Coleman—who I worked with in Chad, and the other people from the office. I am feeling a bit lost and threatened by the possibility of culture shock. We finally hook up and drive over to the hotel, then it's off to the office where I meet all the folks. American manager, drilling engineers and numerous Chinese workers—accountants, secretaries and the like.

Shekou itself is an industrial town of about fifty thousand. The hotel and our office building are nice by Chinese standards—they had foreigners in mind. The rest of the town we can see from our office is white and gray buildings packed in close around narrow streets. I can see more bike riders than car drivers. From my hotel window I see patterns of rectangle-shaped wooden things just above the water's surface in the bay—cultured oyster beds. For some reason I find the view calming.

After work we enjoy a cocktail hour at the company's China president—in honor of the company doctor who was visiting from headquarters. Roger's house had an impressive display of Chinese furniture and art pieces. He tells me he has spent nearly five years in China on two different assignments. After drinks we all have dinner at a village restaurant—Nam Shan Tsui Hang, usually called the Round Restaurant. They serve us a normal variety of food. I'm glad they didn't try to make me eat any fried baby birds or pig skin. After dinner some of us walk over to the expatriate bar—the Snake Pit, for a nightcap. I'm in China now.

Upper Level Management Politics & Hash

It's been overcast and rainy since I got to China. As I get into work, we find out management had called and said not to start drilling the well. That's all we know. It might be a corporate shakeup. We just don't know. All we know is that we already spent over a million dollars moving the rig out into the ocean and setting the anchors. The following day it turns out it was simply upper level management politics. All the things needed to approve for drilling hit a senior vice president's desk at once with the rig already on location. He blew up and called the big managers in HQ for a royal ass chewing. We got approval to proceed after waiting only nine hours.

That afternoon, a meeting of the Shekou Hash House Harriers happens at the Snake Pit. A group of us, men and women, hop in a couple of vans and head out of town. We drive by a number of factories and tall apartment buildings and notice scaffolding on most of the new construction is made of bamboo.

The start of the running race, or "event" is out in the country, and will take place over low, rolling hills among some peasant farms. About twenty or thirty of us take off up the trail with the plan of following the trail of shredded paper to reach a check point. If you run and hit a dead end, you go back to take the other fork in the road. I personally manage to run at least three hills that are false trails.

I love getting to see the countryside. We run by quite a few farm folks who stopped to watch us crazy Americans yelling, "On. On." We yell to encourage the people behind us that we are "on trail" as we emulate an old-fashioned English fox chase. I see some boys pedaling bicycles with baskets on the back packed with chickens for market, farmers tending their fields, and women drawing water.

The biggest drama of the afternoon comes when a dog that is running with us chases a chicken and manages to get a mouthful of feathers before I stop him. He also jumps in a baby duck pen, but I grab him before he can make the catch.

The race takes about an hour, and I come in first. All of us are covered with mud and are very wet, but we are all enthusiastic as we make the traditional circle to make people chug beers for various violations of the rules. I only get nailed for five violations.

The party moves back to the Snake Pit where we have some food, lots more beer, and even some dancing in our running outfits. It's pretty wild; but I enjoy it while I can, because I will be stuck on the rig soon enough.

Offshore, it takes a few days before the waves settle at sea and I'm able to travel to the rig. I tried to make the best of it—waiting onshore; getting a haircut and enjoying the scenery and the people—us Westerners are still a bit of a novelty in the mass of Chinese people. Cemented into the beach area near the hotel is an old cruise ship with a number of shops and restaurants built into it. I take long runs through the local areas of town past fishing boats and the local shops. I stand out in my bright jacket running through the rain; most of the locals wear a lot of black relieved only by some white and gray. I rarely see any colorful clothes, but aside from being poor most of the people seem happy.

Soon enough I'm off to the rig. We get out of the car at an industrial shoreline staging area where we board a chopper, a hefty unit capable of carrying some supplies and eight to ten people.

The flight out takes about an hour and a half through the clouds to a spot just over one hundred miles from shore where we land on the helipad on the offshore floating rig.

Offshore

I've just about gotten use to the swaying motion of this semi-submersible drilling rig I'm sitting on. They tell me that whales have been seen swimming around the rig.

The rig is a bit old and small but it's still interesting. Built in 1974, it has seven huge anchors holding it in place in just over four hundred feet of water. A system compensates for waves and tides so that the rig can go up and down and not interrupt the drilling process—amazing. Even though it's "small" it still sits seventy feet above the water line when anchored down. It is semi-submersible, which means we are floating. Expatriates like myself hold a few leading roles, but the Chinese supply the drilling crews. Add the Australians and folks from the United Kingdom, and this is truly an international outfit.

One of the Australians, Chips, gave me an earful during a bull shit session about one time when the rig got blown a couple hundred yards off the hole during a typhoon. It took them forever to find the marker with the ROV. He says not to worry, though, if a typhoon whips up, geologists (non-essential to the operations part of the business) are evacuated from the rig on the first chopper out.

I'm enjoying meeting the people aboard. The head mechanic, a Scottish fellow is named Billy McGregor. As soon as we meet he says, "Hold the Star Trek jokes about Scotty, the engineer on board the

Enterprise." Ha. He gives me an earful about how Scottish people invented TV, hospitals, and have been president of the United States eleven times. Later he gives me a fine blue wool cap that says "The Bruntsfield Links Golfing Society, 1761,", which is from the third oldest course in the world. Luckily, I have a white American Golf Club hat to trade him. He says he was going to give it to me anyway, but when he took my hat, he laughed and said, "Ha ha. Just like all American stuff—crap."

Life at Sea

I am looking over the railing one morning and see a couple of fishing boats working the area. Even though we are one hundred miles from shore, apparently this isn't uncommon.

Billy walks up and says, "Yep, the Chinese are good seaman, but soon it will be time for the Vietnamese boat to show up—tiny boats packed with people all trying to get on the rig saying, 'USA.' They think we are all Americans, so watch out—they may try to give you a baby. 'Here, you keep.' It's a sad thing to see."

"When we first took over this rig, it had boxes of guns on it," Billy explains. "The Chinese and the Vietnamese have argued for years over disputed waters the ocean borders. The damn British, who control Hong Kong, say the Vietnamese boat people are economic refugees, not political, so they send them back. When they get back to Vietnam, they get tossed in jail for five to ten years. Sounds political to me."

We stand there quiet for a few minutes, and eventually he says, "We will try fishing off the rig when the seas calm down. We can pull in big sharks, tuna, and other big fish. The crew boys like to dry the fish with salt and take them home."

I'm entering my cabin as the young Chinese boy who cleans the cabins is leaving and I finally get a chance to talk with him. He knows just enough English to try to ask me a few things, such as where I'm from and if I am married. It's hard to puzzle out what he's saying, but his English is better than my Chinese. I show him a picture of my wife, and he says, "Pitty." ("Pretty"). Our conversation reminds me of my very first trials in speaking Spanish—the uncertainty in the pauses between words. Still, I enjoy the exchange.

Chinese geologist crew change: two geologists take the chopper out after Shen arrives. A sunny day. I celebrate by running an extra mile. Ha. About twenty-five times around the helideck is one mile. I also have my jump rope and Greg's golf club to practice my swing. It is still like being in prison here—not that I know that first hand, I just imagine it from what I know of prison life from the movies.

Our brief window of sun is gone fast, and clouds and rain move in. The wind picks up, and soon the waves are rocking us. Of course, the drillers say it's nothing, but, the barge master, gives me an orientation—shows me around the lifeboat hoists, engine beacons, emergency air, water spray system, provisions, water, rope, guns, radios, bilge pumps, and the like. It pays to be safe.

The days are creeping by, and I've been working from 4:00 a.m. to 4:00 p.m. every day with the Chinese geologists covering the opposite shift. At 10:30 p.m. I call my wife—it's 8:30 a.m. Houston time. I'm glad to hear all is well there. She is working, keeping herself busy and her mind off being alone. We are both more than ready for me to get back.

The food remains a sticking point—they try to serve us Western-style food most nights, but sometimes the Chinese catering crew pulls a fast one. I skip the ox tail stew and eat fried rice one night and am happy to know I missed the braised tongue and French Fries they served for the midnight meal.

The last few days creep by, and I'm just praying there are no storms on my departure day Thursday.

The day I leave I get to live twice. It goes like this: Up before the sun to write my geology report on the rig. The chopper lands and Greg my replacement is aboard. We change over and I take off at noon Thursday. We fly an hour and a half landing in Shekou on the Chinese mainland. I stop by the office to pick up some stuff, pick up my ferry ticket, and say hello and goodbye to everyone. After a little shopping, I ride the ferry back to Hong Kong and from there I'm flying across the date line. I wake up in San Francisco and it's still Thursday.

Heading West to Get East

I have a good break back home in Houston, then it's off to the Far East—for offshore rig duty. The time at home was nice, the house seems to be in good shape, chores are done, repairs made, cars maintained and taxes paid. Lucky for me my wife can take care of herself.

"Will passenger David Allard please come to the gate area?" This comes over the intercom in San Francisco—oh no, what has happened. Turns out it's just a United Airlines agent to walk me from the Continental gate to United's first-class lounge in the international terminal. I'm fixing myself a drink when I get another surprise: "David Allard?" I turn around to see Chip Miller, the drilling rig supervisor who I worked with in Guatemala. He is on his way to China too.

We sit together on the flight out and talk about our passion; golf. Chip is good, a two handicap. Two movies, two meals, and fourteen hours later we are standing in Hong Kong.

I get a fourteenth floor hotel room with a partial view of the harbor. I got enough sleep on the flight between the two movies and meals that I feel like going out and doing some shopping. I bargain for a few good deals but still end up buying someone else's shirt from the tailor—it still has their initials on the sleeve.

I get a suit from a Pakistani tailor with Chinese workers in the shop, then I pick up some frames and lenses for about $80 that would have cost me twice that in Houston. Camera in hand, I take the ten-minute boat ride across the harbor to Hong Kong Island Central District. I really want to walk in the Western District, a regular Chinese shopping area, to take some photos. I leave the Central District and start to see more high-rise apartments and small Chinese shops, I even find the "thieves" market where people spread their stuff on blankets on the ground right in front of very nice stores.

I find the Man Mo Temple. This temple is dedicated to two gods that are generally to protect the well-being of men—Man (civil) and Mo (martial). King Emperor Man and Holy King Emperor Kwan were at one time real living persons who eventually became regarded as gods or saints.

Cheung Ahtse (alias Tsetung) was born in 287 AD in the Chin Dynasty. He had jurisdiction over government officials and was later an emperor of the Yuan Dynasty, which titled him Kin Emperor Man Cheong. Holy King Emperor Kwan in life was Kwan Yue (or Kwan Wan-Cheung), born in 160 AD. He was dedicated to the support of the Kingdom of Shu. He was a famous warrior hero, becoming the personification of loyalty and righteousness. The temple was built in the mid 1800s.

They use two elaborately carved chairs with some gold plating to carry statues of "Man" and "Mo" when there is a parade. There is a center shrine at the back with the two figures and an elaborate red tapestry hung at the sides and top. There are a lot of lights across the shrine. Its various other statue figures are brass with gold decorations. There are offerings of fruit left by people in front of it. Another table is covered with burning candles and incense. Locals and tourists frequent the temple. Three old beggar women are by the door hunched over, one sporting only one eye. I give them some money.

I have to cover the office at Shekou for a week, wrangling the phone and calling back and forth between the rig, where Greg is, and Houston, which seems to want constant updates even though the extra information rarely changes what we are doing on the operations side. We probably spend a couple hundred dollars a day talking to Houston and faxing pages of reports.

The weather is still overcast but warmer. Looks like good golf weather. There is a course in the neighboring town of Shenzen. The accounting controller, Jim Wozniak, is an avid golfer—we leave the office at noon to go play. We meet up with two other guys, Doug from Chevron and Rick from Weatherford Pipe Company. The course is fairly nice—surprisingly, sitting here in an industrial area, which ten years ago was just a fishing village. We have female caddies who wear uniforms. I shoot a 92, which is not my best.

Nan Hai West and Nan Hai East are Chinese companies that help us with people at the office. They don't get paid much, but we pay them a living allowance that is more than their salary. This makes them loyal, hard workers. My secretary, Xiao Dan, stays an hour late to finish some typing, no problem. Heck, the radio/fax guy worked straight through supper until 9:00 p.m. with me one night.

Chang Kuang, the geologist, is from Nan Hai East—on loan to our company for this operation. We pay Nan Hai East $500 a month for him—certainly he is paid much less than that. Even though his wife works here as our receptionist they can't even afford to live together—Chang Kuang has to share a place with three other guys and his wife with three other girls. It may be a short assignment for me, but it could be as long as ten months.

Before I leave for the rig, I get another round of golf in. I get someone to cover for me at the office—I've been putting in late nights, so I don't feel bad about this at all. I meet up with Jim downstairs to get in a quick eighteen holes. It is overcast and they're worried about rain, but it's warm. It looks liked I was going to win some money from Jim, but he comes back on the last three holes. One particular incident occurred when I took a mighty swing on a par 3, only to see the club head of the six iron fly farther than the ball—both of which plopped into the water hazard. I asked for a do-over shot and Jim was quick to say oh no, play it as it lies—that's the rules of golf. I took a drop, hitting 3, lost that hole and the bets of the day.

Floating Hunk of Metal

On the chopper flight out you can see the coastline winding around Shekou out to Hong Kong, and I can see Macau off to the right as we fly away from the mainland. Goodbye land, hello floating metal hunk that I will live on for the next two weeks. Being a well site geologist is not always glamorous.

I'm under pressure right away—should we take another core of the reservoir rock formation? It costs upwards of $80,000 a day to operate, and pulling the sixty foot core of rock will take a day and a half. We have already cut two cores on this well and have not seen any really good oil shows. The prospect-generating group in Houston is not keen on spending more coring money unless we see a good show of hydrocarbons.

57

After replacing our worn-out bit, we drill about a hundred more meters, with no shows. This was the primary target, and I am the first person to realize that we have probably drilled an $80,000,000 dry hole.

Talking with some of the guys on the rig gives me an interesting understanding of how the Chinese see Americans—as a mixed "mongrel" race of inferior barbarians. The Chinese have been isolated and an unmixed race for thousands of years. Their high opinions of themselves don't make their workers any happier—many are very unhappy, and the government tells them their jobs and even splits up their marriages as it sees fit for job placement. Some couples may only see each other once or twice a year.

My Chinese geologist friend, Chang Kuang got married four years ago. He lives in Guangzhou where they have been waiting four years for an apartment. The company was to find a place for them. Chang says that is an unusually long time to wait, but there seems to be a shortage lately.

Chang and I have a plan to visit Guangzhou when I get off the rig. I hope it works out. The other geologist, Qian arrives to replace Chang. I tell him that this well looks bad and that we may be done here in a week and probably won't drill another. He says, "That is good for me. I will get to see my baby. I went abroad to London for training for a year then I have been working for my company. I have not seen my baby for a year and a half."

Liang is a very smart, university-educated man. Amazing, only five percent of the general Chinese people have the chance to go to college, yet even with his privileged education, he has never heard of the Rolling Stones or The Beatles.

Things are worse in-country—living conditions are third-world primitive, the technology and techniques are seventy-five years out of date. Some areas in central China are used to send workers (deemed as bad citizens) for "re-education." Glad I'm here on this rig.

Jim, the mud engineer, shares some stories from when he was on a team for a drilling company hired to go help drill wells in Central China where nearly every well drilled blew out. Blow outs are sudden bursts of pressure that can push pipe out of the hole, burst into huge fires and kill people. He says the Chinese in this area drill into the target and let the wells blow out on purpose in order to encourage oil production. They are not concerned with safe well control practices. They divert the blow out to a side pipe into a large pit in the dirt and let the oil spew into it. Trucks then come and suck it out of the pit. If the pit over flows, they just try to dam up a ravine down the mountain side and catch some of it for trucks to get there. Jim says when you drive up to this mountain you see black spills all over it. Trucking is much more expensive than setting a pipe line, not to mention what is lost in the dirt.

Jim says when they tried to teach them blow out prevention the Chinese laughed and said, "You scared?" "We have many more men in China." Oh yes, and the local town sheriff made many visits insisting that the expatriates say how much they make so they can pay the sheriff forty-two percent in "tax." Corruption. At the end of the job, they were not allowed to leave until a Drilling Company Manager came from Beijing with cash in a briefcase.

A Sneeze

One day when I sneeze, the Chinese geologist, Qian, says, "Your family misses you." That is the Chinese saying when you sneeze. Love it. Well, he is right. I talk to my wife today, and I can't wait to get back home myself.

I saw a large school of fish off one side of the rig today. Even though it was eighty feet down to the water's surface you can still see the shapes moving in the water and occasionally the shiny flat side of a fish reflects the sun. Then I spot a Chinese guy on a lower deck with a line in the water. He later pulled in about a fifteen pound fish. He had managed to yank it away from a group of sharks—most small but a couple were five or six feet long. Makes me glad for the work boat that sits within site of the rig in case we have to abandon it because of a blowout or fire.

We keep drilling and start getting ten to fifteen units of gas show out of the first part of the drill break. J.D., the company supervisor, says, "Crap, who farted? Let's drill." But I say back, "Let's wait for it all." It takes over an hour and a half for the stuff we just drilled to get to the surface. The last two meters came up, and boom—sixty, seventy, ninety-four units. That's usually not much, but on a relative scale, that's more than they ever saw in the offset discovery well eleven kilometers away. Let's core.

Sunday night when I'm on the rig floor while we were cutting the core, I am standing in the drillers control room. There are all kinds of levers, gauges, etc. but there is also a video monitor screen. They have a camera four hundred feet down under water at the well head on bottom. This camera is so you can actually see the well head so if there is a blowout or leak you may see it on the screen. All I saw was about a five foot long fish swimming by. There are buttons to push so you can move the camera around.

It gets frustrating sometimes here at the well. We figure out where we are in the stratigraphy or how we want to run the logging program. Then you tell the guy in the venture office and he talks to Houston, who then has to have meetings about it and let you know what they want to do. If the managers in Houston want something or are interested in an idea, it's no big deal to call in the middle of the night. If it's real important, at least you hear about it the same day. They want the answers quick. When we are logging they have to have all the data faxed to them to make big decisions. These are big money wells, but I'm used to the old west Texas days when I would evaluate the whole well myself, call the office, and recommend to test or plug it.

We get the core up, out, and described, then packed to send back to the Chinese oil company. We need their evaluation as soon as possible, so the rock core is boxed up and on the chopper in the afternoon, but I'm still working away till early evening.

The core effort is the hardest I have worked on this hitch; I may leave before we start the electric logging. This work is interesting but this rig reminds me of a floating prison, and I'll be happy to leave.

GuangzhouTrip

I get away just as another coring operation begins, leaving that for my relief to figure out, and get back to Shekoh.

Chang is there and ready for our trip. I go to get the driver and hit the trail. It's a long ride to Guangzhou. It's only 120k (seventy-two miles), but traffic makes it slow in the afternoon.

We drive along through town after town, rice paddies, fields with an occasional water buffalo, and some small hills. All the towns look similar. Guangzhou has 3.5 million people and taxis may not be ready at the exact time we want to rush to another place, so we keep the driver with us as we pull into Guangzhou about 8:15 p.m.—four hours or so travel time to go seventy-two miles.

Guangzhou has a long history—it's 2,800-plus years old. We would know it better by the name Canton. In the mid 1800s, big sailing ships—mostly British—traded for silk, tea, and opium in huge volume here. The Chinese are right—in America we have only ancient Native American ruins with any comparable long term history.

After a great meal of dim sum food in a place frequented by locals we go to Chang's apartment—he has roommates. It's very small and basic—I somehow expected him as a government geologist to live better.

In the morning we drive along the Pearl River into the Shamian area, which is separated from the main town by a canal. This is the actual place where foreigners were allowed to be in a compound years ago for trading. The old buildings in this area have European styles unlike the rest of Canton. Chang points out the old office and living quarters where the company was for the drilling campaigns in the 1980s. After breakfast we go to the Qing Ping market, something I had on the top of my list of things to see in Guangzhou. The market is actually just some closed streets with people selling things on both sides of the street. It's hard to walk because of all the people here to do their shopping. Make no mistake, this is a locals market with an impressive variety of vegetables, red meat, live animals including dogs, turtles etc. Oh my, I try not to stare. We then drive to the Six Banyan Pagoda Temple. Chang even has an itinerary typed up for me, and last weekend he checked to see when things were open and how far apart they were. Since we have a car, we can easily make it to everything; what a guy. He was really glad to have me visit his town. He even bought me a gift of Chinese cork art.

At the temple, we buy tickets to enter and climb the temple. Time is running short, so we go straight into the center pagoda structure and race to the top—eight stories up. This gave a good view of the city. Buildings are packed closely together in every direction as far as you can see. This Liurong Temple, the Temple of the Six Banyan trees, was first built about 537 A.D. during the Liang Dynasty. At one time it was named in honor of the nearby banyan trees. But originally, it was built under orders from the emperor as a pagoda under which Buddhist bones are buried.

Next we go to the Guangzhou temple. In the courtyard on the inside a policeman is standing by an archeology dig. This temple is the oldest and biggest in South China. In the second century B.C., it was the residence of the King of the Southern Yue Kingdom. An official from the state of Wai was in exile in the south and lived there during the period of Three Kingdoms. When this Yufan died, the place was donated as a Buddhist temple about 400 A.D. A high monk from Pakistan came to Guangzhou and had a Buddhist hall built on the site.

We walk in the entrance and up to the main hall, where we stumble upon a group of monks in some kind of service inside. They're chanting with the beat of a ceramic drum, standing, kneeling, and saying things.

I buy a few pieces at the souvenir shop, and then we're rushing out to the driver who's waiting outside so we can get me to my train. There's a lot of traffic but just as I'm getting nervous it breaks and we're suddenly at the train station. The driver leaves us at the curb and I put some cash in his hand when I shake it. He tries to give it back but I make him take it. Chang walks me over to the entrance gate and I say goodbye to a great host and new friend.

I walk up a ramp area by a gate. Maybe I should show my passport to the guards on the side? But I hear Chang yell, "Keep going, Dave." I turn raise my arms and then walk on.

Customs gets a little hairy, but finally the lady who is checking me through—she knows just enough English to give me trouble—lets me through just in time to catch my train back to Hong Kong.

All of the stuff I ordered before I got to the rig is ready, so I get busy picking it all up—my shirts and glasses, some Cuban cigars, and a few other things. I have tickets for the hydrofoil boat that evening to Macaw. It surges to a roar and zips across the water, by the harbor, the many islands, across the huge mouth of the Pearl River, and into Macaw. It is a small, coastal section on lease to Portugal. It's over four hundred years old and was a trade center at some point. Now, it's known for gambling. It's getting dark quick.

I walk around and get a couple photos and then go into the Lisboa Casino and Hotel for a steam in the sauna and a massage. In the room are two women in white nurse outfits. Half the time they use their hands, and the other half they walk on me with various levels of foot pressure by holding onto the bars on the ceiling. It's so good I fall asleep on the jet boat back to Hong Kong. I didn't gamble—the only game I recognized was blackjack with a minimum bet of 100 HK (about $12.50 US.) It's hard to win when you run out of money after a few bets.

I fly out of Hong Kong the next morning and land in San Francisco sixteen hours later but the same time as my departure—10:00 a.m. Saturday Ron, a former co-worker of mine in San Francisco, is there to meet me. We drive across the Bay Bridge, which is still standing after the earthquake, to Walnut Creek and played golf at Diablo Hills. It's a little nine hole course but we play through twice. Later I see the quake damage on some buildings in the area. That night I stay with my brother Bill Allard and his wife, Margaret. It is great to catch up.

I take a 1:30 am flight—what an odd time.—and get home early; in time to walk into my front door at 7:45 am and surprise my wife.

Typhoon Alert

I'm home just a few weeks and it's time to go back to China. Hanging out in Hong Kong after I land, I get a call from Greg that the offshore operations are shut down for a typhoon alert. There's a strong storm north of the rig, and they evacuated. Even when they do get back on the rig it will be two or three days of work before they can drill ahead. "You may as well spend another night in Hong Kong," he tells me.

Well, don't mind if I do. I enjoy a long run through the streets followed by a rooftop swim. It's cloudy but warm. I take the Star Ferry across to Hong Kong Island and from there a cab to the other side of the island to visit Aberdeen. As we drive out, I take note of Central and Wanchai areas of interest for the way back. From what I had read, I expected a small town with thousands of house boats in the harbor. When we pop out of the tunnel, I see tall high-rise apartments. The taxi lets me off by the boat clubs at the end of town—I can't even see the water.

I hire a motorized sampan, a low, and narrow boat, to drive me around on a tour of the harbor. She asks for 80 HK, but I get her down to 60 HK. We go by the marine shops and boat builders with raw timber piled outside their shops. The boat builders work by eye, no plans. The harbor is packed with boats, and people are working on their boats or just hanging out. Some kids are swimming. I see a group of young men taking out a long boat, a dragon boat, with paddle power and a large drum at the front. A light rain falls as we make our way back, stopping in front of an ornate floating restaurant, where we dock. I'm tired, so I call it an evening.

In the morning the pool is closed as a precaution for the typhoon alert. The ferries are running so I catch the 10:15 to Shekou. After checking into my hotel I bring by a stack of newspapers to Greg and his wife so they can see some current news. They live in a very nice apartment provided by the company. The offshore rig is still evacuated, but the storm seems to be headed back out to sea.

We will send men back on Saturday. The drilling guys have to test the blowout preventers and new casing before they can begin to drill. Geology people won't need to go out until next week. I wish I could have stayed in Hong Kong a while longer.

I get to run a hash and generally take it easy while we wait for things to get settled down. Even when we head to the office we aren't there long. Greg and Janie have me over a lot, which is a lifesaver while here in boring Shekou. I get in some golf with Greg, and Janie who just likes to go for the walk. I send Chang and Qian out to the well on Friday, and because of some setbacks I won't go out until Wednesday. Sometimes days just add up while waiting to progress with drilling operations. That's ok, I am happy waiting onshore instead of on the floating rig.

Thursday June 31, I get back out to the rig. I brought line and hooks I bought in Aberdeen (China) two weeks ago, but the new camp boss, Ben—probably no relation to his Chinese name—says the forty-pound test line I bought won't be strong enough. The fish I would catch here could be huge—even an average fish would be nearly three feet long.

We start drilling Friday afternoon and by Saturday we have worn out our bit and are tripping out to get a new one. We are over fifteen thousand feet deep now, true vertical, so it takes nearly twenty hours to go all the way out and back in. The temperature is about 350 degrees at the bottom.

I try some fishing using the line I brought with me, and sure enough, it's not strong enough. Specifically, these fish have teeth, and they bite through the line. I keep getting a nibble and then nothing, and the fish gets away with my bait and hook. I try to use a metal coat hanger to keep them from biting through the line. Ben the camp boss comes out with one hundred pound line and a big grin.

"I tie this one because I am fisherman." he says. And, promptly, we get no more bites for the day.

The really great thing is that because of the typhoon warning and the time I spent on land, I'm already almost done on the rig. Yay! I'll soon be headed back home.

This looks like the last time I'll pull a hitch on this well. Things have changed here in drilling operations. We began drilling at 4,877 m in the 6" hole and it took off. We've drilled to 4,910 before the trip gas starts coming up. We are so deep that it takes over two and a half hours for something drilled at the bit to reach the surface. Gas shows came up in 1,500 units in the surface detectors, and continued after reaming to the bottom of the drilled section. So we stop at 4,910 to circulate and build mud weight from 11.3+12ppg. We drill a little deeper and are moving pipe up and down when the drill string rips apart leaving the bit and some pipe stuck down hole.

We go in to pull it out only to find it has broken off lower down as well. So we go back in with an overshot and grab the remainder of it— we hope. They are coming to surface, but we fly out on the chopper before we can see if they have it all. We should be able to drill the last

300 meters and run logs before I need to come back for this well. Things get tough when you are working about three miles deep and in a six inch hole.

Greg says he doesn't think we will drill another well based on the late info, but you never know for sure until the last minute with exploration.

I'm so eager to leave, a restless night before I depart. I definitely don't do as well on a floating rig as on a land operation. There's not much change in scenery and no opportunity to explore the surrounding area. I can't wait to hear the sound of the chopper landing on the helipad above us.

And then it's here, and I'm off again. One last stop in Hong Kong then on to San Francisco where I visit my brother and his family on my layover. I catch the 1:30 am from San Francisco after a great dinner and land in Texas just after sun-up. It is so good to be home.

Chad oil field landing strip

People of southern Chad

Hong Kong family fishing boat

David Allard

Golf swing practice on an offshore rig, South China Sea

Qing Ping market, Guangzhou, China

Ocean Sunrise over oyster farm and Chinese junk, Shekou, China

Chapter 5
Thailand Temples

November, 1990

I am waiting in Taipei, Taiwan, to board the last flight of my journey to Bangkok, Thailand. From what I hear, Thailand is a great place to visit. Word is that there will be working in Bolivia, Pakistan, Trinidad, Russia, and West Africa in the next year or so, so I have no idea where I will go.

My wife and I just finished a nice four day vacation with her family for Thanksgiving. I will fly from Texas to San Francisco and on to Thailand. This one is not as hard a goodbye, even though I'll be in Thailand for Christmas, because on December 7 she will join me there for a visit—which I'm excited about.

I've had lots of practice sleeping on airplanes now, so I'm able to get some rest and enjoy a few cocktails on the flight—it's more than thirteen hours. I fly United at 1:00 p.m. Monday to arrive Taipei, Taiwan on Tuesday at 6:45 p.m. The three hour flight to Bangkok goes fast because I'm sitting next to Tom, an international marketing manager who travels all over the world and spends a lot of time in Southeast Asia and the Middle East. We talked about culture, and government corruption like he experienced in Indonesia, where the guy he was to be in contact with was thrown into jail before the deal could go down.

As I'm clearing customs in Bangkok, I'm glad to see someone waiting for me. He has my name written on the sign, and he has a car ready to go. By 11:00 p.m. I'm in the plush Dusit Thani Hotel in downtown Bangkok. My body is telling me it is noon, so instead of trying to sleep I walk over to the world-famous Patpong Road to see the nightlife. Even at this late hour, the streets are jammed with vendors and people milling all over. There are all kinds of things for sale, but I settle for having a couple drinks and going back to the hotel. It's still hard to sleep, but I manage to get a few hours.

The hotel staff shows me a 1.6 mile loop in the park, and knowing that it is important to run early in Bangkok because of traffic and pollution, I decided to go for a 6:30 a.m. outing and find a surprising number of other people working out. A girl on top of a truck leads hundreds of people in aerobics to the beat of loud music blasting out of a big speaker system, and during my entire jog there are no fewer than five people on either side of me. I see older people doing tai chi and many others just enjoying being outside.

Later among the din of heavy traffic I walk down the busy streets to work arriving in time for the morning meeting of geologists, drillers, engineers, and management. Afterward I'm able to give my wife a call and tell her I made it ok and will pick up our tickets for her visit. My visa situation is complicated but by simply leaving the country and coming back I can reinstate my fifteen day temporary visa. A shopping trip to Singapore is in the plans.

I watch a number of locals greeting one another, and I notice how they put their hands together in front of them like they were praying. I learn that the higher you hold your hands, the more respect you have for the people you are greeting.

The day after I get in I hop on another flight about an hour long to northern Thailand, Khan Kaen province. The driver meets us at the airport for the twenty minute ride to the rig, which is just outside the town. The area here is mostly covered with rice fields; I see cows and even water buffalo. Its harvest time, so there are a lot of people out in the fields.

Ronnie is the geologist I am here to relieve, he has been here almost two weeks and is ready to go into town. He introduces me around and brings me up to date.

We are currently at 10,411' trying to run logs before we set casing and drill ahead. The hole is deviated as planned but is a bit crooked, so we can't get the logging tools below 8,360'. By early afternoon we give up so the drillers can run the drill pipe back in the hole and try to clean it out. Before he flies out for Bangkok, Ronnie showed me how to run the little computer we have here to do our reports.

The well I am on is deviated because our target depth in the subsurface lies directly under the village of Baug Wuan Huang (which translates to mean "village of sweet mango"). Rather than hurt the village, we just located off to the side and are drilling at an angle to reach deep in the sub-surface under the village. The first well was a discovery with high volume gas production from a big structure. The company is building a gas gathering plant and has a main work camp near here.

I start getting to know some of the guys. Nigel Walker, the head mud logger and I take a jog from the well through a couple villages and end up at the base camp. Nigel, who speaks fluent Thai, now lives here but is originally from England—this saves him a lot of taxes. He lives in Udonthani, which is about eighty kilometers north of here (a little more than fifty miles) with his Thai wife. Another fifty kilometers north of there is the river and border with Laos. Nigel said there are a lot of ex-U.S. Air Force guys living in Udonthani. During the Vietnam War, the US had a big air base there and many of the guys just stayed there.

While the drillers set the casing, the geologist has time to explore the countryside. I meet some of the locals, and all I can understand from them is the word "American." I hate not being able to understand anything. I will need to learn some Thai words very soon.

We will be drilling soon and everyone in Bangkok and Houston offices will be interested in what I see. In the meantime, luckily for me, golf is becoming popular in Thailand. I find a driving range with 50 covered hitting areas, and they are building a second floor. The funny thing is when I manage to get there I'm the only customer. It's not super expensive, so I borrow some clubs and hit a couple buckets of balls.

After that I walk the two miles back to town and poke around in some shops. It gets a little cool here at night, so I buy an inexpensive long sleeve casual shirt because I only brought a couple of T-shirts to wear on the rig. To get back I negotiate a reasonable price for a tuk-tuk—a three wheeled motorcycle-like thing with a brightly colored fiberglass roof. At first it seems fast, but not fast enough. Cars whip past us on the open road; sometimes we have to go onto the shoulder. We make it back to camp just before dark and the driver smiles as I wave—after my first few feeble attempts to speak Thai.

Before breakfast I take a long run. I go through a neat little village where the little kids stare and older girls and women yell at me—a few good-natured sounding comments I don't understand—the rest of the people ignore me. I go down the small dirt road around some curves and by a couple of water reservoirs. I see a few guys with water buffalo, some sugarcane fields, wood floors raised off the ground, planted fields and lots of rice paddies. There are a few gently sloping hills with the occasional trees on the edge of the fields. It is so beautiful that I push my run from three miles to about five.

After supper, the fellows and I stop for a beer under the light of the full moon. The waitresses at the place are funny. Apparently Scooter had promised to take them to see the rig and didn't come when he said he would. They crowded around him, poking him or pointing at him saying "Bo hai,", which means Liar. They nicknamed me SA, after some famous Thai entertainer. After a couple of beers and stories I got the check and we headed for the rig. We should be drilling again before the sun comes up so I'll be busy tomorrow.

There are currently three seasons here; hot, from March to June, rainy July to October and cool and dry from November to February. "Cool" here means it is a comfortable heat in the day instead of absolutely baking.

Coups and the Silk Festival

When we do start to drill we make slow time. The drillers want to drill faster and make more "hole," but their gamble didn't pay off—it delayed us even more. We geologists, of course knew better but why would they listen to us? Ha! When we resume drilling, the rate is only five feet per hour, which I can keep up with pretty easily.

Just as I'm settling in, I hear something distressing from Ronnie. The latest word from Chad is that rebels led by a former army chief have overthrown the government. The president was killed while trying to flee. I'm worried for the people in the capital—but I learn everyone we know is safe, as far as we know.

The people in N'Djamena were taken to the French compound and later flown out to Europe. Operations people in southern Chad were flown out to Cameroon with the Twin Otters. My geologist friends Paul and Greg are cooling their heels in Amsterdam for a couple of days until the company decides what to do. The risks of international operations are real, but quick reactions by the company kept our people from harm's way.

The drilling here has slowed down so much that they think the drill bit in the hole is shot. We decide to go into town to see the silk festival. It's common for these towns to have a festival around the time of the rice harvest when the locals actually have some money. I take a couple pictures of the rice fields and the people threshing rice by hand. They give me two sticks tied by a rope so I can try threshing too. I think they get a kick out of our visit—very friendly people.

The men beat bunches of rice on the ground creating piles of rice, and the women gather the leftover rice stocks to feed the cattle and water buffalo. The silk festival in Khon Kaen is interesting and has a lot of stuff for sale. I buy a Bow Khan—"something you blow in" is the translation. It consists of various lengths of bamboo tied together with a mouth piece in the center of carved wood. It's a wooden flute/whistle instrument native to this local area of Thailand.

The next day is a holiday in Thailand. It's the king's birthday. Buniphpol Aduluday is in his early 60s, I think. I see a shield-like symbol surrounded by colored lights at various businesses in town as a decoration. Christmas, of course, is not a national holiday here, and I think it would seem out of place even if it was.

My last day on the rig dawns clear, but where the top of the objective is going to be is not. We are drilling deeper than we were supposed to and have not found the top of the rock formation we seek yet. I guess it will be up to Joel who is taking over for me to find the top of the Permian carbonate and pick the core point.

My wife in Thailand

I wake up a little slowly—slight hangover from having a couple of beers with my co-workers Bob and Andy last night at a bar on the strip.

I'm still in early enough to get Joel's report from the rig—still nothing—and I find out that Mike will be traveling back from Singapore tomorrow so I'll have to go in to do the morning report for Houston even though my wife will be here. It seems odd to me that I'm in this big city (eight to ten million) halfway around the world and she is going to show up at the airport tonight.

I have a busy day including a visit to the immigration office to get an extension on my fifteen day visa. It's hot with a confusion of lines and lots of waiting. The Thai like to keep tight control over their visas. While I'm waiting, I catch site of a sign written in three languages—Thai, English, and Chinese. It read:

The Minister of the Interior issues by virtue of section 16 immigration act BE.2522 (1979) the following order to identify an alien with hippy characteristics.

1. *Singlet or waist coat with no underwear worn*
2. *Shorts not in respectable condition*
3. *Slippers or wooden sandals when not part of a national costume*
4. *Silk pants not in respectable condition*
5. *Long hair worn in an untidy and dirty manner*
6. *Person dressed in an impolite and dirty looking manner*

Persons identified with these characteristics should be prohibited from entry or immediately deported.

I get upstairs to the last room, where I obtain the visa. I guess I don't have any of these characteristics today.

I'm excited to see my wife, but they can't confirm her flight—even though it should be in the air already. I leave with a hotel car and driver who will wait with me and take us back—now that's service. Waiting for an hour for a taxi at Bangkok airport is not unusual. At 9:30 p.m., I walk into the airport terminal, look at the board, and spot United from Taipei—estimated time arrival 12:15 a.m. Arrgg. So I have a couple drinks and write some postcards.

Finally, it's time to stand by the arrival area. I have to stand behind barricades in the main terminal area. I am looking at the people coming out the door. It's packed with drivers holding signs and other Asians four or five deep in front of me—but I stand flat footed and see over them all, no problem.

And there's my wife looking a little tired but darn glad to see me. And I'm glad to see her too. We make it back to the hotel about 1:00 a.m. and trade stories until 2:00 a.m. She brought me some special treats: Cheetos and some homemade cookies. Yeah. She said she had no idea how lavish the service was in First Class.

We both really enjoyed getting to catch up. In the morning I get up and walk to the office to send out the morning report. I am back by about 10:30 am, and we go sightseeing.

I find us a cab driver who speaks enough English for us to haggle over price and tell him where we want to go. Instead of him just dropping us off, we work out a price where he will wait for us at each place we want to visit.

Our first stop Wat Tramit, a small temple with a big treasure. It houses a solid gold Buddha that is five and a half tons and over nine feet tall. Gold gleams brightly, and it seems brighter than even most displays I've seen in jewelry stores.

Next Chumpoon, the cab driver takes us to one of the bigger temples we planned to see—Wat Pho. It is so big we agree to hire one of the guides that provide an English tour for the two of us. The buildings on the grounds are ornate, and there are a number of different temples with Buddha sitting and meditating, standing, teaching, and reclining—or preparing to die. We also see the urns where the cremated ashes of past kings are kept, shrouded halls, shrines, and more statues. We see a sacred tree that Rama II brought from Shi Lanka and planted.

We learn some basic things about Buddhism from our guide. A monk's father and mother shave his head in order to symbolize the serpent. On earth, man is an animal, a serpent, and he must live ten lives on earth before he or she can become a man in heaven. For each life you have lived, there is a curled round part of your fingerprint on a finger or toe.

We go into the huge temple of the reclining Buddha where they built the building around the image hundreds of years ago. This Buddha is fifteen by forty-six meters long. His ten toes each have a circular curl, and he is reclining, ready to die and go to heaven. Also depicted on his feet are the 108 auspices that Buddhists believe are part of the person. If any one of these go bad, they teach you must go to the temple and pray, light incense, make sacrifices (donations) and hopefully repair the bad part to remain in good health and spirit.

Our guide looks at our hands and concludes we had lived no previous lives, due to the lack of circular print markings.

Our guide shows us how the bases of the structure have a convex shape, boat like as our tour guide puts it. This is by design to allow for the soft soils of the area; this interests the geologist in me.

At one spot in the tour a monk blesses us. He is wearing the traditional orange robes and is seated in a chair. My wife and I hold hands together while he mumbles some jargon, splashes some water on our heads, and then ties an orange string around our wrists. He gives us a small gold colored medallion, and I give a donation.

This temple was actually the first University of Thailand in the 1700s, but it is no longer a school. Some boys become monks as a way to get an education if their families are too poor and otherwise cannot afford it. I find it interesting to learn that monks do not have to remain so their entire lives. In fact they may only be in for a few months.

We meet our driver outside and he takes us to another major Temple, Wot PhreKew. Here we see the famous jade Buddha as well as a bunch of other beautiful buildings, statues, shrines, and so forth. The other main part of these grounds is the royal palace, but our tourist tolerance is wearing down so we pass on hiring a guide this time and just wander around the grounds viewing the grand halls and main royal palace. The king does not live or even work here—it's just for show. We find a small museum containing a few artifacts and a lot of things being restored.

It's getting late so we drive to the hotel and pay off the cab driver after agreeing to meet him at 12:30 p.m. tomorrow for more sightseeing. I can see my wife is tired; the jet leg is catching up with her so we call it a night.

I can't even describe how nice it is to not sleep alone in the hotel. We miss each other terribly when I am on a hitch, but you can learn to live with it. After a jog together through the crowded park, we end up taking a river trip. We are the only passengers. Our boat's motor is not one of the giant Toyota ones that's fast and noisy, for which I'm grateful.

Our first stop is Wat Arun, the Temple of Dawn. We climb the steep stairs on the outside of the towers and have a fine view of Bangkok across the river. A man let me hold his six foot long python so my wife could take a picture and yes, there is a small price for this and even a docking fee when "Mr. Thai," the boat driver—his obvious name for tourists, dropped us off.

Mr. Thai slips through to pick us up when we're done. A little further up the river we turned west into a small town area, which is a pleasant part of the trip as we wind through small houses, fields of grass, and teak wood structures that Mr. Thai points out to us. I'm especially interested to see the small boats filled with prepared foods and sometimes small cooking stoves that dock with houses to sell their stuff.

Around noon Mr. Thai stops at a small market where he buys sautéed pork on a stick and small bags of cooked rice for us and himself. Normally it's best for expatriates to not eat street food, but he gave it to us and it tasted great. We return to the Dusit Thani Hotel for a brief rest then meet Chumpoon, the cabbie downstairs. Our first destination is the Vimanmek Teak Mansion, built around the turn of the century and used by Rama IV as a summer home for a five year period.

Next we ride about an hour southwest from Bangkok to a place called the Rose Garden. We enjoy a one hour tourist show with demonstrations of local music, dancing, Thai boxing, cock fighting, martial arts, and even a mock wedding ceremony. Afterwards we see an elephant demonstration moving logs, etc. We skip the elephant ride and go back to the hotel. After dinner, my wife is down for the count—still working on the time adjustment and perhaps suffering from the pollution in Bangkok.

Phuket Island

In the morning we fly an hour south of Bangkok to tropical Phuket Island, a popular destination that attracts tourists from all over the world. Phuket Cabana, one of the few places that is right on the beach and not across the road from the beach, has cozy rooms with twin beds, bamboo ceilings, a covered porch—and no TV. We check out the pool and then walk out onto the white sandy beach.

Patong Beach salesmen jump on us right away—"Jet Ski, man?" "Want to parasail?" Rather persistent fellows. We walk down the beach and cross the main street to see what is around. We notice a lot of foreigners with Thai girls—more than normal couples and immediately obvious are the great number of European women going topless on the beach. This is a wild place.

In the morning we rent a motor scooter, pack our snorkel gear and go north to explore the island. We see all kinds of beaches. It's beautiful and tropical green so we just keep motoring along. We stop at Singha beach where there are few tourists. They charge a little to get in, more if you want to use the chairs. We picked this beach because it was small, secluded, and a good prospect for snorkeling—the snorkeling is great. We see a good array of coral and tropical fish and really enjoy our time in the water. The beach had a shower, even a bamboo chute with water running in a little stream over a small waterfall, so we're able to get the salt water and sand off. Back on the scooter and headed south we find a lookout point near Kata, then drive on through dense jungle hills, rubber tree plantations, resorts, cheap bungalows, local towns, and big and small beaches—some great views. We spy a "sea gypsy" village down at one end of a beach and find the prices for tourist stuff to be much more reasonable at Raiwan Beach than Patong Beach.

We get caught in a warm tropical rain shower on the way back— not too bad, so we push on back to the hotel. After dinner and a couple of beers, we are through for the day—it was a fun day.

The variety of people here is interesting. We have run across German, Italian, Swiss, French, British, Irish, Indian, Spanish,

Australian, Norwegian, and of course groups of Japanese and other Asians.

The Thai concentrate on learning some English to deal with the tourists, so it's easy for us sometimes. It's funny all Europeans have to speak English—and for some it is their second or third language—to get by.

Unfortunately we also see some demented things—signs for "Uncle Charlie's Boys for Men." Sadly, child prostitution (for both boys and girls) is still a reality in Thailand.

The next day, Wednesday, I play some golf. Phuket Golf and Country Club is a fantastic course but the price is high enough that my wife didn't want to play. You have to use a caddy—all girls, wearing blue jump suits who actually carry the bag. I start off paired up with a couple from Canada and two guys from Norway—soon I leave them behind because of their slow pace.

The course was in excellent condition, palm trees, flowers, small hills and lots of water. I had more good holes than bad and ended with an 88. One funny sight was the Japanese foursome flaunting their wealth. Each player had a caddy and another caddy to just hold an umbrella over each of them to keep the sun off. So a huge group of twelve is walking up the other fairway towards me.

The next day we are back on the scooter and headed to a beach we had spotted Tuesday on our scouting trip. We take it carefully, but it is still fun—the wind in your hair and tropical breezes.

We're the first customers to hit the beach, and we have a peaceful morning. I dive spotting coral, fish, and purple starfish, while my wife picks up shells on the beach. That night we hit a Thai place with reasonable prices—Sabi Sunu Bakery. We share a table with a nice German couple and enjoy talking with them. They speak English, like many Germans, and we talk politics and the crisis in the Middle East. (When is there *not* a crisis in the Middle East?). The next day is our last full day on the island and we sail for the Phi Phi Islands—pronounced "pee pee"—with a bunch of other tourists to the sounds of "Yellow Submarine" on the stereo. We cruise out by a few islands and past an offshore tin mining operation that looks like a giant tin house then on to the "Pee Pees." We arrive in a cove on Ko Pee Pee Don, the bigger of the two islands we would visit, then transfer to a boat that takes us to shore.

This location is beautiful. There's a huge curve of white beach fringed with palm trees and a low jungle-covered hill to the north with huge cliffs to the south. We go snorkeling and we see a brilliant variety of coral and other sea life. After a decent lunch of sea food and fruit and a trip on a glass-bottomed boat, we just hang out on the beach—no, my wife doesn't go topless like some of the gals nearby. It's time to go, and our group makes a trip around the smaller island, Ko Phi Phi Lee, with its shear rock cliffs. We see the caves where they collect small sparrow bird nests two times a year—the birds make their nests from saliva. The Chinese use these for the gourmet birds nest soup and grade the nests for quality (white, red, black) and price them accordingly. Apparently you can make a decent living from this, which explains why they risk climbing rickety bamboo pole ladders high into the caves to get them.

Saturday is our last day, but we don't have to be to the airport till 1:30, so we lounge around the pool. I haven't given in to the temptation to rent a jet ski or go parasailing, but I do get a massage. I pick one of the big older ladies, and she does a great job. She uses a few different oils and some stuff she says is better than tiger balm—some secret potion. At the end she was funny saying in a hypnotic voice, "Oh, you come back and see me. Marina, only Marina—bring your wife. I'll do her first, then you. See only me."

Back to Bangkok

Instead of going back to the Dusit Thani Hotel, we stay with Mike and his wife Nikki. Mike is a colleague of mine, and they have been living here for a year and a half. "We have the space," Mike had said, and they sure do. They're on the twelfth floor in the penthouse, with three bedrooms, two baths, and a huge parquet wood floor living area. I learn that what the tuk-tuk drivers charge is relative to their passengers—the least for a poor Thai woman, more for well-to-do Thais, and "rich" foreigners pay the most. Generally they consider all white foreigner to be rich, which I suppose isn't far off, since compared to the average Thai our net worth probably really does make us rich.

We visit the Thai National Museum where they have evidence of pre-historic man in the region from 500,000 years ago. The most accepted theory of Thailand settlement, formerly Siam, was shown as a migration down from China. The displays then trace the development of the kingdom's various battles against the Burmese through the centuries and the ancient Thai capitols Ayutthaya, Thonburi, and Bangkok (established in 1782).

Monday I fly to Singapore so I can renew my fifteen day visa. While I'm gone my wife is going to check into the Dusit Thani and do some shopping on her own. I'm impressed with Singapore—a cleaner city you won't see anywhere. Yes there is a fine for spitting on the sidewalk. I'm there just long enough to window shop and fly back to Bangkok.

I find my wife at the Dusit Thani, and we celebrate my birthday a day early. We have a nice dinner on the twenty-second floor, the top of the hotel, in the Tierra Room. With just three glasses of wine and no dessert, the bill is still over 2,000 B ($80 US), but it's nice. At the room we eat some cake my wife bought and I open some cards she had brought from the USA. The cards from family are a very nice touch. I have a great wife.

The next day, my actual birthday, we go to the airport. Time to say goodbye to my wife, but not for too long. I'll be home soon. I watch her head through passport control. Then she's gone, and I'm alone in Thailand again. We had a great vacation though and I now turn my thoughts to work.

Back to Work

I meet Mike at the office later Tuesday, and we discuss what needs to be done. He is taking vacation for the rest of the year, and I will cover the office in Bangkok. Joel came off the rig and arrived at the Dusit Thani about 9:00 p.m. We have finished the well—it is a dry hole—and we will not test. The rig will be moved to the next well location.

Tuesday night, Joel, Andy and some of the other guys take me to Kings X II, where Joel buys me too many beers for my birthday. It's 2:00 a.m. as I struggle into my hotel bed. I settle back into my routine of walking to the office on Rama IV, just a few blocks from the hotel, and running in Lumpini Park in the mornings. I pass most people, but a few Thai runners help challenge me—maybe even hurt myself—keeping up. We never say a word; we just understand—it is always a race.

We have the company Thailand Christmas party in the Dusit Thani on Friday, and some of the guys who went last year don't plan on going this year. "It's not what you expect for a Christmas party." They're right—my company has a lot of expatriates doing special jobs, but most of the workers are Thai. It's an odd, if festive, party—announced nearly all in Thai, so my table of Mike, the head accountant, an engineer and their wives, just watch the proceedings and try to figure out what's going on. There are karaoke singers, impersonators, and it has very little to do with Christmas. Everyone gets a small gift on arrival, and the emcee announces contests and gives out prizes for winners. I've got an early tee time, so I don't stay too late—I see what those guys who had gone last year are talking about.

We are almost late for our Saturday tee time because we have trouble finding the course, but the car has a phone, so we are able to call one of the other guys we are meeting. There are ten of us, and we tee off in three different groups—walking, with female caddies carrying the bags. Most of these guys play together regularly, and most work for oil field service companies in Bangkok. I play a good round of eight-four.

Sunday I meet Bob at the office and together we go to a snake farm where we see an impressive display of poisonous snakes. I thought they'd just take the snakes out, show them off, and maybe milk some venom—but no, they put them on the ground right on the walkway, move them around by the tail, cause them to rear up, hiss, strike, and generally scare the crap out of the bystanders.

Later I go to see some Thai boxing with Bob and Mike's son, Randy. The intensity of the fighting style is hard to imagine without seeing it. They kick, punch, hit with elbows, throw each other down then the referee breaks them when they hit the canvas. The fighters were so quick and agile but could take so much. They throw kicks and punches when they lock up. They knee each other in the ribs and stomach. I cringed most when they crack shin on shin. A musician plays drums and a strange horn thing with a tempo that varies with the intensity of the fight. It's incredibly impressive, and the intensity level ringside is amazing. This is Thailand's national sport, and these guys are phenomenal.

Tuesday hits—it's Christmas. I call my wife at her parent's place in Midland, where they're having their oyster stew for Christmas Eve. Wish I could be there. I go by the office but can't really focus on work. Tuesday I head to Khon Kaen for the day to check on the mud-logging crew, but also to see the monk's blessing of the well location, it's nice to get out of the city. I've been in Bangkok for only two days but when I blow my nose it comes out gray from pollution.

At the well site ceremony there is an area government official and a monk who says a prayer. Then all the Monks chant in unison for a bit then we move to the lunch tables. The company guys then set a big basket in front of each monk, walk around to each one, lay an envelope on the basket, and push it toward each monk as a gesture of giving. They take it. I learn that inside the basket are everyday toiletries that the monks will appreciate, but the envelopes contain cash.

A senior monk dips into a bowl of water and throws it on everybody, then on the drill bits, radio room, nearby cars…and that was the end. The monks all climb into their monk mobile van and leave. We all hope that will help the chances for this well to be successful.

I've done so much in Thailand and kept so busy that the time has gone fast. I'm now starting to look anxiously towards my freedom bird flight out of here on January 2. I will be on it in six days—seems like November 26 when I left Houston was such a long time ago.

I head to Andy's place for a New Year's Eve party, and a lot of people show up, including people from our bar, Kings X II. People are calling me "Sam" again and we are all drinking way too much. We are having fun though, especially when Andy brings fireworks and water balloons out on his twelfth floor balcony. Turns out I'm the best shot with a water balloon.

Time to Go

In these last few days, I've been busy with work activities, but I'm going home soon. New Year's Day, I make it to the office, though my head hurts, and manage to bring Mike up to speed on what's going on now that he's back from his vacation. Later I get some packing done—but just feel wiped out. A nap seems better than working out right now.

My last night in Bangkok I go to dinner with Bob and see the contrast of Bangkok and Houston more clearly than when I first arrived. If you drove like they do here in Houston you'd be shot. Lanes are more suggestions than anything else.

Many things are closed for New Year's Day—they take it very seriously here—but we find an Italian restaurant that's different but still good. After dinner I do a little last minute shopping and enjoy taking a picture of a woman serving fried grasshoppers—never know what you'll see.

By 5:30 am I'm checking out of the hotel. I win the big bill of the day award—my total from December 17 to January 2 is nearly three thousand dollars. I've been in Bangkok so long, it seems like I live here.

The day is clear and our flight path take us northeast out of Thailand, over the Mekong River, over the mountains of Laos and cutting across Vietnam to the ocean. Near the coast a pilot announces we are going over De Nang, the river deltas. The coastline looked interesting enough, so I take a picture while thinking of all the Americans that went there for the Vietnam War and never came home.

With all the traveling I have done in the last couple years, I've gotten used to the inconveniences, jet lag, different food, different news, and poor communications. I think the experiences have allowed me to look beyond the little things and see the good, interesting aspects different places have to offer.

Chapter 6
Caracas, Venezuela

November, 1995

I'm on the tarmac in Miami on a plane bound for Caracas, Venezuela, and it suddenly hits me how much things have changed in the three years since I was in Bangkok. At first I thought it would be nice not to travel so much, but I didn't know what else was in store.

Our lives have undergone a lot of changes over the last few years, personally and professionally, and not all the changes have been for the better. My position with the company has seen some changes, and I've worked a lot of overtime and put in other hard hours. I've spent time looking at rocks in eastern Utah, burned out florescent lights in the Houston office, and seen bosses come and go.

Things at home have been the true adventure. It was in February of 1992 that my wife had surgery, which was tough, but they said it would probably help the odds of getting pregnant. I love hearing the word "probably" from medical professionals. And then came the surprise in July—we learned my wife was pregnant. We welcomed our little blessing, my son, into the world in March.

I didn't waste any time introducing him to air travel—he's gone to Midland, Texas with us to see my wife's family, to Colorado two years ago and Florida for Christmas the past two years. Soon he will be old enough to require his own ticket. I smile as I think of it—my son, world traveler. I now have two people to miss while I'm gone. At least I get to have breakfast with my two favorite people and leave on a later flight. My role is a little different than trips years ago. This new job I have is quite different from being a geologist where you have to grind out technical details. My new boss is focused on environmental and public affairs. I am the geologist on the team. For the next year or so our main goal is to put safety, health and environmental procedures in place for the international division of the company. We need to adapt the corporate framework to include the operations integrity and safety management system for our Russian operations (OIMS for short). We will develop detailed written guidelines that are to be endorsed by senior management and do risk assessments for safety issues and set plans to avoid major accidents and environmental issues.

This system really was adopted by the company to avoid such disasters as the Piper Alpha incident in the North Sea but it has also been adopted to try and better manage environmental regulations and responsibilities. That sounds great, but we are trying to adapt a system in countries that are using technology that is twenty or thirty years old and has various degrees of industry maturity and that covers huge geographical areas, cultures, and peoples.

I can expect to travel to Russia by this winter to do this work and look over various operations and places, but for now I head to Caracas, Venezuela to wrap up some previous business.

I left some important maps in Houston, but my wife and my son brought them to the office. The secretary gave them to Larry, the project supervisor to carry since he was leaving Monday night; so I will have them for the meeting. We will give technical presentations, hold a workshop, and present to management for one of the Venezuelan government oil companies. We are doing this technical study to show that our company people are good technically and we will make a good partner.

We have the meeting in a small auditorium with a stage. We cover the walls with maps showing our results, and we have two viewgraph machines up front, as some of us are showing two things at once. Thirty to forty Government Co. people attend. They have a few questions but not too many as our presentation was clear. I think it went really well.

The next day we start working with the local people and discuss the pros and cons of five potential prospect locations. It's funny—I find out another Petroleum Co. took over as operator for most of the fields we studied. So we helped them pick locations for our competitor to drill. The concepts we developed in the study will only do the company good if applied elsewhere.

We're expecting to have a half -day presentation with their Co. VP. But Thursday night we learn that our three hour talk is being cut down to one hour, and our team's briefing to the director was cancelled.

This vice president review of only one hour is insulting, considering this is a big team project with a lot of work and good conclusions. The background of doing Venezuela is debating how to allow foreign companies to be part-interest owners in Venezuela fields. Oil exports are a key to the Venezuela economy, which is in bad shape right now. They need to let foreign investment of money into their economy; however, it is a political football right now with some politicians against the idea.

They don't have a good idea how agreements would be worked to protect Venezuela and are cautious about protecting their resources. Some locals think US oil companies would come in and drain all the fields in five years, which is physically impossible given the realistic economics of doing that. Venezuelan congress has not approved laws to allow things to proceed. The director saw no need to have the meeting right now, and the vice president decided that one hour was enough to hear the highlights—plus he wanted to leave after lunch and go on vacation.

Venezuelan oil companies Maraven and Logoven were originally Shell and Exxon Venezuela, who discovered some of these fields in the 50s and 60s. In 1975, Venezuela nationalized all these operations and asked the Shell and Exxon operating teams to leave. Being nationalized and kicked out of a country is a political risk that companies carefully weigh as we seek opportunities to invest around the world.

Ten months ago, the VP bet us a case of Polar—Venezuelan beer—that we would not resolve enough issues to make clear sense of how to drill for oil in the Cretaceous Cogollo Carbonates in Venezuela. We accept a lunch on Friday as payment for winning the bet. He says he's impressed with our work. Companies have done studies for them before, but ours was clearly the technical best.

The trip goes well, and I am actively involved in the meetings with good contributions on the pertinent issues. My operational experience of recent years gives me a different perspective from the research guys.

The Venezuela group supervisors put in a good word with my Russian group leaders for me—"Thanks for letting Dave work with us to finish our project. He came up with some good new technical things." Always nice to be appreciated.

Explorer

That's enough technical stories; what about Venezuela—the country? When you drive over the mountains and into the Caracas Valley, the multi-colored square adobe brick of the lower cost houses covers the hillsides all around the city. They build on some fairly steep slopes, but people say in earthquakes almost none of them are destroyed. The ramshackle sprawl makes an interesting contrast to the more normal looking buildings of the city in the foreground of Caracas.

At night, a beautiful spread of lights traces up into the hillsides around the city—Venezuela gives electricity to the poor. I don't see any homeless or street people during my stay.

It's interesting that Venezuelan cuisine does not have a lot of spicy food like Mexico. In fact, Mexico and Thailand are some of the few places where they typically eat very spicy food. Beef is very good in Venezuela, and I'm surprised to learn pasta is very popular, likely due to the large European influence. Seafood is also good since we are near the coast. One of our better meals out was to El Clupe's Peruvian Restaurant. Clupe is a thick soup, typical of Peru with seafood or chicken recommended by the large Peruvian host in his black jacket.

The steakhouse we visit is excellent. There's a weekends sports bar, which we visit to catch the Houston Rockets and San Antonio Spurs in the NBA playoffs, they have great beer but not so wonderful burgers. By Friday, we are celebrating the end of the project even though we have some reports left to write up.

The people here are beautiful, with a large mix of races and characteristics. The local Indians mixed with European settlers, and the result is that lighter hair and eye color are fairly common, even among some of the darker complexioned people. Due to their exotic facial shapes Venezuelans will commonly tell you they have the most beautiful women—women who dress provocatively and want men to notice them to a degree that a woman in America would find insulting.

Driving around is very interesting. Jorge, a cab driver who spent ten years in the US, is able to answer a lot of my questions. No, they don't have speed limits. If you have an accident you don't typically get a ticket—but you may get to claim your insurance money. Technically there are some traffic laws, but a small bribe can fix it if a cop should pull you over, and even if you don't, most people simply throw their tickets away promptly thereafter—there's no tracking system.

My trip to Venezuela is wrapping up—two of my coworkers and I fly to Isla de Margarita for a quick two day and one night breather. It's just right for a short trip, northeast from Caracas about half way to Grenada with beautiful beaches and blue water. It's hot and dry and I see people burning quickly—considering the numerous topless ladies on the beach.

Things are expensive on Margarita, except for the traditional tourist junk, so I didn't do much shopping. The focus is to swim, relax on the beach and try to unwind after the presentation. The island has gambling as well, and while my co-workers were too tired, I went out long enough to blow a few thousand Bolivar on blackjack. (The exchange is 170 B to $1.00 US, so it wasn't too bad).

It feels odd vacationing without my wife and my son, and I'm glad to start back for home. After a stop off in Florida to visit Mom, I'm back to Houston just after Memorial Day.

The plan for my next trip is to Russia. It will be interesting to see how the country is transitioning from Communism after getting a taste of Venezuelan socialism.

Chapter 7
The Former Soviet Union

October, 1995

It is Sunday, October 1, and I'm about to board a flight with my old friend KLM airlines. During the ride to the airport it's great to hear my son's high little voice as he sings songs from church. We hold hands riding to the airport, and they come inside with me—those were the days non flyers could go to the departure gate. After several hugs and kisses we're saying our last goodbye and I'm through the gate.

The nose of the big plane is near the windows, and I can see my son is smiling and waving when I look out the small seat window and wave. When I was saying goodbye to my wife, I thought about how far I am going this time and the places in the former Soviet Union I'll be visiting. I think, "What if I don't come back—what if the plane crashes in the Ural Mountains or shooting starts due to a government take-over in Azerbaijan..."

Naw, I'll be back.

Typically I have a hard time sleeping on planes, I'm usually too excited but I manage two or three hours on the flight to Amsterdam and then about six in my day room at the Schipol Airport Hilton. I even get a couple of hours on my way to Almaty, Kazakhstan, (which is eleven hours ahead of Houston time).

I awake to bright sunlight over desert as we drop down to Almaty, but I soon see streets and plenty of trees. It looks nice from the air as most places do. I look out the other side of the plane and see the huge mountains, the Tian Shan Range, which are very steep, jagged, large, and snow covered. Almaty sits at the base on a sloped area just off the foothills.

As we taxi across the tarmac, I see the President of Kazakhstan's plane and Kazak Airlines planes with the blue and yellow Kazakhstan flag. We enter the small airport, where I quickly pass through passport control—glad I already have my visa, so I can avoid that line. I get my bag and clear customs with my blue form. This form asks if I have any guns, narcotics, other declarations, but the focus is the written summary of how much money you are bringing in. Since the hotel we will stay in takes only cash, I note $1,100. The main thing for departure is that you should note less cash going out than when you went in.

A driver with a sign with my company's name meets me. He luckily speaks English and I enjoy getting a feel for Almaty on the twenty-minute drive through town. A city of about 1.5 million, most of Almaty's people live in apartments—the many trees are just starting to turn fall colors. My hotel is a very plain, one-story building with an adjacent Chinese restaurant. I meet Yuri, a dark-haired Russian who has just arrived from Moscow and will be working with us. We're expecting a car to pick us up at noon, but it doesn't arrive and we end up getting in a van with a number of other guys for lunch at an old hotel.

The Trista is a bulky grayish building. We pass through a large front gate with an overgrown grassy area and up the lobby stairs to a very fancy second floor dining room. They seat the eight of us at a large round table. The waitress asks me if I would like water "With or without gas." I say with. She says we don't have any, so I get plain water after all. Most of us order hamburgers, except for Yuri, who orders a rabbit dish.

Yuri acts as our translator when needed, but he's here from our company's marketing department and specializes in lubricants. I learn that he was in the Russian army and worked with missiles as an air defense specialist. It is strange to meet these people who not many years ago could easily have been our enemy in war if the "cold war" ended badly. My how things change.

After lunch, a few of us catch some of the speaking presentations at the Oil and Gas Exhibition. There is an earpiece that has a translator you can listen to, and although I try, the jet lag catches up and I blink out a few parts. Dinner is at the hotel's Chinese restaurant; it's not terrific, is expensive, it has garlic overload and the chicken and duck still have bones.

I'm able to sleep all night, but I'm not quite over my cold. I know I'm close enough that if I run, I might blow out the rest of it. Brian, Eric and I decide to go for a run at 7:00 a.m. The air is cool, and we see a few other people on the trail. I soon realize that we are steadily following a stream and going uphill. We finally get to the top of our run, where we see a clear morning view of the Tian Shaw mountain peaks—we run back down. Glad I went, I'm feeling great.

A group of us in suits pile into a van to go across town. I take in the sights of Almaty waking up and leaving their old, over-crowded apartments. I see a lot of old women with home-made brooms sweeping the streets. We arrive at a different hotel than the day before—it's full of display booths from different operating and service companies. Our company booth is one of the largest and located near the front. It's ten by twenty yards of colorful pictures, a front desk running a promo video, and has four local women handing out posters, pins, and brochures as well as three translators standing at the ready. I am the "Environment and Safety Representative" along with others such as Yuri a Dutch guy who is into chemical sales, and someone representing Coal and Minerals. The basic idea is that the girls pass out stuff to everybody and when someone stops to visit that has legitimate business we are available to have business discussions on the specific topic as needed. In fact, we all end up going outside to wait for the President of Kazakhstan to arrive and make an appearance. He's half an hour late—he is after all the president. He arrives with an entourage of people, including non-uniformed security people with piercings and a general tough-guy attitude. We all trickle back in after the president enters, he had already passed our booth when I get in. Our Region President, Randy got to shake his hand and say a quick hello as he passed by.

All of us company folks have dinner at the Marco Polo where Randy is staying. He held court after we were all seated, asking the higher ranking guys how they thought the day went. The food was an amazing buffet lineup, and we were serenaded by live piano and flute music throughout dinner.

After dinner a few of us go to the restaurant bar for some overpriced beers, and eventually it's just Yuri and myself talking about the transition from communism to a free market. Understandably, all their newfound freedom is quite a transition and will take some time.

After the morning run—I feel even stronger today—Eric and I walk over to see the War Memorial Park. Gates under the communist star and sickle/hammer lead to a memorial for World War I and II. A large flat stone walkway leads to a huge statue of army figures in a flamboyant exaggerated pose—Russian style. Behind it is a large Russian Orthodox Church with big bulb spires that look hundreds of years old. A quick lesson in Russian history—that up until the 1800s, Russia was ruled jointly by church and state and had been for eight or nine hundred years. Before that, it was feudal and suffered constant attacks from Mongol tribes out of northern China. Russia has always faced geographical challenges in its defense, it has heavily influenced their culture.

After our morning outing, we're dressed in our suits and headed back to the conference. At the booth, I review the Safety System with our local office leader, Wayne Holmes, and his staff. I show the video and give a short presentation as I have done with the other company offices.

I find out on my last night in Almaty we will have a group dinner to celebrate recent progress towards making a Kazakhstan oil and gas deal. We are to have a group dinner up in the mountains. This group dinner includes all of us—staff plus interpreters and girls who worked at the booth.

We ride far up the mountains, past the place where locals go for picnics. They have a small ski area up in the mountains. We arrive at the Yurt in three vehicles—a yurt is a round tent with a dome top held up by long sticks, with a smoke hole in the center. At least that is the basic nomadic style tent carried on camels by the ancient Kazakhstanis. We have a large cozy tent with four round tables covered with the first rounds of food. We sit and the vodka, beer, and wine begin flowing. We have large, round Kazal bread loaves, plates of sliced house meat, lamb, cheese, fruit, and nuts.

The most important part of this party is the toasts. There is some protocol dictated that highest level people make the first toasts, but basically there is a long string of toasts involving vodka shots, wine, and so forth. Toasts are about this great county, how wonderful all the people are for helping make the exhibition a good event, how we enjoyed the company and we should all be pleased that our company has an active deal in progress. Plus during this week, negotiations are successful in that we have an agreement that should lead us into an integral piece of the high potential offshore Caspian Sea Exploration Consortium. We made an agreement with the Kazakhstan Government Oil and Gas people to do a lot of training, pay some of their bills, and eventually acquire a portion of their WI in the offshore consortium. It's a major breakthrough, and vodka, beer, and wine flow in celebration.

Moscow Bound

We are scheduled to fly to Moscow today on Transaero Airlines, which is approved for employee use and is a Russian operation. Our current policy is not to fly Aerofloat, Russia's older airline, because of their incident rate and maintenance records. Although we had Transaero business tickets some time ago, our reservations had recently been cancelled for some unknown reason. Our local office admin had gone to their office each day and reinstated a seat, although only economy was now available.

Four hours of flight time take us to Moscow, home to about twelve million people and now a very expensive place to live. It's obscured in fog, I think at first—no, not fog: smog. A few buildings poke above the gray-white haze.

Under the smog blanket, the trees are changing colors for fall. My hotel is very grand—the Metropole Hotel, built at the turn of the century and renovated right after the fall of communism. My hotel in Almaty was nice but basic and cost equivalent to $100 US dollars a night. Here, this lovely hotel with its marble floors and high ceilings is $360 a night. My room is elegant, and I have a great view of the Bolshoi Ballet Hall. The Kremlin and Red Square are just down the street.

Three of us plus the Moscow security man Mike, head for the largest open air market around Ismaliva, where we spend a couple of hours and I buy some Russian nesting dolls, hand-painted boxes, a metal truck for my son, and some post cards. I pass on the fur hats and military gear.

We walk the short distance from the hotel to Red Square when we get back. Since it's a warm day, there are a lot of people out. We step out onto the large open cobbled stone area; to one side was a large stone reviewing stand for military parades and also Lenin's tomb. The near end consists of two large red brick structures with gothic styling, which are currently museums. The far end is the ornate Russian Orthodox Church, which is now a historical monument built in the 1700s by Ivan the Terrible after finally beating back the Mongol invaders. It's just strange standing here imagining all the armies and tanks that passed this place.

The next day is Sunday, and some sightseeing is on the agenda. I'm too tired for a run, but I make the 10:00 a.m. guided tour of the Kremlin. We see the flame for the Unknown Soldier and pass through the walls—the remnants of an old castle wall that at one time had a moat to keep the Mongol invaders out. We pass by the government buildings and on to a huge church area that actually houses five different churches built by different leaders dating back to the 1600s. The iconography is amazing, with depictions of biblical events but also local saints, other people, and events important to Christians the world over.

The front has ornate doors open only during services that represent the way to paradise. I find it interesting that the back wall has paintings of symbols for hell, serpents and more—for people to see when they leave the church, sending a message. The congregants would stand through services; the only places to sit were for the bishop or Peter the Great or whomever was ruling at the time.

We go on the armory tour—well worth it. We see gold plates and a few jewels from the fourth century, and samples of king's jewels, crowns, and gifts from other countries representing periods right up to the 1800s. There are ornate carriages, jeweled thrones, weapons and armor used by Mongols and knights, and exotic guns from hundreds of years ago.

On the way out, it's just Edward, our guide, and myself—the others have dispersed. I ask him about the new government; he tells me it's hard on him and his parents but the young people are adapting. The older people remember the cheap prices under communism, but forget the long lines they had to wait in for anything good.

On the way out of Red Square we see workmen on the spires, the red brick buildings facing the street placing gold two-headed eagles onto the spires where once sat the communist star; it's very symbolic of the changes. CNN I notice thinks so as well, I see the event on the news that night back in the hotel.

Monday I visit the Moscow office to give an Operations Integrality orientation to all the employees. There's some confusion about how I'm to get to the office, and by the time I get there at 9:40, it is five minutes before my scheduled presentation. I set up fast and try to calm my pulse. Luckily I've got the eighteen minute video to show before my safety talk and Q&A.

After my English presentation, Randy thanks me and it's on to the Russian presentation—given by someone else of course. I've worked hard to get a Russian language version together, complete with graphics, voice-over, and clips of Russian scenes. Show time.

The Russian presentation goes great, and any comments I have are translated easily—I even get some questions at the end, which is a good sign. The security guy Mike, goes over safety and security procedures…and we are done. Afterwards I run into some guys I know and we go to a restaurant that's been recommended to us, Uncle Gillys. It's down a dark side street and down some stairs—good thing we had excellent directions and there were four of us, otherwise I'd feel very nervous. The food is amazing and so is the service, with an English-speaking waitress happy to help. In the morning, I'm away to another office in Baku, Azerbaijan.

Baku

I fly from Moscow to Baku—my third destination on this trip. I can see the Caspian Sea through the clouds—really a giant salt lake with no shipping pathway to open ocean. Baku is on the western shore, and it takes some time to fly over the Caspian.

The South Caspian Sea has offshore operations, and producing wells. On land nearby there are spills around some fields, the ground soaked with oil—even some pools on the surface in places. It is amazing the Sturgeon fish of the Caspian and the caviar business is still so big.

At the airport, a sharply-dressed young man shows me a company pen—a signal from my man. It seems like it would be easy to get kidnapped in a place like this, but Murad's the real deal. On the drive from the airport, I get a good look at the very arid and scrubby brush countryside—nearly desert. I can smell the oil in the air.

We turn out of the airport and onto the main road and haven't gone far when police frantically wave us off the road! We sit for a moment, then a motorcade with a couple black cars and another couple cars all surrounded by motorcycle police and followed by a just-in-case ambulance zip by. Our driver Famil starts us up quickly behind them; we enjoy a smooth drive in from the airport by tagging along behind the procession. The traffic police wave black and white batons to direct traffic. I am amazed that every 50-100 yards all the way from the airport to our office in town an officer stands on either side of the road. People are gathered at intersections, still looking. We are close enough to see the police lights ahead at times, so it feels like we are part of the show.

I learn later that the Amoco president of Azerbaijan came in on the company plane with food for the refugees of the Armenia-Azerbaijan War. The motorcade had Azeri government officials and possibly the president, who rode with the president to catch his plane out. Murad tells me they don't see the motorcade driving around that often, so it is a special event.

There's not a single reflective glass building anywhere. They're all Soviet-style apartments and buildings hunkering down next to buildings built by German WWII prisoners. The company office in Baku is actually a renovated apartment on the second floor of a building that is over one hundred years old. I saw photos from the Bolshevik Revolution of this same building with cannon ball holes in it.

Just behind the office is the old city, which was originally surrounded by castle walls. The locals call it the "Inner City," and this section of town is over a thousand years old. Moscow, by comparison is a mere 850 years old; and the USA of course is just over 200 years old—a world youngster.

I eat breakfast in the main restaurant but somehow, even though I was in the lobby at 8:30 a.m. the group leaves without me. The driver comes back for me at 9:00 a. m. When I get to the office, I try the "Where were you guys?" but they piled on me saying: "Nice try on the offensive move, but you crashed and burned anyway."

We gather the few employees, and I launch into the safety orientation meeting. We decided to just use the Russian film and Russian view graphs.

I have another presentation the next morning, mostly office manager types for various Western companies in the AIOC Consortium: Azerbaijan International Offshore Consortium, and exploration venture. After discussions with the group, we decide to just adopt this group's plan rather than write a separate plan. If things get really chaotic we may be better off with this group of experts. Our current evacuation plan is for our employees in country and any visitors, but in the future we could have a larger operation and need to make new plans. In case of civil unrest, natural disaster, etc. The basic plan is to trickle out on commercial air, take a charter plane or, if it gets wild, hop on the work boats and head out into the Caspian Sea. The two boats can hold up to six hundred people. We would try to cross over to the Turkmenistan.

After lunch Famil, the driver, and Layla an interpreter agree to drive me around some sights of Baku. We take a winding drive through the narrow streets of the thousand year old "Inner City," a portion of the city that is contained by a castle wall.

We stop at an old mosque. Layla tells me to wait by the car while she checked it out, then waves me in. From the small twenty car parking area, I can see a couple of mounded roofs and a couple spires that were all stone. The two of us walk around to the main center room area where the first king-type lived. Prior to the 13th century there were no unified kings. The king had a hole in the floor to put people in if they were wrong, bad, or maybe just threatening. The hole dropped into a prison cell area that contained a tiger.

We walk through the main mosque, the open-air bathhouse area, some different sized areas for social events, and see a couple more holes with iron gates over them. On a back patio are a variety of stones with ancient Arabic writing and inscription—large, bold, curvy, and odd-looking stuff. Some of the stuff here was dragged from an ancient (13 th century) city that is under water in the Caspian. This mosque site is where the first real regional leader/saint type was buried.

We get onto the main road and drive five miles out of town. We leave the congested building area and drop into the next valley, which is dominated by an oil field. I see ditches stained by crude oil on the edge of the scruffy town, adjacent to the oil field. People live right next to what Americans would call a waste zone.

From the hilltop we look out over an incredibly bizarre sight. Metal skeletons of old rigs are in various spots all over the place, and a few on islands in ponds. Dirt, oil, grease, rust stains, pits, tanks, and metal junk is laying everywhere. Words are hard to find—to understand this, people will just have to see it. It looked so strange to my eye, even though I am used to seeing some oil field equipment in the field. It looked like a movie set—almost unreal.

It is real, Layla says. She sees it every time they head to the beach—but the beach area is now under water due to flooding—and closed.

They also show me the cemetery. Since 1990, hundreds of people have been buried here, the majority from the war with Armenia, which is still going on. They tell me that when Azerbaijan and other countries claimed independence from Russia, Azerbaijan gave some land to Armenians, as they didn't have any. Now reportedly Armenia has continued to push for territory and has taken twenty percent of Azerbaijan. The war has lasted four years now and generated many refugees—they say one million, many of which have come to Baku. Baku is a city of about four million people.

Layla and I walk through one section of the cemetery that is all grey stone. In 1991 when we saw Moscow coverage of the coup, there were other things going on across the region. Reportedly, Gorbachev sent Russian soldiers to Baku, who ended up shooting unarmed demonstrators and innocent bystanders—at least one hundred of them, all on the same night. This row we walk has all their portraits etched on the stone—mostly young adult men, but many young and old women, and even a couple children. They are heroes to their people, but mainly this is just a sad place to me. We head back to the office, but Layla has one more thing to show me. We walk to an old, twelfth century tower castle and to what was once a festive boardwalk area when she was a girl, when she would come with her father. I see only a few reminders of those times—a kid's merry go round, tennis courts—but the shoreline is full of weeds. When I look closer, I see a thick twenty-foot wide area of oil and sludge. Oh, how sad. It's a disaster area that would require a major excavation to clean up.

Layla tells me the Caspian is recognized to be a rising water level, so maybe another five feet will put all this under water and eventually bury it. It's my last night here, and after calling my wife and son from the office, I travel back with Roger, the area manager, to his apartment—a nice and spacious two-bedroom flat with high ceilings. The most striking things are the ornate ceiling decorations and the detailed wood-inlaid living room floors. He seems to be happy living in Baku, it's charming. Although I could be offered an overseas assignment it's hard to imagine living with my family in a place like this.

I stand looking out at a busy street, the boulevard that runs along the Caspian shore. To the right is the ornate white building that is now a puppet show place. With dusk the car lights are coming on. In the distance is a Ferris wheel at the amusement park. From the second story I see across to another old building painted a dull yellow, like a number of buildings here and in Moscow. Soon this place will be a memory for me—after I am transported to another world.

The next morning I'm out the door at 4:20 am. I leave my keys at the front desk but the driver, isn't here. Uh-oh, this is not a good way to start the day. When he hasn't shown by 4:45 a.m. I call Roger. He said calming things and says he'll get a hold of the driver, Roger calls back a few minutes later to say Akief had overslept but was on his way.

At 5:00 am, I see headlights cross the bridge and come up the hill—going fast. Akief pulls up to the curb quickly, jumps out, and helps me with my bags. "Sorry, sorry," he says as he tosses them in the car. Nothing too fragile, luckily. We race across the city to the airport. Luckily this early there's very little traffic. Since we are driving through town so early, we don't have to worry about pedestrians. Funny thing here—people lean out close to the street and sometimes try to run across at busy times. The drivers forge on sometimes using the "brush-back" technique and making even me jumpy. I understand the car population has grown quite a bit since the break away from Russia, and people seem to not be great judges of the on-coming cars' speed—also some people drive like they're crazy. People just weave all over the place and squeeze into places at lights…if they stop. I hear most never take a driver's test. They just pay off a fee and get a license.

We arrive by 5:30 a.m. My flight is scheduled for 6:25 a.m., so barring trouble in customs I should be okay.

There's a first class section at the airport. I see the owner of Moghan's Restaurant—where I ate while here. Akief stays with me until I leave, and as I do so, he says goodbye and a hands-in-prayer sign to me with a somber head nod. I think he still feels bad about being late. I could have made him feel a little better if either of us could speak a second language worth a damn.

I fly about five hours to Frankfort, Germany, without any trouble. First class on this flight is just a regular seat…but we each get our own row. I'm supposed to be on first class all the way, but I find out I'm business class on the ten hour flight back (actually, a little more, because you're flying against the prevailing wind).

On this trip, we pass England, fly over Scotland, and then over water…before the Captain says, "To save a passenger's life, we need to make an unplanned stop, a bit north, in Reykjavik, Iceland." "I'm sure you all understand and would do the same thing if you had to decide." We eventually start dropping in elevation, come in low off the water, and finally reach the shore of Iceland. It looks barren. Near the coast I see a few steam puffs from some hot springs, which I understand are common around Iceland. There is not a tree in sight; just stark, dark-colored tundra. I can see a line of snow-capped mountains to the north. We sit on the ground about an hour and take on some fuel—without deplaning and without smoking. Ha, good thing I don't smoke. We stand in the open door of the plane off the front section for a view and some fresh air, and then we're off again.

It turns out to be a clear day, so I watch as Greenland looms up, and...wow I can see dull gray peaks and glaciers spilling out of valleys and ending at the waterline. There is snow covering all the other land and icebergs dotting the water 30,000 feet below. The scenery is amazing. Ice choked rivers and more glaciers and icebergs. In one area the snow is so deep it completely covers everything. All I can see is a great depression for a valley that ends at the water with a glacial wall that must have been hundreds of feet tall, in all white. One valley is covered with cracks or small faults in the snow that parallel the water line and follow the valley back maybe ten miles until it disappears. The scale of things is hard to judge, but I know it is massive.

Arriving in Houston, it has been about twenty-four hours of consecutive travel since I left my hotel before dawn Saturday in Baku—seventeen in the air, plus layovers and delays. Ouch!

I fly through customs and my baggage comes out pretty quickly. My wife and son are just outside. I duck under the rope, turn left, and run right into two of the biggest and best hugs with kisses a guy could wish for. It's good to be home.

Chapter 8
Stories from Azerbaijan

May, 1996

M y wife and son like to bring me to the airport, My son loves to see the planes take off, and my wife and I get a little extra time to talk. The three of us hang out and have a snack but soon I have to say goodbye and walk down the ramp to my plane. The jet way ramp blocks my view out the window and my son likes to wave to me. I can't get to another window easily, so I ask the stewardess if there's another window I can look out. At first she says there isn't, but then I mention a three-year-old is involved and suddenly she's trying to bend some rules for us. A few moments later I am leaning over the copilot and waving to get my son's attention. Maybe he can't see me; the stewardess grabs a white cloth and waves out the side window getting my wife up out of her chair, she lifts my son so he can see, and the copilot says, "Houston, we have contact." It's a special moment and a great way to start my trip.

I will be gone for about ten days. Actually, I just returned from a two-week training school that involved days driving through canyons between El Paso and Carlsbad New Mexico, flying to Utah, and driving into Wyoming to look at rock outcrops and study stratigraphic concepts that may be applied to oil and gas exploration. That is the fun part of being a geologist, working outside "in the field" as we call it.

Not only that, I'm scheduled to head back to Russia in June. In the wake all this time away from my family weighs heavily on me. I hope my son and wife can stand it, I sure miss them. When I get home, I will probably be exhausted from all the travel, time changes, too many airports, and road meals. The things I do in this industry are interesting but tiring.

During the eight-plus hour flight from London to Moscow, I do not fall asleep because I am busy watching a movie. In first class, they now have small, six inch square pop up TVs for each seat. British Air also offers a selection of 8mm movie tapes to check out to your seat, in addition to the movies and shows on channels. I stay up and watch the 1970 *Isle of Wight*, filmed on an island off the south shore of England. It's about a concert festival that attracted 600,000 people and music acts including rock legends The Who, Jimi Hendrix, The Doors, Moody Blues and others.

I look down to see patchwork German forms over the northern portion of the Alps, which are still covered in snow, then across Hungary and the Danube River basin at more farms. This takes us in to Bucharest, Romania, for our pit stop.

We land in Baku late Saturday night, and we are greeted right on the tarmac—the same treatment our executives might get. Maybe the local staff is practicing. Ron Hall, a coworker who has shared my whole journey with me, and I are not tired when we check into the Hyatt Regency Baku, so we check out the hotel casino and I bet on a little blackjack.

Things are changing fast here in Baku; as I can see from my drive across town between the airport and the office. Renovated buildings and new banks with dark glass windows herald the coming of change, and new money is already here. Baku was a cosmopolitan place at the turn-of-the-century, with the Noble brothers helping import the oil industry and turning it into the major production area of the world at that time. The primary market was kerosene lamps.

Most of the large old buildings in Baku were built prior to 1900. Then the Bolsheviks came in 1917 and burned much of it, destroying the Nobles' business. They also brought irresponsible oil practices—which in the old days were normal practices worldwide. The concepts of conservation and environmental responsibility did not exist as we know them today. The Russians built Caspian area production to a peak in the 1970s to over one million barrels per day to help meet the needs of the USSR. The simpler Russian buildings stand out from the old ornate Baku era buildings.

Ron and I are here to do workshops for safety, health, and environmental practices as well as management systems for the Caspian Sea area. Ron is one of the company experts on assessment. Two Azeri officials recently visited Texas to see our company wells in the Gulf of Mexico in action—and our safety management process, specifically. They were impressed with the high quality of our operation.

On the offshore platform, they said, "Where are all the people?" In Azerbaijan (and Russia), they use equipment that is twenty years behind Western industry technology, and that means they need more people to do jobs. Typically, their offshore platforms are full of people. Western technology has automated much of the oil production process. The concept of jobs for everyone in the communist era is still evident in Azerbaijan's national oil company. SOCAR currently has 75,000 employees yet produces only about 225,000 BOPD today. That is a stark contrast to the smaller staff levels of a western company relative to production volume.

We catch up on local news with our company resident manager. Lots of little things are going on at the office, but the big news is an attempt to kill the president of Azerbaijan by blowing up a bridge that his motorcade was about to cross. Apparently they found the explosives before that could happen.

Workshop

Tuesday is the big day—eighteen companies are represented at our safety workshop, which is hosted by SOCAR the national company of Azerbaijan.

Some of the people who attend seem to be defensive initially. They may have thought SOCAR would adopt some ridiculous plan that would hinder their own progress in Azerbaijan. When it becomes clear we did not have a hidden agenda, everyone seems more relaxed. Everything has to be translated into English and Russian, and it is a bit chaotic at first.

The next day, Ron and I go to the office to start risk assessments. We have a meeting with all the Baku staff to explain how we do assessments and hear their ideas. We ask them to think up hazardous scenarios: what is the worst thing that could happen? What event or chain of events may happen to cause serious injury, death, or significant financial loss to the company? Then we try to plot the risks by severity of consequence in the probability that they will happen to get a relative ranking of all the hazards from high to low. We make the high-priority risks our first orders of business.

Our Baku staff comes up with some very good ideas, and we cover everything from disabled vehicles to terrorists, from air travel, to communication breakdowns to slips and trips at the office. It was also interesting to hear stories of their youth describing the local culture. Murad talked about his school boy days when they dug fox holes and dirt banks to hide behind—military style. He also joined a Boy Scout type group so that he did not have to join "Young Pioneers"—a pro-communist party primer.

After flying back to London and landing in Houston, I'm excited to see my family at the airport to meet me—they even have a sign that says, "Welcome Home Daddy." Some hugs and kisses are a great reward for a job well done; at least another safe trip under my belt.

The only thing to bring down my spirits is that I know I'm going to have to leave again very soon. I have to finish the rest of the risk reports prior to July 1, which is a steep goal. It gives me about two weeks to do Kazakhstan, Northern Russia, Moscow, and of the Sakhalin Island offices—that's eight or ten more flights.

Mother Russia

Two weeks later on Saturday, June 8, I am back flying from France to Moscow into the former USSR. It takes me an hour to clear customs, and when I do a man holding a sign that says, "David Allard," relates with virtually no English that the company security man who was supposed to meet me will not fly to Arkhangelsk as we had planned. So I get the jet plane to myself for the two-hour flight over northern Russia. It is odd to think about my days as a child, hearing about the "cold war" and the potential for the USA and Russia to become enemies in a war; and now I am flying over the vast Russian lands.

As we touch down in northern Russia, I see over a hundred Russian fighter jets and a big bunker system as well as the fair sized commercial terminal. Jacob and his driver pick me up at the airport. On the drive in, I notice some large wooden houses built during the

Stalin era, they once housed four families each with one kitchen and an outdoor bathroom, -the water pump was out front, imagine that in the winter. The large square apartment buildings I see have no cars parked outside, which seems odd.

It's only a few minutes' drive to the office, and I notice the small-town feel I was told about despite the town's population of 400,000. I didn't sleep well and didn't get up early to jog or eat breakfast, I'm a little nervous. I try to distract myself by looking at how few cars there are and the people walking or riding the trolley to work. Everywhere I look, I can sense how far north we are—snow and cold are common nearly year round—the lush green grass is a sign of summer but seems out of place.

The ancient history of this quiet town is interesting. In 1584, Ivan the Terrible ordered the founding of New Kholmogory (, which would later be renamed after the nearby Archangel Michael Monastery). At the time access to the Baltic Sea was still mainly controlled by Sweden, so while Arkhangelsk was icebound in winter, it remained Moscow's sole link to the sea-trade. Arkhangelsk continued as the chief northern seaport of medieval Russia until 1704, when Peter the Great founded St Petersburg.

After some office small talk, I jumped right on to business. The Russians actually seem surprised that our company is concerned for their personal safety; the old Soviet system focused on the business. At first they don't understand the point of the meeting, and a driver, revealed an apparently fatalistic attitude, of the people here. "I do not think of these things," he says. He finally admits that his primary worries are about robberies and heart attacks.

A classical concert is the only thing going on tonight—Jacob goes to shows like this because it is all that's happening—it's actually pretty good. The performance is by a rather famous guy, Harvey Goldberg. The old remodeled church is full. The solo organ concert show Harvey's virtuoso skills and is impressive if you like classical music. I especially enjoy watching the local people during the breaks, including a lot of young people there with their mothers.

After dinner at Jacob's apartment, we walk back to my hotel. It's 10:30 p.m. and it is still light out. We talked for a while about the region, following from a book Jacob is reading about Russian history. It is sobering to think about the Gulag system of persecuting people for anti-communism. Millions of people died in work camps during the period 1917-1970s. Stalin's time also caused another estimated forty million deaths due to military mistakes of WWII.

We manage to get everything done over the next couple of days for my report on area resources and risks. I get to the airport with five minutes to spare—heck, they would wait for me anyway, since it's a charter plane and I am the only passenger. It's a funny feeling to associate with a plane ride. I of course thought, "This is what it must feel like to fly as a rock star."

Kazakhstan

The next stop is Almaty, Kazakhstan, where I meet the local office staff and hear stories about the Russian mafia.

I arrive at my hotel, the Marco Polo, have a quick nap then a work out, which usually sets me straight after some jet lag and lack of sleep. Almaty is three hours different from Moscow and Arkhangelsk. Russia has a staggering eleven time zones.

First thing in the morning, I call my wife and my son from the office—Houston is eleven hours earlier, so Thursday morning for me is Wednesday night for them. All is okay, and they are doing well.

On the way with the area manager Bill up to the mountains for a dinner, I get a real taste of the dangers of driving here. I look left from my position in the rear seat and watch a lady driver pull out of the side street headed right for us. She is supposed to yield, but it doesn't look like she sees us... I watch with my mouth hanging open as she just misses where I was sitting half a second before and smashes into our left rear. We're all thrown for a jolt, and Yuri our driver hops out to exchange information and discuss how the lady will pay for the damage. Nobody wants to call the police—they will only cause things to drag on and on for weeks.

So instead of heading out to the yurt restaurant, we end up having lunch at a nearby hotel while the other car shows up. Despite the accident, we elect to go up the mountain anyway. Heck, the only people we have to answer to are all asleep in Houston right now anyway. We drive up the mountain canyon, pass some landslide barriers, and pay a small fee to drive into the national park. Last time I was here it was a cool October evening, but now the hillsides are grassy, the trees are in bloom, and there are mountain flowers. I take some pictures. I even buy a small stuffed animal—made locally, of camel hair.

I go over my assessment and then we go to an expatriate's bar, where I meet with two other geologists who will be flying out with me in the morning—I have a 2:30 a.m. Wake-up call….. With a jolt, I sit up on my bed. I fell asleep. I haven't packed yet—what time is it? A quick look at the clock shows that it's 11:45 p.m., and relief floods over me. I do not miss my airport departure time. Luckily, my inner clock saved me. I pack, but have trouble falling back to sleep while thinking about everything.

Getting into my seat on the plane automatically relaxes me after so long in the world of the former Soviet Union. It's like stepping into a first world oasis. Soon I will be back to my world. I have six hours to Frankfurt, Germany, and then ten or eleven hours to Dallas before I hop to Houston.

To Russia with Love

It seems I've been traveling forever by the time I roll into Moscow at 4:00 p.m. local time. I managed to get about four hours of sleep in there somewhere. My hotel, the Metropole, is as nice as any I can remember.

The entire presentation is maybe forty-five minutes, and then it's time for one-on-one with the various office folks. We have the standard twenty-five hazard scenarios for the Risk Assessments done in Azerbaijan, Kazakhstan, and Northern Russia. After some discussions, we plan to add a couple new scenarios for the Moscow office.

Recently in Moscow, a number of bombs have exploded at random times and places; some politics—Chechen Rebels, or the elections—with some related to the Russian mafia. Some new hazard scenarios for Moscow include a nuclear accident and/or radioactive release. Around Moscow, there are nuclear power plants, weapons, raw materials, and labs that work with nuclear material. Another problem in Russia is the hospitals have limited supplies of medicine—it's up to the patient's families to buy medicine at drugstores. An expatriate guy was recently mugged, beaten and left unconscious with no identification. They put him in a Russian hospital, but nobody in his company could find him. He was effectively a missing person, and he almost died before he was found.

The next day, I get with a driver for a bit more sightseeing and for some dinner. He is very surprised that I was willing to buy dinner for him. Usually drivers just wait in the car while we go to the restaurants. I asked him to take me to a restaurant with good Russian food, and he drives to a quaint little place across from a church with their main dining rooms downstairs in the basement. We enjoy authentic Russian food while a group of Gypsy musicians played for a nearby table.

The next morning (my last full day here) back at the office, I inspect the Arctic survival kits and we discuss where we may place a generator. Our communication system has no really good power backup other than the battery box with the surge protector that will provide six hours of power in case of an outage—probably not long enough if there were a national emergency. The Moscow office is aware of the problems, and our assessment is one element in an effort to fix them; or at least reduce risk.

I say my goodbyes and leave the office, then stop to buy a couple things to bring home. I come back the next day and find a carved bear toy and statue—with plenty of time to catch my ride it to the airport and my flight to Amsterdam.

I buy some Dutch tulip bulbs for my wife, though the timing is not great and they will stay in the refrigerator until this fall when we plant them. I love coming home, no matter how long the flight. I am finally home with my family where I'm supposed to be.

The former Soviet Union seems like a tough place to try establishing oil production for Western companies, but their reserves are huge. The idea is injection of western capital investment and some newer technology and working with the host government may develop stranded value. Azerbaijan presents one of the best chances for success, which is why all the major oil companies are there. The other major world reserves are in the Middle East, much of which is not accessible to Western companies. It will be interesting to see how various companies' efforts in the former Soviet Union pan out.

Other problems with exploration areas of the world are: Algeria has Islamic extremists trying to overthrow the military government and have killed expats and westerners. Vietnam exploration acreage in the South China Sea is also being claimed by China. Papua New Guinea has headhunters not far from new discoveries. Places like Columbia and Russia have serious organized crime, and in Nigeria there is corruption clogging the system. Some companies purchase risk insurance from the U.S. Federal Overseas Private Investment Corp. From 1992 to 1996, this federal agency sold $1.6 billion in insurance for forty different overseas oil and gas projects. The agency will not currently help in certain countries. Other sources for political risk insurance include the World Bank and even some private insurance companies.

It is hard enough to explore, handle the risk of geology, and find a significant volume of oil and/or gas. The political risk adds up such that usually only larger companies can handle the added expenses and risk of loss. Sometimes it's many years before wells start to produce hydrocarbons and companies sell and begin to get return on their investments.

Chapter 9
Baku Business

December, 1996

O n my way back to Baku, and things have changed a lot—I have time to reflect on how things have come full circle while I wait two hours at the gate for my British Air flight to take off. While they are replacing one of the hydraulic pumps, I consider the series of jobs I had to cycle through recently—being banished back to the log analysis job a couple years ago, then to a safety environmental staff job and now finally back working as a geologist for the South Caspian Basin project. If anything, I seem to have more credibility now. The old Co. way was to question most of the things professionals like myself offered, but now in Team Azerbaijan I find my opinion is respected... at least a little bit.

We plan for delays so no big problem that we are leaving Houston three hours late. However, there are actually twenty-three people on the flight from Houston trying to make the connection to Baku—this just shows how much oil industry action is going on there.

British Air actually holds the flight for us in London for about an hour and usher us all over to the right gate while announcing, "Sorry to keep you waiting for the departure to Baku, but we had air traffic problems on the flight from Houston." I guess we are the troublemakers. Another six hours in the air, some food and a movie later, I land back in Baku.

They meet all of us on the tarmac again; a handful are flying in this time. One of the last flights brought in an Executive Vice President, who, along with a group of people, toured a number of locations in the former Soviet Union this past summer. What he saw really encouraged him about Azerbaijan, so here we are. There's nothing like getting a vice president to meet with the president of the country, Heydar Alliev, to get things moving.

The message to us then, is to not miss any opportunity in Azerbaijan. Negotiations for Exploration blocks means there are: 1) A defined geographic area, which may contain an undiscovered oil or gas field, 2) Need to decide on what fiscal terms there would be, if a discovery is made (royalty percent profits to the government and taxes) and 3) What we as a company must do in the Exploration phase: number of wells we will drill, square kilometers of seismic we will shoot, and 4) how much we will utilize the host country labor force in our work, both "blue collar" and professional level jobs.

We pile into a company van and a four-wheel-drive vehicle to ride to the hotel for a drink or two before getting some sleep. Being the savvy traveler, I have a basic rule that while on international trips if I cannot sleep I work out. I get about six hours of sleep, and then hit the Hyatt gym for a quick workout before breakfast. Baku is ten hours ahead of Houston time, so my body thinks that 8:00 am Wednesday is 10:00 p.m. Tuesday.

After breakfast three white new Mitsubishi's are waiting to whisk us to the office, but Azerbaijan has strict rules about overtime, so we will have to watch the driver's hours. We spend the morning at two different meetings, then we drive up the hill to the University area to meet with two research-oriented groups—the Geologic Institute of Azerbaijan and the Institute of Deep Oil and Gas (IDOG). My group also gets to go to the office of the vice president of Azerbaijan, Mitott Apasov, where we meet two men with whom we will work directly for this study. Dr. Yuri, head of geologic studies, and his co-worker Rauf Alijrov who will be helping us create some basin cross-sections.

After a catered lunch at the office, Jake Long, a young geologist, and I go back to work with Yuri on our study plans. We get off to a good start because the IDOG received an outline of our proposal and had written up a more detailed proposal we began to review that afternoon. Overall, the plan sounds good, but we will work out all the details in the next few days. It quickly becomes clear to me that this Institute has a lot more to offer than just well logs and correlations; they have a complete understanding of all the offshore fields discovered to date and more. This group is the research group used by the now National Oil Co. (SOCAR) to defend the field assessment volumes to review by experts in Moscow during the 1990 reserve update prior to the breakup of the USSR. I plan on returning on my own with a translator in the morning.

Front Line Efforts

After a brief meeting, I'm off to meet with Yuri and Rauf, though I'm not really "on my own," as I have a translator with me. Marco is more than just a translator; he graduated in nineteen ninety-two from the Academy of Science in Azerbaijan with a degree in geology, but couldn't find a good job. He actually translated for foreign journalists during the war between Armenia and Azerbaijan. (Actually, the threat of more violence is a big item on our risk assessment for Baku. The war between Armenia and Azerbaijan began in 1990 as a guerrilla war. Armenia moved to take territory in Western Azerbaijan and in 1992 it escalated into a large-scale war.)

When the various teams meet back at the office at 5:00 p.m. it is funny to watch us all scramble for a computer since there are only a couple of shared computers available in the office. We all have documents to create, plus our computers are hooked to satellite communications in Houston so we can check and send (email) messages. After we get some stuff done, a couple of us rally and decide to check out the new restaurant called Dolce Vice. They serve more than milk. It's actually an Italian place just up the street from the office near the Old City castle wall. I can't sleep, so I work for a couple hours and hammer out the first pass of the write up. The group we're working with seems to do good work, and we will get some sub-surface data and good science observations, but we will give them back a published, quality report.

Our area manager, Ray Nichols, had an adventure planned for after lunch, and with our driver and interpreter, we head off for Peshcanny Island. We head east and were soon driving through an old oil refining area. I have never seen such an amazing collection of rusting steel arranged like so many Tinker toys. Beyond the city over a small ridge and a bend in the coast line, we are driving through a grove of olive trees. They follow the coastline to the Peshcanny Island field. We passed through a wasteland of oil stained pits, rickety old pump jacks, and other debris. The land around Baku, except for the garden areas where they have imported plants and soil, looks a lot like West Texas, with no trees just scrub brush and dirt. Beautiful.

In the middle of this wasteland is a building, and as we roll up Ray says, "This is it." In an upstairs office is Rafik Mamedov, who runs the Azerbaijan well log trust. He seems to know Ray well and trust him, so after some small talk, we go look at the logs with his chief geologist. We tell him what we want to see, and the geologist calls out to an older woman who brings in a handful of paper logs. The Russian logs are recorded on paper in the field and then hand traced onto graph paper. We digitize these paper copies after we purchase logs for a well to load into our computers.

SOCAR isn't used to Western companies asking for all the logs from each well. We have asked for this information before but miscommunication at management levels changed the request. We reviewed the data, which I take over due to my knowledge of electric logs. Later in the afternoon, Jake and I go to IDOG to hear the last part of the proposed work from Yuri. Marco and I work late together, and as I work on the English version, he is creating a Russian version. My boss needs to approve it so we can get it into Yuri's hands to forward to their boss in the Azeri Institute by Monday. After dinner at a steakhouse, we go for a big night at the Chinese restaurant, which later turns into the ten-dollar disco. I see quite the mix of Western oil company expatriates, airline people, and locals with money. We stay out until about 3:00 a.m.

Despite the late night, Saturday is another workday for us, and somehow even though I did not get a wake-up call, I magically wake up in time to get ready and downstairs in time for our departure. Sam takes note when someone is late, and after he hears of our exploits last night, he laughingly referred to us as "drunken ass holes." We end up working hard all day creating a work program outline, describing the project including cross-sections and field studies; and then translating it. We don't get done until about 7:00 p.m. We deliver it to Yuri's apartment on the way back to the hotel.

In the morning, we depart from the office to visit a boss at SOCAR—the Azeri State Company. Then Jacob and I go off with Nazar, a SOCAR geologist, to see a core. Nazar speaks no English, and neither does our driver, however we manage okay by asking for help, where critical, along the way. We go to a large plain yellow building on the edge of town towards the airport, walk down along dark hallways to a dusty old auditorium. The window at the back looks out over an industrial complex and a refinery in the distance with a gas flare. The core is small broken pieces, so we knocked out a description in two hours.

A little bit later a few of us decide to check out the casino that is part of the Hyatt. We stand around and observe for a while then notice some high rollers tossing $100 chips at a large stakes black jack table. A British guy comes over and asks what we were doing. Once he realizes we are regular working stiffs, he tells us that those guys are Georgians—(actually Chechen Mafia). Then he offers to sell us a tanker of oil, black market style—I think he was serious. We decide to keep our distance.

I try my hand at blackjack—five dollars per hand minimum. I start off by winning then start to drift, so I switched tables. I end the night forty dollars up, not bad for a couple hours of fun.

Touring Baku

Sunday morning, I force myself to get up early and work out for an hour before breakfast—that snaps me back in line. Sam has a plan for touring Baku. The guide, Fuad, turns out to be a fantastic host. The oil boom in the 1890s left many buildings behind, but much of the area's history was raised during around fifty years of communism. Now that Azerbaijan society is free, they feel like they can share their history.

Fuad has done genealogical research to learn about the famous people who built these grand castle homes and buildings and what happened to them. He tells us how they got rich and their personal stories, which, typical for Baku, involved tragedy. Fuad's delivery of the stories is great. He is enthusiastic and tells them with humor, romance, and even poetry. He carries many old pictures with him of the way the buildings originally looked and old pictures of the people he shows us as we stand in front of each building.

We left the hotel at 10:00 am and didn't get back till 4:30 p.m. In that time we toured the city, went to an overlook, and ended up outside a Zoroaster Fire Worshiper's temple. I find it interesting that tankers carrying oil back to Russia at one point had to bring soil to Baku. The dirt was used to build garden areas with imported trees. Baku is in such an arid area that it could not support gardens and trees without this.

Even more interesting to me is the origins of the city. Over a thousand years old, it sat on the Silk Road trade route that linked Europe, Asia, and North Africa. Imagining the history of a place that goes back that far is amazing to me.

Fuad regales us with tales of Mukhtrov's Palace—sometimes called Suicide Palace—and an Oriental mosque-style palace built in 1899 by Rothschild that he defended from the Russians in 1920. He tells of oil baron Tagiev during the time of the last Russian Tsar, Nicholas II, hiring architect Muhammad Fuzuii to build the first girls school in the orient in 1901-1918. The Russian army gutted the building in the 1920s, and it's now the location of the Academy of Science. He tells us of Sabil, now lost beneath the Caspian Sea. The Maiden's Tower, built in the 10th or 12th century—also called the Tower of Ma'Sud, son of David—and how the intended maiden threw herself off it rather than marry her father. An odd excavation near the Maiden's Tower is dated 1 BC, and it is a tomb containing seven or eight people buried in a circle in a seated position. No known religion or civilization can be tied to this example of a burial style, Fuad says. Was it a quirk or evidence of another civilization of people?

One of my favorites is a palace in front of the Maiden's Tower, built for an oil baron at the turn of the century. The construction was going slowly, and the oil baron would ask about where the bathroom was. "It's in my head," the contractor would say, but in reality he was pilfering materials to build his own palace. This embezzled, troubled construction is now home to the US embassy in Baku.

I love the history of it, the culture. Fuad's tour was amazing, and we told him that he needed to change his card from "amateur tours of Baku" to professional tours.

Seek and Sign

Monday is back to work—the IDOG documents need revising, and we're aiming to have the document signing ceremony with our manager and IDOG's VP on Tuesday afternoon. Some pieces are out of my hands, like the technical attachment to the contract that the lawyer is writing, as well as the Russian translation.

I'm able to make a couple meetings we had planned. We went as a large group to see the Vice President of Exploration for SOCAR. The next meeting with Ali the vice president of production went well as he was ready to meet with us to review some geology and an overview of their work in order to write a joint study proposal. We need some of their oil field interpretations for this area and to purchase wells. We call this our "gap area" because we have no well data from these fields southwest or northwest of Baku.

It is difficult to explain to Ali, via our interpreter, that we only wanted to see a very brief overview of the fields for this area. They prefer to show the most complicated field in as much detail as possible, which required a lot more time. Words can't really describe how proud Ali seems to be of his work—it's obvious he has lived with these fields from the 60s to the 90s and is a very organized, detailed person. For each field, he shows us hand-drawn logs with pen and ink, beautifully detailed maps, again by hand with sketches of cross-sections showing distribution of oil and gas in the fields.

We also have to make a cold call and visit Farkhad, the new chief of the offshore exploration drilling company we are working with. He and his lead geologist seem receptive enough of us, but after some introductions, it's clear we are not going to see the actual data today—they are going to make a list of all their reports and data to send us, which is better than nothing. He gets an interesting phone call from a rig in Iran. While they are talking I look at the giant wooden wall map with location symbols for his operating drilling rigs on both sides of the border. After he is done yelling at the man on the phone, we learn that though the well was almost completed, the Iranians have not paid their bills. "Bad partners," he tells us.

After getting to take a break on Monday, Tuesday sees me feverishly working on the document again. We are able to get it done and deliver it to Yuri, but they said Mitat is not available this afternoon for a signing ceremony. Looks like the ceremony will be at a restaurant Wednesday night.

Wednesday is finally a slow day until Rauf calls with some last-minute changes. In fact, he has to come over to the office to make the changes the very hour before we are to leave for the celebration dinner. Wow, we just barely make it. The dinner itself is at Mogham's, which I have visited before—it used to be an ancient camel caravan stop. Sam and Mitat sign the English and Russian copies, plus initialing each of the fifteen pages of the document while the rest of us watch and take pictures. An Azerbaijan tradition is to make long toasts at a formal dinner, starting with the most senior person present and then going down the pecking order.

I even get to make one, and since I don't want to buck tradition, it's a bit long as I mentioned our custom of verbally abusing one another when someone is dumb, and some of the things I liked best about their culture. What I really want to do, though, is to toast Yuri and Rauf for being so smart and easy to work with. They made it easy to develop something we could all be proud of.

Thursday, my last day, we have some office stuff to do, but I still manage to slip out for some souvenir shopping with fellow geo-scientists Jake and LeAnne. I find some WWII-era goodies. Namik came along to translate, and with his help, we went to the rug factory where the weaver ladies sell small hand-woven rugs on the side. A few people had asked me to get them some rugs, and I negotiate on all of them together to try to get a better price. I had to use what I call the "Mexican walk-away" technique—I walk out the door like I was leaving, wait a few minutes then walk back in and make a good deal.

At the airport Fuad, the Baku security man, helps us clear customs, and then I'm on British Air to London. I breathe a sigh of relief as I board the plane again—I'm so ready to go. I fly to Houston on Friday December 13th, without incident, and I'm really looking forward to my birthday on the 18th, Christmas and a visit from my Mom. But especially my welcome committee, waiting for me at the airport.

Your Houston Host

I get to spend a week in Houston relaxing before I have to entertain Yuri and Rauf on their visit to Texas. We get some work done on the joint study, but we also have some fun. We catch a Houston Rockets game, go to dinner, visit Galveston on the Gulf Coast, and attend the Houston Livestock and Rodeo. The guys were intrigued by the huge scale of the rodeo, various animals on display and the cowboy skills. I have a car and driver available and a beautiful blond Russian woman Natasha, the translator assigned to help me. The company provided our visitors with daily living expense money—which I handed them in cash. Taking the guys shopping in Houston is an adventure and Yuri's wife got a nice dress.

I go back to Baku in February to describe core with Dr. Roger Vaughn, who is a sedimentology specialist—i.e. skilled in detailed rock description and original depositional environment interpretation. I arrive in Baku to an unusual four inches of snow, ice coating everything and a slow ride from the airport. The office guesthouse power is out, and it's cold. We use flashlights to get around, and I end up having tea in the dark with Vidadi.

On the way back to Houston we arrive late in London—at 11:45 p.m. yet still have time for a couple of Carling drafts at the Forte Crest Hotel in the Gatwick airport. They're only two pounds and twenty pence each (about $4.00 U.S).

The next day we are flying over Northern Canada, on the way to Houston and they let me go into the cockpit and chat with the pilot of this old DC-10. He explains what some of the instruments are, radios, air speed, and how when you push the throttle the autopilot brings it back slowly like cruise control. He actually let me try it. The third pilot's main concern is fuel controls and handling some of the panels that look like hundreds of buttons, but most are actually fuses.

It doesn't feel like I'm at home very long at all. By Friday, April 11, I'm in Houston in a meeting all morning, at work and then race home, get my stuff together, push my broken fence off the driveway, and speed off to the airport.

I'll be gone twelve days this time, and when my wife and son take me to the airport, it is a sad goodbye. My son says, "That's a lot" when I tell him how long I will be gone. It's extra hard leaving them this time for some reason. In fact, my head is out of it as I'm putting up my bag, crash. I knock the VP's glass over, and it breaks and spills. He and my boss give me some crap, but luckily Ronnie is easy-going. The Continental flight from Houston to London gives me some time to decompress and get ready to be back in Baku. My boss, Brian Russel, and Vice President Jack Brewer, are both on this flight, along with lawyer Ron Hall—all headed to Baku for negotiations with the government company SOCAR.

The Baku-based office staff is working like crazy because the corporation CEO has decided to fly a corporate plane over and visit St. Petersburg, Moscow, and Baku. His group will visit Baku for two and a half days, and he plans to meet with the President of Azerbaijan. The travel and security planning for our executives is unreal—meals, seating charts, security, background checks, back-up plans, agendas, phones, and fax machine access. My group will try to demand as little as possible from the Baku office staff during our visit as they prepare for the executives' arrival. It will be fun to be on the scene and see what is going on with that, but we have work to do.

I feel lucky that I wake up right before the plane lands, as it makes a circle on approach out over the Caspian Sea—a beautiful view. We get checked into the Hyatt hotel, and I wind down by losing some money at blackjack. Off to bed.

Sunday, we all agree that it would be fun to drive north into the mountains. Five of us pile in the company minivan and head north out of Baku, passing some small lakes. We see some derelict oil equipment rusting away to nothingness and pass miles and miles of the old Soviet-style collective farms.

This region is famous for apples. Roadside stands are flush with buckets of apples, red and yellow, all stacked as pyramids in each bucket. We also drive by acres and acres of vineyards. The grape vines look brown and lifeless. Gorbachev reportedly ordered the vineyards burned in an attempt to suppress the Azeri breakaway. What a waste. My guess is that happened between 1991 and 1992. Grapevines take seven years to develop. Azerbaijan had some good quality vines in the old days, but not now.

As we drive further into the hills, we see the massive snow covered Caucus Mountains—fantastic views. Just north of Quba, we drive through a thick forest of deciduous trees. The road shrinks down to one lane through a narrow river valley.

Our lunch stop is a shoshlick (shish-k-bob) restaurant set among the trees. They cook the meats over a smoky, open pit fire and then serve them at the guests' tables. The tables are set at various levels on the hills around the main restaurant buildings, and each table has its own roof covering. We have a great lunch and then make the two-hour drive back to town.

Back to work—meetings, coordinating with other oil companies, and settling back in to the time zone here in Baku. Tuesday, I head to Villa Petrolea for meetings. It is quite a sight to see representatives from all these competing companies gathered together in a project. Make no mistake; what we are here to do is a long term project. We're planning thirty years' worth of work and an estimate of producing five billion barrels of oil. I get to go out into the field, too—we caravan out to oil field locations in the productive series of rock outcrops that are the main producing reservoir in Azerbaijan fields. I see a couple of long-haired, two-humped Bactrian camels, reminding me just exactly how far away from Houston I am. We spend the day looking at the rocks and getting sunburned. I find some hand-dug wells from the old Oilers days with wooden casings.

Mike and Evona are seconded by the company to work for AIOC. He and Evona—who grew up in Moscow—moved to Baku in January. Four of us get cleaned up after a second day out in the field and head to their apartment for a nice, talkative evening. It's a good change of pace from hitting a restaurant or bar.

Monday morning I'm feeling all the wine I drank at Mike and Evona's last night, so instead of working out I sleep in a little—I'm trying to rest up for the big trip home that's almost here. I'm the only representative from my company attending a really nice dinner Akif Narmanov, the SOCAR VP, threw for the people putting on the meetings and courses this week. We eat fine appetizers to surprisingly good live music—the ensemble, playing jazz, includes a piano player, standup bass, and a guy alternating on sax and violin. There are some substantial musicians in this region of the world; many who were career trained in the Soviet system and are now available as support for that system has declined. We have five or six toasts, each with a shot of vodka. A fine evening albeit a bit cloudy on the ending. Despite my late-night, Tuesday is get up and go day. I actually don't fly out until later, so I roll into the office as normal for the morning routine. I have a few emails to send and a proposal to type up before I leave, which gets written, translated, and delivered by 1:00 p.m.

I get to take it easy before going to the airport. Jacob and I catch an early steak dinner because we know it will be a while before we eat on the airplane. As I'm going through airport check-in, I watch the customs guy try to get some cash from a British couple who are heading towards Central Asia with a couple of rugs. I had to give them kudos for sticking to their guns; they hung tough, and didn't pay him anything. Without all our local connections, we would probably go through the same thing.

I fly into London and find out that the day before there was an IRA bomb scare that shut down the airport. It had direct impact on travelers—backing up like crazy. I manage to catch some sleep on the flight, and I'm feeling good—but I feel even better when I meet my wife and son at the curb in front of the airport. Home at last.

Back to Baku

It is now June, 1997, and this is my sixth trip to Baku. I just realized that I have had more offices (twenty-three) than years of industry experience (seventeen). Oil prices have been high lately, and the demand for geologists has increased. In the last year, the company has had many professionals quit and join other companies. I even floated my resume to a couple of job search firms in January—I have now had two job interviews with independent oil companies for geologist positions. Both companies are in it for the long term, I would have a chance to have more impact and the money would be good. It does feel funny to think about actually leaving the company where I have worked for sixteen years. I recently got a pay raise but have been overdue for a promotion for years now.

This trip to Baku will be for one week of training workshops for the Azerbaijani scientists. Dr. Vaughn will lead four of us putting on a workshop, my boss Sam has some technical meetings planned in addition to this, so we will be visiting a lot more people than I had planned. The Company Soviet Union area president Randy will meet with the President of Azerbaijan, Heydar Aliev, and proposes a joint study SOCAR with our company on how to develop, build an infrastructure, and export the huge gas reserves of Azerbaijan. Heydar responds with a "Let's do it" type of response, and says he will be in Washington in July and would like to sign something at the political ceremony. The company's production sharing agreement (PSA) for two offshore exploration blocks is what he wants to sign. Negotiations on that have been dragging on for a year.

Back to the training school. We do a quick scouting trip out to the field to prepare for the class trip we will lead—on the way back we go a different route and take a wrong turn. I find myself in a forest of old well derricks, dirt mounds, oil and brine pools, electric wires, and rusting steel equipment everywhere. It's all a testimony to how aggressive business has been done in Azerbaijan in recent years. Monday morning I wake up early for work—I need to be sharp for the big opening day of our training class. Scientists start showing up; they are from the national oil company, SOCAR, the Geologic Institute, and a couple of university students thrown in for good measure. Sam our Region Manager, kicks it off with welcome words. I'm up next and provide an overview and the logistics of the workshop, then Roger, the main technical leader, begins the first lecture. We also have two translators.

Out in the hall, I get cornered by four people from the news media who all want Russian language press releases. I grab one of the translators from inside, and the next thing I know I am being interviewed with tape recorders in my face. The reporters ask questions about the school, what we think of Azerbaijan's scientists, and then ask sensitive questions about the company's negotiations for offshore exploration blocks. I need to be very careful about answering these last questions especially, because the company has designated spokespeople for media and government relations. I do ok—as evidenced by what we read days later.

The workshop goes well with a lecture or two and a lot of exercises to apply the concepts taught in the class about sedimentation concepts—many of the students are doing well. I enjoy answering questions via a translator, but a lot of the time I am out dealing with various planning issues with the Hyatt, and making phone calls. I have a cell phone from the company to use while I'm here…my first time to use a "mobile" phone (at this date, still a rather new thing for the general public to use). I slip out and visit Ali at the Field Production Group office to follow-up with him since our December visit, and review the April proposal I sent him for oil field studies and log data. We need to visit them before too much time goes by, or they will think we are not serious. He isn't worried about obtaining a big money fee, so it's hard to keep him focused on the plan, they keep showing us various maps and diagrams. After an hour or so we settle on a plan for us to send back a proposal, which is good.

Sam and I return from visiting with Ali in time for the dinner we are throwing for the workshop attendees. An Israeli journalist is there as well, and Sam talks to him poolside. Our dinner is set up under five large umbrellas with tables to match. We snap the class photo by the pool and then Rauf, there to say a few words on behalf of Akif Narmanov, makes a few nice statements.

Friday is the last classroom day for the workshop, and again we slip out for a meeting—this time with the offshore exploration drilling company. Farkhad and his geologist Akif, are much more open for this visit than they were in December.

Sam and I are back in time for him to present each student their certificate at the front of the room. We all shake hands, and I enjoy seeing the smiles on students' faces. The company team then has a nice dinner at the steakhouse to celebrate—classroom side has gone perfectly well, and tomorrow is our field trip.

Saturday we load onto buses and two four-wheel-drive vehicles, which go to the office by mistake, causing an hour delay. Some of the students have never been to Kirrmaky Valley or to any rock outcrop before. We point out a few detailed features and explain stacking patterns and sequence stratigraphy on the outcrop—I can see that some of them get it and some are lost. To be fair, some of the folks sent to this class do not fully integrate geology interpretation on the job; some I suspect are lab workers. Now that the class is over, we spend another few days in the field—geologists are not meant to only write reports and live in offices. We are really in our natural environment working in the field. I originally got into geology to work outside, but now I find myself mainly in front of a computer. First stop is Kirmakau Valley near Balakhamy field.

That night Roger and I have a drink at the Britannia Pub. We talk to the bartender Marina, who says she has a degree in astrophysics. She just has not figured out what to do. She, like most young Azeri's, would like to leave but have no means. They are the generation in transition during the times of change from the Soviet rule to an independent Azerbaijan. Stability and opportunity take time to develop.

Nick and Jacob arrived last night and plan to join us in the field today. We go back to Kirmakau Valley and climb to the top of Balakhamy Hill for a look around. We see some old mud volcanoes and more hand-dug wells. Instead of going back to Balakhamy Quarry, we go to Lake Masazir to see a shallower part of the rock section.

I have really enjoyed my time in the field, including watching an old Azeri guy ride his skinny brown horse to herd his cows and sheep around the area. We give him a sandwich and an orange when he is working near our outcrop, he is very thankful. He rides his horse up on the outcrop to pose for us to take photos.

Despite getting my blood pumping by actually winning a little money in the casino, I manage to get a couple hours of sleep before my 3:15 am wake-up call to get ready—the driver is in the lobby. I pay my three thousand dollar bill and we climb into the company car to race to the airport in just over twenty minutes.

In Frankfurt, I try to find some toys for my son; I already have some perfume and a hand-painted tea container from Baku for my wife. I told my son I had some neat rocks for him when I talked to him on the phone, so if I don't find any cool toys, perhaps I will be okay.

With my job applications in play, it's possible this will be my last trip to Baku. Regardless, I hope I do not have to travel internationally again for a while. I have been gone from my family too often for too long; in interesting foreign places that just aren't home. Whatever the future brings, I hope it is bright and that we are together a lot more.

Chapter 10
Meetings and Sites in Egypt

October 1997

I have turned over a new leaf and am beginning an exciting (and intimidating) new job with a new company. I am now part of the HEET Team—Houston Egypt Exploration Team. With this new job comes a new set of challenges and new people to meet—I think I am up for it.

As the plane came in from London, circled by the pyramids, around downtown and into the airport, I was able to see Cairo's lights spread out in all directions. When we land an expeditor whisks us through customs. We pile into the two four-wheel drive vehicles with our luggage, and we are off. Two soccer games are being played in deserted areas of the airport parking lot under the street lights. I can smell the dust in the air. Our driver, Big Said, spoke no English. He laughed when I asked him a question.

It was an exciting reality check, but I was landing in an incredibly historically rich location of culture dating back many thousands of years. It's intimidating to think that I am now in a city of ten to fifteen million people, I speak no Arabic, and am starting a new job.

As I settle in my hotel room on the banks of the Nile River in Cairo, Egypt I finally have time to reflect on what's been happening since I resigned from a major oil company and joined an independent oil company.

In the morning, the driver meets me at the hotel to take me to the office. On the front steps, I meet Don Valentine, a tall thin man with white hair in his sixties who has worked in Egypt for many years with various companies and has been involved with success in the Western Desert. I get to meet a few of the other expatriate workers at the office, then get briefed on an afternoon trip plan to the duty-free store for some key stuff, like liquor.

I'm a bit zoned out as we make our stop at the duty-free store and buy a couple bottles of liquor and a case of beer for each person, as well as supplies for our upcoming trip. Egypt is trying to control alcohol so they note the purchase in your passport and try to limit you to two visits per year. This is why the guys living locally want to use our visitor's passport stamp. It takes several people to accomplish this process. The guy who writes the ticket, three women at a counter who look at my passport, another guy who approves it and finally a guy in a booth who actually collects payment.

Finally, at 10:30 a.m. we hit the road, a four vehicle caravan heading out of Cairo. At Ismailiya we catch a ferry across the Suez Canal to the Sinai Peninsula, and are in wide open desert flatlands. We stop to look at an Israeli tank left from the war with Egypt (1967-73). During that war Israel took the Sinai Peninsula and threatened to take Cairo, but other countries stepped in to halt the action. Israel dug in across the Sinai until 1973 when Egypt attacked and took it back, breaking the myth that the Israeli army was undefeatable. As we look around I think about my new co-worker geologists, a cast of characters, whom I think I will get along with very well.

We continue our journey north along the coastline of the Mediterranean Sea, a sparsely populated area with a few scattered towns. We go through military checkpoints and Hamed, riding in the lead car, presents the soldiers with a list of our passports and of the cars' plate numbers. Hamed, a geologist with our company, is the only native Egyptian with us and has done a lot of work to prepare for our review of the rock outcrops in the field. He is doing a great job leading our trip.

We arrive at El Arish and check into the ocean side Hotel—a modest looking, sandy colored stucco-type two story hotel along the beach. I join Doug Eller and James Adams for a run on the beach, which I hope will help stave off jet lag. After a group dinner I am having trouble staying awake through a lecture on the structural setting for the Sinai Peninsula and the Western Desert area of Egypt. I pass out the instant I hit the bed.

After a skimpy breakfast of white toast and coffee, we drive into town and then South back into the desert. The desert gives way to some large hills, but there is no vegetation anywhere. Oddly, once in a while I see people in the middle of nowhere; these are Bedouins. These nomads somehow scrape a living from the earth where most anyone else would die.

Our geology goal today is to see the hills in the northwest central part of the Sinai. These hills are anticlines set up by inversion faults with occasional strike slip movement, so they say. The late Cretaceous Continental Collision of North Africa with Europe caused inversion on what were originally normal faults. We will visit the Gebel (mountain) El Maghara and Gebel Yelleg to see what these structures look like. In order to visit this area of the desert, we had to acquire desert passes to get by the military road blocks. This northern part of the Sinai has a large Egyptian military presence. After the checkpoint, we turn down a road with a sign that says, "Road Forbidden to Foreigners." I see military bases and bunkers built into the hills, reminding me that I am in one of the most volatile regions the world has ever known—the Middle East. OK, technically we are in North Africa, but Egypt and Israel form the western gateway to the Middle East.

We spend the day looking at various structural features in an area near a former Israeli army base. All that's left are some roads now, and I see a Bedouin woman with a herd of goats milling around on some rocks—I can't say "grazing" because there is no vegetation in sight.

We check into a hotel and enjoy some drinks, cigars, and spend time getting to know each other. The four-man team I am part of is new to the company; all the Cairo-based people arrived about a year ago, and while receptive to us, they have built this from scratch and are possessive of their turf.

We check out by 7:00 a.m. and are on our way. Hamed gives us an overview while we look back across the road at the mountains or at the Red Sea. We discuss the details of structuring in the Red Sea and north in the Gulf of Suez where the big fields are trapped. Eighty percent of Egypt's oil production comes from the Gulf of Suez.

We head south to our next geology stop, a large subsurface fault that cuts through the area. A little hot spring trickles onto the beach here, and they tell me this is perhaps where Moses parted the Red Sea. A little further down the coast is Sharm El Sheikh, which Israel originally built in the 60s when they occupied the Sinai. The main attraction is the amazing snorkeling and deep sea diving. The Egypt State Park outside town is called Ras Mohammed. The park area is more arid rolling hills and no vegetation. Soon after passing the entry gate we see the coastline, which is rimmed with some of the most spectacular reef I have ever seen.

Underwater Fun

In the morning we check out the structural geology of the area, then get down to the business of snorkeling. Paul Miller and I hit the water first, tracing a five foot deep shelf about ten yards wide that ends in a sixty to eighty foot drop into dark blue water with fine white sand at the bottom. This precipitously dropping vertical wall is covered with coral of many varieties and fish swimming all around. We swim the wall for about an hour and then recess is over—back to the cars.

Our group breaks up; some of the people living here go back to be with their families in Cairo, while the rest of us check out more geology, then head in-land to Mount Sinai, where Moses received the Ten Commandments. We arrive at St. Catherine's monastery at the base of Mount Sinai that afternoon, and even though there is not much here, I find it moving. The monastery is nestled in a canyon above a valley with a small town. Built by the Greeks in 337 A.D., it reportedly marks the site of the burning bush from which God spoke to Moses. In the sixth century, they built a wall around the church, and now it is a complex of buildings with a resident staff of monks. Unfortunately, we are too late to go in, so I don't get to see the rare icons and historical items from the tenth and eleventh centuries.

I look up at the top almost wistfully. The hike to the top of Mnt. Sinai takes four to five hours and we do not have time. We do not want to drive after dark if we can avoid it because apparently locals believe their headlights will burn out, so they drive with them off at night. Also, when they break down, Egyptians will place a rock in the road to mark where they had trouble, and they won't always remove the rock after they fix their car and drive off. Put the "rock flares" together with slow-moving donkey carts in the road and the scary drop off at the edge of the blacktop; it just isn't a good idea to drive after dark.

We make it to Moon Beach for dinner, and I am somewhat amused when I have to share a two bedroom villa with the other guys from my team, Brian, Dave, and Greg. It seems like college geology field camp days; with roommates and driving around looking at rocks.

Back to Cairo

We spend the morning at the beach, and I get in some more snorkeling. I find a patch reef not far from the shore with some cool coral and fish, but this area is most popular for windsurfing. I see at least twenty sails up with folks zipping out and back—I want to try that sometime. We plan to have lunch and then drive back to Cairo.

Things get more complicated when Doug wakes up sick with some type of virus or bug and starts vomiting, feeling lightheaded and achy. It's a five-hour drive back to Cairo, and apparently it is best to get him back in case he needs medical help. We have to stop frequently for Doug to puke during the drive, and the closer we get to Cairo the more frequent the stops. He can hardly talk and just raises his hand every time he needs to stop. I feel really bad for him, but there is little we can do. We make it to Cairo that night and Doug recovers in a couple of days. I feel fine.

First thing in the morning I have a meeting with Vince Keller, our boss and the Egypt VP. My team has a lot to do before we fly back to Houston; technical meetings, data to gather and attend the company reviews for Stock Analysts in Cairo next week. We are supporting a plan to drill a well and perhaps drill other prospects nearby. It sounds almost laughable, but due to growth here in Cairo we struggle to find any office space. Eventually we find a company apartment across the street to layout out stuff.

We complete our review the next morning, and then Vince calls another meeting. After lunch my team goes with our local co-worker to an informal meeting with representatives of our partner company. That night, Vince offers to take us out for dinner, I get my first taste of downtown Cairo.

Traffic is unbelievable, it takes us an hour to drive the few miles. There are few lights but many traffic cops, both of which people seem to ignore—the drivers are as crazy as anywhere I have been. There are no lanes, cars just squeeze into any space available, cutting each other off with six inches to spare. People step off the curb right in front of you. Traffic may be slow because a guy with a cart pulled by a donkey or horse is in the road. Drivers constantly honk their horns, even if just sitting still, so the melody of Cairo is a cacophony of car horns.

We manage to find the restaurant—The King of Shrimp. From our table on the second floor, we look out the window and see a man on a ladder fixing a lamp on a post. Typically, Egyptians work on electrical things with the wires exposed—electricity on. Wow! Running "hot."

Since we plan to move to Cairo with our families someday, we try to see a Community Liaison Officer (even though we heard that the US Embassy in Cairo does not support US citizens, other than embassy employees). We get a little bit of information, but apparently the rumor is correct—we get no use of medical facilities, no counsel, and there are no functions open to US citizens living in Cairo. It turns out the reason the embassy officer agreed to meet us was he thought we were US military. As soon as we said we were an independent American oil company, he said, "Oh, be sure and register with us, but we can't really help you much." United States expatriates are on our own in these lands.

The Cairo operation of Geology & Geophysics seems chaotic, with so many wells drilling and political demands and regulations to keep up with. The work week here in Egypt is different, and since the Muslims prayer day is Friday, the company honors the schedule and we get Friday and Saturday off. The first destination is of course the Pyramids at Giza—could there be any doubt? We meet up with a co-worker and his family at the horse riding stables. There are actually thirty-eight different pyramids along the Nile, the Giza locations are the three largest and most famous. I have to say that seeing the pyramids for the first time on the back of a horse is a great way to experience it.

We next visit the Step Pyramid, entering through a long hallway lined with thick columns and emerging in a large courtyard at the base of the pyramid. I walk around and look at the hieroglyphics and tombs, most of which are cut in limestone. The carved blocks and glyphs are in granite, which must have taken forever to carve. Most of the statues from here are now in museums. I learn that this area had people living here as early as 2600 BC.

A passage to an underground area with painted hieroglyphics is locked. When Ryan asked the attendant "how much to open" it didn't work; so we figured something was wrong—turns out the lights weren't working. Another guy convinces us to follow him across the dunes to see something "good." Mohammed, our driver translates and we follow our "guide" to an area not yet open to the public. We see some low structures, columns, and a lot of glyphs. We tip him, of course.

Memphis is on the way back to town, and was the seat of power in Egypt for hundreds of years—2850 BC through 2180 BC, the second through the seventh dynasty. No large buildings are here, only statues and blocks with hieroglyphics. The featured piece is a statue of Ramses II laying on the ground, inside the two-story building built around it to preserve it.

We meet for dinner at Charlie and Cathy's house, and Hamed—our field trip leader is there to deliver a traditional Egyptian dish his wife has made. Kushari is considered to be the Egyptian national dish; it consists of pasta and tomato sauce, among other items, including rice, lentils, caramelized onions, garlic and chickpeas. It is the most popular lunch item in Egypt for the past hundred years. After dinner we have a few more drinks—and backgammon of all things until 2:00 a.m.

Saturday we head for the Egyptian National Museum, which is crowded with buses outside when we arrive. We spend a few hours taking in the sights, but I easily could have spent all day there. It was amazing to see King Tut's treasure, the many statues, preserved chariots, and artifacts. After the museum, we go to a downtown shopping area called Khan el Khalili, a tightly packed area with shops lining the streets and alleyways covering a number of blocks. It is very old, over 1000 years as a market. I buy some of the area's specialty, perfume bottles and other shiny trinkets.

Meeting Investors

It's Sunday—back to work day. After two days off, it seems right to be at work. We have a lot to do and won't be here much longer. I am preparing something to present to Vince (Egypt Exploration VP) later in the afternoon. I end up presenting our group's study results and the essential part was looking back at the last two years of results from an exploration drilling program, and explaining, technically, why some turned out to be oil wells while others—in fact a bad string of twenty wells—were dry hole failures. Predicting correctly when all the elements for hydrocarbon accumulations come together such as trap shape and adequate hydrocarbon charge, are things petroleum geologists worry about.

Monday the entire day is consumed by stock analysts, and investors visiting us in Cairo from the USA for a three-day review of Egypt activities. We arrive at the Mena House located near the pyramids and march in the front door in our suits. I look at the tourists enviously—from their expressions, I bet they are wondering what we are doing all dressed up. We will be in all day meetings Monday and Wednesday, giving an overview of our status, or potential production, and prospects for additional discoveries. The talks are upbeat and hopefully have a positive impact on the company stock price.

When I was with the major oil company, I only heard about meetings with investors at the corporate level, but here we talk directly to them. The talks are by geoscientists and engineers who are experts in their field, not corporate or PR types used to buttering up investors. At my last company, a staff of professional presenters would have written scripts and generated displays, and lots of eyes would have looked everything over. The company's trusted employees are free to say what they want, it's quite a difference in corporate culture. Some of the analysts are quite knowledgeable, but they basically want to be clear on where additional reserves are likely to be found, what volume of HC flow may be established, new cash flow, and the costs to develop the new reserves.

Tuesday is one of the key reasons I made the trip to Cairo, a technical committee meeting for the block operated by another company. After the meeting the Operations Management team will vote on the 1998 budget proposal—a big deal.

After lunch, back at the office we pack up our data to take to Houston for analysis—which is incomplete, so we make various arrangements for getting the missing data from Cairo to Houston, time is now short. Wednesday we have more meetings with stock analysts and we fly out Thursday. That night the company is entertaining several stock analysts and employees on a Nile River dinner boat cruise, it is quite an experience. All of the Cairo expatriates and their families get to go on this festive outing. As we get off the bus men in Pharaoh costumes and girls throwing rose petals greet us. Our party takes up one entire deck of the boat with a cocktail party and then dinner.

The sites from the river as the boat cruises up and down are beautiful. A belly dancer works the crowd. Later a whirling dervish spins in circles, twirling colorful cloths long after I would have fallen over and thrown up. I had heard of this, but didn't really know much about whirling dervish, which originated as an ancient sect of Islam that is known to work into a religious frenzy.

We meet up with Vince for dinner that night to discuss any remaining issues about our work plans before we leave in the a.m. We also talk about this crazy new adventure and how growing this operation will be fun.

In London, we rent a car and drive south to the Copthorne House Hotel. Doug Eller lived in London for a few years, so as the only one capable of driving on the right side of the car, he is our designated driver. Copthorne House Hotel was originally a farmhouse in the 1600s but is now a rambling hotel in the countryside. It's fun seeing where Doug used to live. We drove along narrow old country lanes to Dougs's old house located near a mansion. On a nearby hill was a fort run by William the Conqueror during the time of the Crusades.

We crisscross the area and then stop for dinner in a pub. At one point I have a rock station on full blast while Ryan bobs and weaves along in the back seat of our small Euro-car. He passes out a few minutes then re-surfaces with his un-lit stogie still in his teeth—awesome. It is interesting to think about what life was like through all the generations and centuries that passed through this area and these buildings.

For me, this closes out my Egypt work in the short term, because when I get back, Ryan and I are supposed to switch to another project. On the nine-hour flight back I watch some movies and try to sleep in order to be fresh when I get home. I'm thinking about seeing my wife and son and enjoying some family fun.

The Cairo life

I'm back in Cairo by May 1998, hitting the ground running with a full day at the office even though we are all still fuzzy from jet lag. The HEET (Houston Egypt Exploration Team) traveling team this time is four. We arrive at the company apartments at 1:00 a.m. Monday night, and we put in a full day on Tuesday.

A lot has changed since I was here last year. A building was added across the street, the basement remodeled into "the Bunker" and full computer workstations setup. The team will be here for about twelve days, but on the second day we find out Doug's sister in-law is dying—he hops on the first plane back. I will present his work at the partners Technical Committee Meeting ("TCM").

Jet lag is weird. I have been awake since 2:30 a.m. I read for a while, listen to music, lay in bed with the lights off for a while, get up, and lie down. Well, I think through a lot of stuff in these odd hours. I hope I remember the good stuff the next day.

Wednesday is packed full. We work until about 6:00 p.m. getting displays ready for the technical meeting. Thursday morning is a fun surprise. Hank picked me up to go running at 5:30 a.m. at Wadi Digla (a dry desert canyon). We head out of town, dodge trucks, and then leave the car to jog down the canyon just as the sun starts to come up. What a refreshing start to the day. We are back at the apartments by 7:00 a.m. to get ready for work.

Today is the last regular workday to prepare for our Sunday meeting where we plan to propose some new well locations and change the previous seismic program proposed and approved. During my meeting with Vince to discuss our strategy, I lean back in my chair to make a point—and it breaks, landing me on the floor.

We are off Friday so we head to the Kattamaya Country Club, which is very nice and may be the key to living in Cairo. We drive up some hills overlooking the city, and it is one of the clearest days I have seen here yet. I can see all of Cairo and across the desert to the other side of the Nile River, with a clear view of the pyramids at Giza. It takes my breath away—so different from Houston.

Another company couple living in Cairo, their son and their three dogs and I are all headed to the Cairo Hash House Harriers run. We actually go out to the same canyon where Hank and I ran a few days ago. Over a hundred people show up and after sign in and a few announcements, we take off racing across the desert. There are two different trails, with runners and walkers meeting at checkpoints. I also find out that most of the wives are going to take the entire summer to travel and stay away from Cairo.

Saturday we visit the company's field facilities outside Cairo in the Western Desert. We drive out Pyramid Road and outside of town we see a fledgling golf course community, a huge grave yard, and an abandoned Sadat City with maybe one hundred partially built buildings that we are told was a project by Anwar Sadat that was abandoned after he was killed. Sadat City is now a ghost town. Around Cairo, there are many partially built buildings. They say it may take years to finish; some have stopped in the middle due to a poor financial plan and/or for tax reasons—an unfinished building has less tax consequences. They remain incomplete at the top with people living below.

Three years ago there was nothing here at this remote site in the Western Desert. Now there is a huge oil and gas processing plant, three huge storage tanks capable of holding 350,000 barrels of oil, living quarters in permanent buildings, and the working rigs nearby. I've never walked through a production facility, so this is interesting and state-of-the-art, with touch sensitive screens and shiny metal equipment—an engineer's paradise.

The Field Manager welcomes us and gives a brief overview of the plant layout and functions. Before the oil can be put in the pipeline, it has to have water and gas stripped out. Gas is compressed to match the needed pressure to go in the output gas pipeline. Condensation from the gas is mixed with the oil to increase overall viscosity (flow) of the pipeline output product.

The Big Meeting

Sunday is the first day of the work week in Cairo and the day of our big meeting with the operating oil company of our block. We find out they have canceled the meeting. They received a letter from our president, which stated we should be operator of the Concession Block due to their poor management, and that the company was unhappy with progress for production operations. They responded with, "There is no need to have a technical meeting on the 17th, we have already agreed to the company's proposed wells." The situation is getting interesting, because the executive levels of our respective companies have a feud.

Every Monday the company's Egypt office has an operations meeting and all the expats attend to review all company activities. The conference room is nearly full. An informal air is maintained anyway, with various people chiming in when they know something about an area. A couple people roll in late. The amount of activity managed by this room of people is really impressive. There are hundreds of Egyptians that work in the fields, and the company is currently producing 70,000 BOPD from two concessions. There are discussions of two other concessions with discoveries to bring into production, operations, various wells drilling, seismic shooting partner, and government meetings and negotiations.

Later that morning, I meet with Vince to discuss a few things HEET is trying to do and what is happening here. I complete my topics and stand up to leave. "Don't leave yet," he says. "We have more to discuss. How would you like to move to Cairo later this year and start your overseas assignment?"

Ryan had warned me that this day was coming, so I'm prepared... A bit. It's still shocking to truly think about. The job Vince has in mind for me is very good. The company is ready to go to the next level of technology, which is what the HEET brings. With Don departing, it will be easy to slide me in as a replacement geologist manager and avoid seeking approval from the Egyptian Government Petroleum Company. I will be pushing the regional study and work my way into northern concessions activity; a ton of work.

I ask a few questions but understand that the details will come later. Part of me dreads the hassle of change and moving, but it is an amazing opportunity. I think it will be a fabulous experience for my wife and son to live overseas with me.

Wednesday morning I wake up with a new appreciation for the talk around me and expatriate life here in Cairo. I have a decent idea how a move will go—I've been listening—and it will be a hassle, but others have gone before me. I now look around me as though seeing a foreshadowing of times to come. We will make it fun, and Lord knows it will be interesting to move to Egypt.

That night back at the company flats, I'm looking forward to the fact that it's my last night. I'm thinking about how to pack for the flight home considering I get the short straw and Vince asks me to carry some data back on the airplane.

As I'm leaving the night's card game, Charlie quietly calls to me, "See you in August." So, he already knows of Vince's proposal to me. Oh well, no big deal. I guess it does not matter if everyone knows about it—it's not like I will reject the proposal. Looks like we'll be moving to Egypt.

Chapter 11
The Family Move

On August 3, 1998 my wife and I fly to Egypt via Frankfurt, Germany, leaving our little son with his Granny at our house. It's a sad parting, because we will be gone from him for so long, but he is looking forward to staying with her so at least he wasn't super sad as we left.

It's great traveling with my wife, sharing jet lag and the fun of exploring Frankfurt during our layover. We will be looking for houses in Cairo and trying to figure out the transition; but first we have some sites to see.

In Frankfort we find old St. Nicholas Church then tour the Grand Cathedral Dom Church and Museum. We see robes worn during the 1300s for coronation ceremonies plus chalices and jeweled crosses. We cross the River Rhine on the pedestrian bridge after popping open our umbrella in a light shower.

That night in Frankfurt, we both wake up at 1:00 a.m. due to jet lag. We watch a movie together and get to sleep by 3:00 a.m. We oversleep and almost miss our flight.

Looking at Cairo as a place to live opens your eyes to all of the stark differences between here and America—the poverty and giant piles of trash on the street are just one of the differences. I hope she is not too shocked at some of the appearances. Once passed it should be an adventure—not just this trip but the entire three-year assignment, we start to see signs that it could be fun too. The company HR Administrator gives us an overview and a tour of Maadi, the section of Cairo the company offices are located in and where most of the expatriates live. We hear about life in Maadi; the culture, activities, school, work, and the details of our living expenses deal with the company. We tour the Cairo American School and the areas of town where other expats live.

On all my other trips overseas, it was easy to explore and enjoy the idiosyncrasies of the places I visited without really thinking about what it would be like to live there. Now all the details stick out because we plan to move here. One day someone said, "I noticed a lot of things when I moved here, but after a while they begin to seem normal. You might write down things you notice early on here and they will be interesting to read later."

We quickly learn it may not be easy to find somewhere to live. We spend time with a number of different "real estate agents" who do their best to show us different places. Most of the flats we visit do not have the air conditioner on—and it is over a hundred degrees. Whew!

After seeing about thirty different places, we have a better idea of what is available on the market—we have some possibilities, but nothing that really works. Especially not the grungy one story villa with bloody hand prints on the wall—left over from a Ramadan goat sacrifice. We get a chance to let our hair down on Thursday with Hank, his wife and their two boys, and take a big sailboat ride on the Nile River. It's a great break from the hustle of the city. We drink a couple beers and watch the sun go down while the old man sails the large wooden boat with a huge canvas sail. We talk of life in Cairo and listen to music.

Friday we tour the Egyptian National Museum, and my wife, with her anthropology and archeology experience, finds it very interesting. Saturday we enjoy dinner together at the Grill, the hotel's finest restaurant overlooking the Nile; a great way to end her visit.

We leave the hotel at 12:30 a.m. for the airport, and I am surprised how busy the streets are at this time—the Egyptian people stay up late and go outdoors because it is too hot to stay in their apartments, most of which do not have air conditioning. I get my wife to her gate, and then she's gone… I am alone again in Egypt, where I will continue the house hunt and start working.

I spend a Sunday, the first day of the work here, with Paul Miller, discussing the situation I am about to enter. He is strong technically and he worked in Cairo with a major oil company before joining ours. He spells out that the Cairo office is not well organized—their data isn't organized, people's areas of responsibility overlap, and every day seems to bring a new crisis from within the company, our partners, or the government oil company. It's crazy, but I find myself actually looking forward to juggling these challenges and the opportunity to make a significant impact myself. My new schedule starts to take shape, working with the Cairo office and trying to see houses in the early part of the day. I spend a lot of time with Don Valentine whom I am replacing. He has been here more than eight years and I am guessing is over 60 years old. He is going out a hero, being able to lay claim to some big Western Desert discoveries.

When I arrive in September, workers are adding a floor on top of my office building—no need to move as construction one floor above my office is no problem in Egypt. We need the extra office space, but the pounding noise, the flies, and dust filtering down through the tin covered hole goes on for months. My keyboard turns black from dust stains. The construction process here does not seem efficient. For example, the stairway is done—new carpet and nicely painted walls. Then the electrician decides to carve a channel in the cement wall from the ceiling to the floor to install a main cable. Painters will just have to patch the wall and paint again.

We sure could stand to have oil prices go up to take some pressure off. The company stock has dropped to about half price. All oil stocks are down because the oil price dropped from $18-20/BBL to about $14 with drops even lower. That's the lowest price since 1986.

We talk of mergers and that the company could get bought out; but luckily there is no good fit for someone large enough to do it. Yesterday the biggest oil and gas merger ever was announced. BP bought Amoco.

We are a bit on edge because there were near simultaneous bombings at the US Embassy in Nairobi, Kenya, and Dar es Salaam, Tanzania. The bombs apparently went off near the embassies, not inside, but they were large and the current count is over one hundred and fifty dead, with over four thousand injured. At the company, we pay very close attention to this, since they may go after other US targets. The US Embassy in Egypt has issued a general warning, but it looks like the danger is past, and the company isn't changing any plans—we are all just proceeding with caution.

Wednesday night from the hotel balcony overlooking the Nile, I realize this is the last night of my business travel era, 1991-1998.

When I return to Cairo, it will be to begin a three-year overseas posting. It's intimidating, but not overwhelming. I have a good feeling that it will work out well.

The whole flight home, my one thought is to be home in time to greet my son after his second day of school. My flight should touch down at 2:30 p.m., and if I catch a limo ride from the airport, I should be able to be there before his bus arrives near the house at 3:30 p.m. Unfortunately the airport wasn't appraised of my travel plans, and U.S. Customs and Immigration is handling three other planes. I wait in agony for twenty-five minutes for my second bag to come out of the luggage turnstile—it is now 3:00 p.m.

There's no traffic right now, so we are able to drive quickly. As the car turns onto a road near my house, we get stuck behind a bus. It's turning for my house. It's my son's bus. I can see my wife waiting in the front yard and I jump out of the car just as my son steps down from the bus with his blue backpack.

I yell his name. He turns and sees me and runs to jump into my arms. What a great reunion.

Get Packed

After a steamy hot summer in Houston and making decisions about our stuff at the house—what we are going to sell, store, give away, or ship to Cairo and making piles or tagging things to bring with us on the plane or ship by sea—we are almost set. We have seen the doctor and the dentist, and after enjoying some going away parties, we're nearly ready. Now the big packing job begins—it's hard because we have to survive on what we can travel with while our stuff is shipped.

A family vacation to Coronado Island in San Diego, CA, is time for a few days of fun to celebrate our 11th anniversary, and be together before I depart for Egypt on September 11th. My family will move at the end of the year. I'm packing for a stay of more than two months but planning for a three-year stint. The company will pay for a couple extra bags. I end up having too many checked bags, and pay for the extras.

After landing and meeting the company driver, we roll through the massive sprawling city and arrive at the company apartment. I have no one to call in country to verify I arrived okay. Overall, I have a good feeling this will work out, but my first night is lonely.

Making a difference on the job has already been keeping me up at night, but now I have to build a life for my family here. The plan is for me to steward two concessions plus push the regional study efforts. My boss Vince tells me that since I have already had a house hunting trip, I should look for a place to live at night and on the weekends— not during company time. Great.

A co-worker recalled his first day at work with the Egyptian Petroleum Company in the Qarun joint venture, when the Commodore came into existence.

My first morning in the stifling heat of Cairo was spent in a unairconditioned, banged up taxi careening through the loud and dirty chaos of my new home city. Eventually, the cab pulled a violent 180 degree turn around a donkey cart and slammed on its brakes. Not knowing any better I paid the driver 3 times what I should have, stepped out into the sweltering street. Directly in front of me was a dusty, 5 story sand-colored concrete building punctuated by two dusty green plastic bushes out front. Above the nondescript entrance a sign read Qarun Petroleum...my new office. The next thing I know I'm being escorted by two "security" guards (dressed like turn-of-the-century British admirals) up to the top floor of the building and into a huge opulently decorated room replete with embroidered draperies, Louis the XVI style couches, and elaborately inlaid coffee tables. I admit I was in a pretty dense fog due to jet lag, lack of sleep, and the free booze offered on the international flight; but it was beginning to dawn on me that I had fallen through the rabbit hole. Within moments a middle aged Arab women, cloaked head to toe in yellow, barged into the room barking questions at me in the King's English. One of the questions stumped me, "What is your title?" she asked. I was flummoxed. "Ah...well...you mean geologist?" I stammered.

"Of course you're a geologist." She said with a tone of contempt, "but what is your title?" "Petroleum Geologist." I said with what I hoped was extra weight and gravity. "Yes, yes, we have very many very good Egyptian petroleum geologists here; I asked you your corporate title."

It had never occurred to me to ask anyone that hired me what my 'official corporate title' might be. I must have been giving her a bewildered look because she began doing something amazing. She started clucking....like a chicken! And the admirals standing on either side of the door began to snicker.

I looked at the admirals, then at the clucking woman, back at the admirals, back at the clucking woman, and finally my growing sense of irritation kicked my bewildered brain back into gear. I didn't know much, but I knew I outranked the snickering admirals guarding the door. What outranks an admiral I thought...and then I had my answer.

"I'm a Commodore." I said loudly and confidently to the clucking woman.

However, in the ensuing silence and I noticed a skeptical scowl, so trying to match her tone of contempt; I spelled it for her..."C-O-M-M-O-D-O-R-E."

Two weeks later she delivered 1,000 Qarun Petroleum business cards to me and under my name was my new title, "Commodore".

The company offices are converted apartment buildings, and I have a nice office on the second floor. We have twenty-four hour a day security, and they work hard to be professional, speak fair English, and try to greet people by name. The office staff is a mix of Egyptians and expatriates—many geologists, plus accountants, secretaries, and computer people. At first glance, the Cairo office national staff seems very Western, but the cultural differences are just under the surface. They are devote Muslims, as far as I can tell, and though the people we have hired locally are quite intelligent, they do not charge ahead and do many things on their own. Nearly everyone, except for two women, wears Western clothing, and there are computers in every office. This office has come a long way in just three years.

My title is Geologic Manager and fellow G&G people seem to listen to me. The high-tech training I received from my previous company has definitely given me a technical advantage.

Driving

The day after I land I hop in my assigned car after work, my map on the seat, and start finding my way around town. While I make a few wrong turns, I make it there.

Driving in Egypt is an acquired skill. Cars are left side drive and road flow is modeled after the USA, however things are very different such as the basic rule to squeeze into any space into which your car might fit and move forward. People honk their horns constantly and cut each other off all the time, but no one gets truly upset—it's just the way it is. On any day while driving, you are likely to see a car driving the wrong way on a one-way street. There are no traffic lights, no rules, and sometimes no logic. The police are no help, they just watch. Police pull people over once in a while, but most people say if the police try to pull them over they just ignore them and keep going.

I am assigned a small, white Toyota Camry, which is a fine car, but actually a disadvantage. Most of the expatriates have large four-wheel-drive Land Cruisers, one of which I am on the waiting list for. Egyptians respect a bigger car and are less likely to cut in front of you, but I will just have to make do. Navigating is a challenge because the few signs are not in English, the streets are twisted and narrow, and the traffic circles, left over from the years of British rule are chaotic.

The main part of Maadi is nicely laid out, but around the edges Egyptian dominant areas have grown with tall apartment buildings, narrow winding streets, many pedestrians, kids, and street vendors everywhere. In October, I try to drive to the new Gold's Gym near the overpass. I get lost and end up in an Egyptian area I had never seen before. I drive through kids swarming out of school, about five miles per hour, twisting and turning until I finally hit a large street that I recognize and make it back to a familiar area.

Downtown Cairo is another matter. There are streets that are not even on maps. Typically, we get a company driver to take us into Cairo if we need to go to a certain store or restaurant. Most memorable are the trips to the Khan de Kalili—a trader's section deep in Cairo that is over a thousand years old.

Still House Hunting

Well, I get settled into work, but the difficulty of finding somewhere to live when my family arrives after Christmas, hangs over my head. The company will pay $2400 a month for rent (for a family with one child), which is good but the very nice places are above that price range—so to get them you need to go "out of pocket." I think I line one up, but then problems start; the deal falls apart, leaving me scrambling to find another place.

Local Professions

Boabs are people, usually old men, who live in a small shack around an apartment building or villa and "take care of things." He may wash the car, help carry in your bags once in a while, or keep beggars away, but mainly he just sits and watches the world go by. Do not insult the gardener by calling him a boab. Gardeners are a "skilled" profession here in Egypt.

Garbage collection is a major operation. Most of it is picked up by large rickety carts manned by two or three people and pulled by donkeys. These donkeys are beaten and mistreated beyond belief. Some of the garbage people are young boys and even girls who, I guess, do not go to school. The garbage is taken somewhere and dumped. Unfortunately, not all garbage is taken to a designated area, and there are piles of garbage along the streets of Maadi. Too bad because this area could have a lot more charm if it was kept up a bit more.

Another interesting profession that exists in Egypt are the self-designated parking attendants. In busy areas, they may point at the spot you are about to pull into. They may hold the door after you have already opened it. He may rub a dirty rag over a couple of your windows. He may point to your car and then his eyes as you walk off—I watch for you. The best thing he might do is stop traffic while you back out. He only expects a small tip, or "backshish"—a couple pounds and he is satisfied.

Pedestrians walk close to the road and step out in front of cars all the time. It is as if they feel protected, so they take risks. Some people joke around and say they are not worried because Allah has a plan, Allah will protect them, and they won't die before their planned time. I hear as many as fifty pedestrians a day are killed by cars in Cairo. This estimate may be high but sadly people are hit by cars every day.

Fall

In October and November I am busy at work getting set up, watching a couple of wells being drilled, and setting up a data room to show one of our acreage blocks to potential partners to whom we want to sell some interest. By November 20 when I leave for Houston, I as Plan 1999 coordinator have to gather everyone's displays and my own into the company's Egypt "plan" book. I return on November 30, and have to finalize this plan material for the Region Vice President. I am to take it to Houston for the December review.

Back in Cairo, Mahmoud, my "realtor" seems more like a used car hustler than anything. The more you look, the better your chance of finding something good. Realtors find out about availability by word-of-mouth and just driving around, as there is no listing service in Cairo. Realtors are paid with one month's rent from the landlord when the deal is made.

Mahmoud starts calling me almost every day, saying, "How are you today my friend? I have a special place for you to see." I go out a few times a week during the evening and weekends. By November, I am quite familiar with the area and I know just what my wife and I want: A ground floor place with some grass or garden area, hopefully in a quiet neighborhood.

I go home for Thanksgiving with nothing firm. After visiting sixty-five places over three months or more, we have a couple we liked. I finally find a great place near school, and I tell Mahmoud, "Get me in there." I had seen too many dark, dumpy places in poor locations that needed major work. This apartment is within walking distance of the school and has a nice private yard. We start negotiations on December 6, but it drags on into the next day—talk about pressure. I am returning after Christmas with my family and we need to lock up a place to live—four months of looking. Ugh.

I finally sign the lease on the afternoon of December 7th, then work until 1:00 a.m. and board the plane to Houston at 3:00 a.m. By making the company meeting in Houston my boss says I can stay in Houston, work a few days there and then begin the move, which was originally scheduled for December 18th. This extra time home to help my wife get ready to go is a nice little year-end bonus.

We were supposed to move this past spring, but as I fly back home, I reflect that things worked out for the best. Our move got postponed due to the Luxor murders; but we wondered if it was divine intervention—not long after we found out we weren't going, my father-in-law became ill and passed away in April. We are now thankful that we didn't have to try to handle the move at that time and we were able to be with the family.

Back in Houston I have to work at the office a few days in a whirlwind of things to do there and at home. My wife has done an amazing job and has most of our house's contents in order—what to keep, store or give away. It's crazy how much junk piles up in a house in ten years.

Lots of goodbyes—my son's friends, our friends and neighbors. We celebrate my fortieth birthday on December 18th with a great dinner—my wife surprises me with a party the next day. We have a great gathering of all our neighbors, friends, and new work friends.

Insanity. My mom arrives the next day, and we're pushing for our final packing decisions before Christmas. We are to leave New Year's Eve. A setback. My son gets sick with a fever and bad sore throat the day after my mom arrives. He's down a few days, but by Christmas Eve, he feels good enough to catch a movie—*Prince of Egypt*, appropriately enough. The doc diagnoses him, it's mononucleosis. We are told he is past the contagious part, but he'll be more tired than normal. Life at home is odd, poised to leave as we are. We have no car—we sold both cars. So we have to rent a car. Most of our stuff shipped for Egypt on December 1, while I was gone—except for the stuff we're actually taking with us on the plane.

The movers arrive Monday, December 28, the day after my mom left. In the course of a day, the Crown movers pack our stuff into four giant wooden crates that are loaded onto a flatbed truck. Surrounded by just the stuff we are taking with us on the plane and a few last odds and ends we'll take to the storage unit ourselves our (now empty) house has a very odd feeling. In fact, it's almost a relief to head to a hotel for the last few days—being in the empty house just feels strange.

Goodbye.

Moving day is here, December 31st. It's the last day of 1998 and with a new year we are embarking on what feels like a new life. I have to buy one more suitcase, putting our total at thirteen—plus our dog, Greta, in her cage.

The neatest thing happens as we are doing our final packing. A bunch of our neighbors come by again to say goodbye. We have had goodbye parties and other celebrations, but this extra show of love is touching. Also, I welcome some help loading bags from these two couples—longtime friends, who drive to the airport with us, which is great because the bags don't all fit in the limo.

Lufthansa Supervisor "Olga" gave me more grief (I've had to deal with her before). This time she thought Greta's kennel was too small. We thought we had the biggest one they made and had to sign a waiver not to hold the airline responsible. We knew Greta would be okay, she likes her cozy kennel. It's funny the things that prove to be a headache.

I can't even describe the feeling of entering the Houston airport for what seems like a final time; a door closing on our old life and opening to a new one. That "new door" opens via Frankfurt, Germany late in the afternoon on the 31st. We fly out so tired we are unable to stay awake till midnight Houston time to welcome the New Year.

My son doesn't relax until two hours out from Frankfurt, when he crawls into my wife's lap to fall asleep, which means she got even less sleep. At least he sleeps most of the way to Cairo.

Thankfully, after collecting all our baggage—three carts worth—we sail through passport check, but then the driver isn't there waiting. When he finally does show it's just him in one car, into which we load all our bags; although we had made plans with the office to send two large cars knowing we would have a mountain of luggage. We hire a "local limo"—lucky the airport has some nice cars so we can avoid riding in a local un-air-conditioned tiny taxi. We arrive at our temporary home tired and hungry. We fall asleep but wake at 4:00 a.m. from the jetlag. My wife and son are up reading, trying to go back to sleep, watching Rug Rat tapes, and unpacking. By the time I get up for work in the morning, they're crashing. So begins the first day of our new life.

A New Life

We begin our new life as a family in Egypt on New Year's Day, January 1, 1999. Our apartment number 1 is in the company flats just around the corner from the office. It has a living room, kitchen, one bathroom, and three bedrooms. It is furnished with a television and a sparse set of kitchenware.

Being on the ground floor, is a bit noisy with people coming and going, cars, and stray dogs that roam the area. It's dirtier than we're used to from the States, but it's much cleaner than many other places I've been. The apartment is sparsely decorated and a bit dark but we'll only be here a short time until our place's renovations are completed.

Being so close to the office has its benefits, international phone lines and internet for my computer so we can email family and friends. The area around the office is called New Maadi, fellow company people who moved here before us joke about the company flats. Most have spent time living here and say they got really tired of it.

I've seen how Egyptian workers and contractors move slowly with work at the office, so my fingers are crossed that the renovations will go smoothly. The company rep. says three weeks, but I feel it may drag on longer, we'll see.

I'm glad to see my wife jump in with both feet and adapt quickly to the situation. She immediately gets involved with the renovation, selecting colors, paint, bathroom and kitchen fixtures, which involved a lot of time shopping to find the right stuff. The first week, we go to the Cairo American school ("CAC" College, even though it is K through 12) so we could meet the elementary principle. My son will be in a class of only fifteen children. They will have music, PE, art, and a computer lab twice a week. The computer lab is stocked with brand new mega memory Apple computers. They have a huge library the whole family can use along with a track, weight room, and a heated swimming pool. My son will have swimming lessons the last six weeks of school.

My son's first day of school is Sunday, January 1. We drive and park at our apartment to be then walk him to CAC. It is a large school with over seven hundred students from about fifty countries. It seems to be of private school caliber considering the amenities and quality of teachers. Mrs. Lockner is energetic and seems to be a lot of fun. The classroom is filled with toys, learning games and computers. My son joins right in with his new class, no problem—I am really glad to see that. He is definitely happy to have kids to play with.

Ramadan is just ending, and the Cairo office celebrates holidays along with Egypt, rather than US ones. This means a long weekend coming up for us. It will be good to be away so we don't have to see the sheep slaughtered in the streets. Ramadan lasts for a lunar month and basically it is a month of sleep deprivation and hunger. Muslims fast from dawn till dusk eating large meals after the sun goes down and at late night parties. A man walks down the street banging the drum at 3:30 a.m. to remind everyone to eat their "sohour," a tradition started in Baghdad to eat before the sun rises. People pay him tips at the end of Ramadan. The company lets national employees work from 9:30 a.m. until 3:30 p.m. during Ramadan, and while it seems like anyone could handle the schedule indefinitely, some local parties serve dinner at 1:00-2:00 a.m. The schedule takes its toll, and very little work gets done by the locals during Ramadan. Egypt's drivers are even crazier than usual, made edgy from lack of food and sleep. So stay off the road right before sunset or Iftar—when food is served.

Vacation in the Western Desert

Tuesday, January 19th, we meet up with our Egyptian tour guides on the other side of the Giza pyramids to fuel up both tanks on our four-wheel-drive Toyota Land Cruiser, as well as fill four five-gallon gas cans to attach to the roof. We are part of a caravan of five families, each in our own vehicle sandwiched in between two guide trucks. We pull out in a line to begin our four day excursion into the Western Desert.

Looking west, the landscape is bleak and flat to the horizon. After a couple of hours we leave the pavement and pause to let some of the air out of the tires to improve traction in the sand—while receiving instructions on how to drive in sand and on rocky terrain from our guides. After crossing some railroad tracks we enter the desert—with nothing man-made in sight.

We do not expect to see pavement again until Friday and will travel about four hundred kilometers off road. The remoteness would freak us out if we were not with a big group and professional guides. The flat gives way to long rolling dunes, back to sand flats at times, then vast pebble covered areas—not a body of water spotted in four days.

Sometimes we drive very fast across the sand dunes, sometimes very slow—and occasionally we get stuck. We travel several hours a day, cover great distances, and endure concerns about having enough gas and being careful with our engines to get through such a remote area.

Day one at about 1:00 p.m. we stop for lunch at a small depression with a couple trees. Apparently this is a popular camel hang out, as evidenced by all the droppings. In fact, Ahmed, our number one guide (we call him "the General") says he followed camel treks to find this place. Lunch consists of tuna or spam with veggies and condiments spooned onto pita bread. I see five camels in the distance.

Our traveling group includes: our family including our big dog Greta; the Walkers and their two dogs; three other families and in total nine kids. The guides of Zandora Expeditions are Wael, author and desert traveler/explorer; Ahmed, the "General," a former military man who worked this desert and the great sand sea for twelve years, and chased smugglers both Bedouin and Libyan; Gordon (Ghardoun) from Sudan; the cook and Mohamed, who drives the supply vehicle; Tarae, another helper; and Maha, conversationalist and female friend of the guide team. Ahmed and the other guides seem to know what they are doing.

We drive the rest of the day in sand, and I manage to get us stuck once. We got out without too much trouble, and at about 4:30 p.m. we pull into the shadow of a giant dune to make camp. Kids spring out of the cars and race up the dune before any of the adults can disagree. We set up tents and talk around a campfire until dinner is ready about 9:00 p.m.

In the morning, we all pick a different direction to look in the dunes for a good bathroom spot. After some coffee and an Egyptian breakfast of sliced cheese and more pita bread, we pile back into the vehicles to continue our journey. Late in the afternoon, we stop at a basin with a hole or a crack in the ground—the famous cave Dejar. First discovered in 1873 and then rediscovered in 1980s, some Germans placed a notebook at the entrance with a picture of them discovering it. They also attached a warning not to take any antiquity from the cave and destroy its future scientific value.

Down inside, lots of sand has blown into the opening, so you have to slide down the sand on your backside in order to emerge into a large room filled with massive rock stalactites hanging from the ceiling. Apparently this was once a wet cave, but now it is very dry. The floor is sand. There is little evidence of occupation inside the cave but outside for quite some distance we find flint, some triangular shapes and some pottery that someone says is of Roman vintage.

We make camp a couple hundred yards north of the cave, and just before dark two Egyptian vehicles drive up in search of the cave. Ahmed gives them directions—he loves the local's interest.

The next morning our travel turns from sand to rocky terrain. We come across the two Egyptian vehicles we saw yesterday, broken down. Our group stops to help. Our Guide gives them an engine belt and some oil and explains, it is the rule of the desert that you stop and help. Later, the two Egyptian trucks pass us and disappear. We hit more sand and the pace picks up as we search for our next destination—the White Desert, marked by giant chalky limestone monoliths. The iconic columns protrude up from the sandy desert floor and we camp among them for our last night. The kids really enjoyed climbing on a mushroom shaped one and sliding down on their bottoms, turning their rear ends completely white.

After a windy night, where some tents are blown down and need to be relocated, we drive along a line of dunes all the way to the paved road. At one point we have to cross over a long row of dunes we have been following. We have to circle to gain speed in order to carry us over the top, before going up and over a few more like a roller coaster. We were happy to see the narrow strip of highway when we reached it on the fourth day south from Farafra Oasis. Upon finding pavement, we say goodbye to our guides who are staying longer in the desert. We go on further down the road and arrive at an oasis. The local children, who run to our cars yelling, "Hello," (the only word in English they know) are so cute. It's a long drive home, and everyone is tired. As it gets dark, it's a bit scary since Egyptian drivers often do not use their headlights. A couple times—as we sped along about 50 mph—cars pull out in front of me and I have to swerve to avoid a collision. We are happy to finally arrive at our apartment, even though it is temporary and the bed is hard.

This has been a tremendous experience so early in our Egypt time. We hope to be able to travel and explore many new areas while we are here. My wife and I start Arabic classes soon, my son already has. Hopefully we will soon be able to communicate better with the local people.

Chapter 12
Settling into Egypt

February, 1999

While we get settled into family life in Egypt, work demands continue to grow. My wife and I are enjoying our Arabic classes although I don't have many occasions to use it. The language of business at work is English, however we are learning more about the culture, and the Egyptian people really appreciate that effort.

Our own place on Road 208 in Maadi still isn't done, and I'm doing what I can to move things along. Most of the work is done, but we just can't get some of the final details completed so we can move in. Tamir, our contractor manager is trying… but things are done the "Egyptian" way. Reviews with senior management are looming at the end of February, so my wife has to take over working with Tamir—and even pack for us to move into our place; while I am working long hours. She's done a terrific job pressing forward and getting us ready to move (again). We are sick of the company apartment.

I get to meet the Joint Venture Government Company people I will probably be working with because the company has a working interest as non-operator. I am scheduled to be assigned to that company, which operates many producing fields in the Western Desert for the partnership. I'm intended to influence for the good of the company and will be called a "Geological Expert." It's a bad time for the oil industry—oil prices are in a tailspin and budget cuts are the norm. We hit rock bottom with Brent Oil down to $9.80 a barrel on Feb. 12th, and NYMEX sells for less than $11. Layoffs are occurring—thankfully not many at my company—and drilling rig counts are dropping. Big players are merging on a global scale; BP just bought out Amoco, and Exxon bought Mobil.

Paul Miller has lived in Egypt for about six years—initially with a competitor company and now for our company—he has a dream to do Wadi Digla with music. So one day he rents a big PA system and we have a cookout/music fest late into the night in Wadi Digla canyon. It's surreal to be out in the dry dusty, treeless canyon at sunset; bouncing sound off the canyon walls.

February 28th, reviews with Sr. Management, go well for my parts with the two operated concessions, but not much progress is being made with my Western Desert regional geology project. I give each presentation on Sunday, but Fred criticizes me for not having done more on the regional study. It was still upbeat. Oh well, two out of three ain't bad.

I find myself lying awake at night trying to figure out how to get the Egyptians to do more work with me on the regional study, as the other expats do not have much time to help due to ongoing operations. I start having weekly meetings with different work groups, each assigned to different aspects of the study. This may work well in this culture, since I assign specific things to certain individuals and the weekly follow-up will hopefully resolve problems, delays and so forth.

Life in Our Villa

We sleep in our new place on March 1, 1999. Thank God the wait is over. I don't actually even move my stuff over until after the reviews for visiting Sr. Management, and I work late through March 2nd until they head out of town. Only then could I begin moving the rest of our stuff piecemeal from the company flats to our new place.

We have the entire ground floor of the building and the surrounding garden inside the walls—we expats call it a "villa." The wonderful thing is that it is walking distance—one block—from the American school. It's great to unload our shipment into our flat. As soon as my son's bed and boxes of toys are in his room he's set. He plays all day while my wife and I work to get other stuff in order—perfect.

I use the boxes leftover from our move to build a box maze for my son's birthday party—a Godzilla-themed blast. It was fun watching my son come out in his Godzilla suit throwing party poppers and chasing the other kids into the maze.

At the end of March we're finally assigned a big white Toyota Land Cruiser of our own. We have a metal roof rack installed on expectation of more travels. To celebrate we pack up the car, join some others and drive to St. Catherine's Monastery, at the base of Mount Sinai for one night and then camp along the Red Sea at Ras Mohamed Parks. Seventy days after Ramadan ends comes the Feast of Sacrifice, Eid El Adha, and a three-day weekend for us. The feast commemorates the biblical event of Abraham nearly sacrificing Isaac before God stopped him at the last moment by sending a ram to sacrifice instead. We drive east in our four car caravan through the Suez Canal by way of a tunnel to the Sinai Peninsula, the gateway between Africa and Asia and the bridge between the Mediterranean and Red Sea. We pass by turquoise water in the Gulf of Suez and we turn inland toward Mount Sinai.

St Catherine's Monastery sits nestled in the granite mountain ridges and peaks of Mount Moses (a.k.a. Mount Sinai and Mount Horeb), Mount Catherine (a.k.a. Mount Jethro), and another pair of mountains. This is where the Children of Israel wandered thirty-three centuries ago. There is where Moses escaped to from Egypt at the age of forty. Forty years later God famously appeared to Moses in the Burning Bush and charged him with bringing the people of Israel out of Egypt. Moses later led them here to receive the Ten Commandments.

When early Christians were persecuted, many sought out holy places like this. From the third century A.D., monks began settling in small monastic groups near Mount Sinai. At first they were little more than hermits living in caves in utter poverty, but by 330 A.D. Constantine's mother, Empress Helena, constructed the first church. Sixth century Emperor Justinian built a fortress wall around the early structures and constructed the magnificent church that remains today.

The monks created The Mosaic of the Transfiguration of Jesus Christ at the end of the sixth century depicting the glory of Christ's face and Peter as he said, "Master, it is good for us to be here,"— recorded in Luke 9:33. The monastery became known as St. Catherine Monastery in the eleventh century when they found her remains on the highest peak now named for her. St. Catherine was born in Alexandria in 294 A.D. to an aristocratic pagan family. During the Christian persecution of the early fourth century, she confessed her faith publicly and accused the Emperor of sacrificing to idols.

Reportedly, after her execution her body vanished. The monks claim the Angels took it to the highest peak in Sinai where three centuries later monks found her remains. They brought them down and placed them in a golden casket in the church, where they remain today. The monastery supposedly possesses two thousand priceless icons of immense spiritual, artistic and historical value, of which only one hundred and fifty are exhibited. The most famous is Jesus Panto Crator, Ruler of the World, which was done in a seventh century Byzantine style, a wax melting technique. The monastery also has a library second in importance only to that of the Vatican in both the number and value of manuscripts it contains.

We stay in Saint Catherine Village in a cabin. As we check in they bring juice and hors d'oeuvres. We may have expected more of a "spiritual" experience, but the rooms have cable TV and telephones. Since we hadn't seen CNN in some time, we watch it for a while hungry for news of the outside world. After a cafeteria style dinner, we turn in early—the "thing to do" is to wake up at 2:00 a.m. in order to start hiking up Mount Sinai by 3:00 a.m., which puts you at the top by sunrise.

I don't think we can carry my son all the way to the top, so my wife represents our family on the two-hour hike. About two hundred other people are already in place by 5:00 a.m. when she arrives at the top to see the sun rise. Everyone is very quiet for a few seconds before cameras start clicking, and by the time the sun is fully exposed people have already started descending the mountain. The monks have carved 3750 steps and two stone archways into the granite of the passage down from the mountain. My wife is back by about 9:00 a.m. and ready for a hearty breakfast.

After touring the monastery, we pack up and head for Ras Mohammed national Park, located on the southern tip of the Sinai Peninsula. In the morning we are finishing up breakfast when we see a dolphin leaping out of the water right in front of our campsite—that whet our appetites. We are suddenly all in a rush to don our snorkeling gear and hit the water. We camped in a small bay where the water is calm and clear with very little wave action. It's like swimming in an aquarium—the water is so clear you can see green, purple, and red coral, as well as angel fish, parrot fish, and blue, black, and orange fish. In tide pools, the kids find snails and hermit crabs along with black spiny-armed starfish.

After a great day Sunday, we pack up Monday but get in one last good swim before our group splits up. We're headed back to Maadi, while some others are going to go back for another night at St. Catherine's. We hit a pretty good traffic jam going back into the tunnel under the Canal. We drive into the outskirts of Maadi just after dark with a whole day left to regroup and recover from our trip.

Austria

We have a company Easter egg hunt at the Walker's house; they have a big grassy backyard. A couple fellows and I show up early to hide the hundreds of eggs prepared by the ladies. The kids get started at 8:30 a.m., and then we dash to church.

Tax season follows quickly after Easter, but it seems like the way the company does their expatriate taxes is better than what I'm familiar with at my last company. This year I get one experienced guy who carries us through the whole process. The company pays for the foreign taxes, he figures out what our base salary is and we pay taxes only on that "stay at home" base income. We also get the opportunity to take a real vacation in April—to Vienna, Austria. My son did really well learning to ski last year in New Mexico, so we are excited to have the chance to ski again. As we fly into Austria we are surprised to find it green and lush since we are here to ski. We were still thinking winter, but spring bulbs are in full bloom in Vienna, our first stop. It's dark by the time we check into the Royal Hotel, which is in the center of the old city right next to St. Stephen's Cathedral; it is an old hotel. Our small second floor room looks out at McDonald's of all things, my son for one is happy about that.

We have energy enough to check out the Cathedral, but a protest is going on in the plaza; about what we do not know. The cathedral looks spooky at night because the outside sandstone walls have darkened with pollution. We take a quick walk around the inner city near our hotel, mostly just window shopping. The next morning St. Stephen's Cathedral is not so eerie. We also check out the Hofburg winter residence of the Habsburg emperors, they stayed there from 1278-1918. We walk around the grounds outside and then to the treasury where they have regal robes, crowns, religious treasures and artifacts collected during the Hapsburg's reign. We are doing good to get my son through the treasury; we do not push him by going into any of the larger museums. We search for a place we have heard about for lunch, but construction near the museums makes it hard to find. Since we don't speak any German it's hard to order. We make it back to St. Stephen's for an English tour of the church, which is impressive and interesting. My son likes the elevator trip up to the Bell tower for a good view of the city. Seeing the royal crypt where the Habsburgs are entombed in ornate metal sarcophagi is creepy, but does not spoil our appetite for dinner in a restaurant in the Danube Tower.

The next day, our last in Vienna, we take a bus tour to Schonbrunn, the summer palace of the Hapsburgs. Sunday we hop on the train and head to the green countryside for a ride to St. Johann in Pongau. We stay in an American owned resort called Alpine Land Sports Resort and enjoy communicating easily with the workers who speak very good English. The only trouble, being early April is that the nearby ski slopes are closed for the season. In fact, they closed the very day we arrived. However, we learn that there are some others still open in the region; we have to rent a car to get there. Guess we should have done more homework.

We finally managed to hit the slopes on Tuesday. We take turns staying with my son on the bunny slope. He has a blast learning to ski and playing in the snow. The next day we check out a bigger ski area. The weather is awesome and quite warm on our last ski day. In fact, it's making the slopes slushy near the bottom of the run. I think we cut our trip a little too close to spring.

We tour the fortress of Hohen Salzburg, and it's freezing touring the old castle—billed as the largest preserved castle in central Europe.

It's interesting to see how the fortress has grown in size with additions over the centuries.

As we ride back with the commuter traffic it starts to snow in earnest blanketing the farms and the green valleys. It's extremely beautiful and I try to hold onto the memories as though they can keep me cool and refreshed back in the ninety degree heat of Cairo in the spring.

Spring into Summer

We finally feel like we live in a home even though we have a few things left to do—appliances, a new table, curtains; it is never really done. We join a tour to visit the pyramids near Saqqara. Starting at Saqqara itself—the Step Pyramid, then on to see the Bent Pyramid and Dahshur and other small pyramids in the area, including Teti. We tour temples and see drawings and wall carvings—hieroglyphic writings and even some original red and green paint from 2340 BC. Some of the drawings depict war achievements and the royals' daily life activities.

According to the law, an international driver's license is adequate until you have a work permit, at, which point you are required to get an Egyptian license. However, the process is unclear. It came to a head when police stopped some wives who were driving our tax exempt company vehicles. One got away with the help of one of our drivers, but the other vehicle was confiscated. They wanted a substantial amount to get it back, but our company rep said, "We will pay with a check, and we must have a receipt." That dropped the price to nothing.

Because of that the company is pushing all those expatriates to have an Egyptian driver's license. The process for us is to get a medical check, eye exam, and then go to the police station. You also have to have a notarized letter from the US Embassy saying that you live in Egypt even though our passports have a work visa. It's clear the government is making it tough to get a license. Egypt wants to keep the number of drivers down because the roads are too crowded, yet they deny licenses to well-trained foreign drivers who are paying the tax money.

Charlie fails his one question oral test. He failed to mention that the sign he is asked to interpret meant "merge left into one lane." He forgot to say "left," and the cop said, "You flunk." His wife got her sign correct, but her Toyota Land Cruiser was too big for the driving test track, so they flunked her. They have it all worked out by the time I go for it; I simply have to appear and sign some papers. Whew!

Finally time to play some golf. At the end of May, there is a company versus Joint Venture Group golf match at Katameya—a grudge match. Competition is firm but camaraderie is great. A lot of us expatriates are cycling back to the states or traveling to other countries, so the next day we have a special event, a going away party for the families moving to new assignments. Some are headed back to Houston, others to Poland, and some to Australia. Each family has been here for three years to start the company operations in Egypt, and I imagine they are ready to get back home to family and friends. It's sort of like an Egyptian toga party with men and women alike wearing a Muslim Galabeya robe. My wife has to take a shot of tequila for having the best outfit.

Unfortunately, we have to cut it short when we get a call that our son is having trouble breathing. Matthew, our babysitter, says, "he is asking for his breathing machine."

It's a long night, and even with treatments from the breathing machine, our son still sounds bad. The pharmacy delivers the wrong stuff, and it is midnight before we get a hold of the nurse on call for the company. She has steroids for the machine, so all three of us get in the car to go get them. We have been through this before, but it is still scary. Even more so, this is our first real medical scare in Egypt. We have a network of help, but compared to the states the medical support system is just not as good. We are very grateful to get the right medicine, get home and eventually get some sleep. A few days later, I get to play in another golf tournament. We have seven teams for a scramble and though I play with three guys I don't know we all have a great day. My team comes in third place and I even win some money. My handicap is now a twenty-two my highest ever, I think my game is coming back. A few years ago before we had our son, I was a steady golfer getting down to a 10 handicap. In the past few years, the priority was our little family—they are only young once so the golf skills rusted.

As I am thinking about spending some time stateside, my Houston co-workers show up to begin their assignment in Egypt. My wife and son leave early Monday morning, the day after my son's last day of school (ice cream Sunday). We leave for the airport at 2:00 a.m. I walk them to the first security checkpoint and say our goodbyes. It's hard to see them go; I have gotten used to being here with my family and will miss them. I am back in bed by 4:30 a.m.—it's just me and the dog Greta now.

Work helps keep me busy, as we are getting ready for our company executives visit next week. I work late most nights and am too tired and rushed to work out at lunch or run in the morning.

I wake up early and drive to Katameya to hit golf balls, trying to make use of our membership and trying to be a good golfer again.

The company is trying to get into the Nile Delta gas play, so I may have to fly to London to work on the deal. At first it looks like we'll be headed to London in early July, but things move much faster than expected. Sunday we're thinking July but plans change on Monday by 6:00 a.m. Tuesday we are driving to the airport and expecting to be in London for lunch.

We listen to a half-day presentation on Wednesday and work hard all day, as well as a few hours on Thursday. Rather than the usual downtown London gig, we stay on the west side, in an area of Rock history. Our quaint hotel, Richmond Gate, is located across the street from Pete Townsend's house "The Wick" built in 1775 in Twickenham along the Thames River. Up river is Eel Pie Island where Hendrix hung out back in the day and Mick Jagger's apartment is just up the street past Robucks Tavern. We're headed back to Cairo Thursday afternoon but before heading to the airport, we make a detour to Windsor Castle. The deal we came to see looks good as far as prospects, but the cash flow terms between the oil companies and the government are tough—plus one of the former working interest partners now has an overriding royalty or cut of the profits, which makes the overall deal tough considering risk and economic chance for success. I think we will recommend to pass.

I get back to another surprise. Senior Management have changed their plans yet again. They'll arrive in Cairo in a week and will stay for three days. I work like mad all weekend to get ready for their Sunday arrival. I go from 9:00 a.m. Friday until 1:00 a.m. Sunday morning putting it all together. These reviews are to be full technical updates on all aspects of our Egypt region, and I have to personally present summary updates on two concessions. The main point of pressure is a status review of the Western Desert regional study I am in charge of—that didn't meet expectations last time. VP Fred has been pressing for results on the regional review and it's been stressing me out trying to move forward. I have so much other work to do and the available staff is limited; I guess we'll see how it goes…

The executives show and seem to be in good moods—it helps that our stock is up to almost $40/share. Earlier this year the company purchased $715 million worth of Gulf of Mexico property. Wall Street likes the deal hence the increase in our stock price. Oil prices are also staying up; Brent is $15-16 and NYMEX is $17-18. Egyptian crude is priced close to Brent (Norway Field) prices. I attend a few of the other reviews, but mostly I just have to keep working. I go till after midnight Sunday and Monday, and I can tell exhaustion is starting to take a toll.

I push it aside; I can't worry about being tired right now. Monday night late, I hang maps all over the walls for tomorrow—the regional study review. Tuesday morning, I throw off my jitters, tank up on coffee, and… roll through it smoothly. It lasts for an hour and a half, and many of my peers come to listen. I close with some play concepts and a forward looking discussion. I will use this momentum to move faster now—I hope.

Poor Man's Golf Tour

With all of our wives gone for the summer, some of the other guys and I plan a poor man's golf tour to a nearby east Mediterranean island, Cyprus. An airline pilot strike threatens to cancel our trip, but after the last few workaholic weeks, we persist and arrive late Thursday night to stay at the Sun Hall Hotel close to the airport. Friday in Paphos we play golf at Secret Valley where Randy Jordon and I bet against the other two guys. We all put up some high scores and in the end we tied. We stayed the night in a different hotel and in the morning play Tsada, a very nice course up in the hills. Randy and I went out in front but the others reel us in to end in another tie.

After the game, we drive to the east side of the island and check into the Grecian Bay Hotel, a place overrun with young folks looking for a good time. Clubs line the streets, all blasting different sorts of music, and there are lots of people. Sunday before we head to the airport, we hang out at the beach—I hope to come back with the family sometime.

I fill the time before I get to go home to Texas with work, and now I have more than geoscience to do because Vince is the Egypt office GM and Charlie took his job. I'm now the geologic manager so I picked up the drafting department and the records center, plus all the geoscientists report to me. I find time to play some golf, walk Greta every day, and practice playing the guitar. It's safe to say I don't like the bachelor life.

I spend two days in a major company's data room evaluating their farm out offer for their deep water Mediterranean block. The block is big money, but it may have major reserves and could be significant for the company. In fact, they ask me to take a day while I'm in Houston to make a presentation to Alex, our CEO, on the idea. We also try to get a first-pass version of the Region business plan written before I head home. Busy as I am, I get some satisfaction working on things that actually happen; which may bring the spending of millions of dollars—unlike at my last company; the big bureaucratic major. Now I can't wait for a break. I land in Houston on July 13th, and I don't go back to Cairo until August 7th. It will be the longest vacation I've ever had, over three weeks, and we plan on spending time in Houston, Pennsylvania, Colorado, and stop in Amsterdam on the way back to Cairo. It will be good to see family and friends. It's been a very long month without my family around, so bye for now, Cairo.

David Allard

The Giza Pyramids of Egypt

Goat Lady at Maadi Mall Cairo

Cairo Electric Overload

PJs and the PC.in.Egypt

The Falucca Captain and me along the Nile River

Fruit stand men, Cairo

Cairo Cub Scouts Pinewood Derby

My family at the top of Greek Ruins Amphitheatre Alexandria, Egypt

Desert Dave, Egypt

Chapter 13
Worry Free Life Overseas

August, 1999

O n vacation three weeks in Houston this summer goes fast, visiting friends and family and taking care of items best done in the states, such as doctor and dentist visits. We catch some movies, swim time and try to relax. On the return we have fun visiting Amsterdam. We enjoy a canal tour, visiting Anne Frank's house, a boat tour, the Rejk Museum, and café dinners. We're able to avoid the less family-friendly areas, which Amsterdam is famous for.

Getting back to Cairo is like starting all over again. We were doing fine living in Cairo before our summer break, however now that we are back it is taking time to adjust to things here again. Not just jet lag or my son's new class at school, but some of the people at the company have left. The entire culture and way things work here are just so different. I started working in Egypt full time over a year ago, and I am still learning about different and strange things. We feel like we have been adapting to the culture to some degree, but we will never fully feel at home here.

My first day back at work, Vince says that we have one day to get a set of documents to Houston. Our Sr. Mgmt. needs it for a presentation, so as usual, we bang it out. I'm just getting back into the groove when Vince drops another bomb; senior management will be making a three-day visit in just one week. No one is sure if they know how much disruption the preparation and presentation time takes from our day to day quest to handle operations. We scramble to prepare for the visit, and when they get there I learn that since prices have stayed up, it is now time to add more wells to drill. In the first half of the year we had no extra money and drilled almost no exploration wells. Now we are going to have to scramble to drill more wells this year. In spite of the scrambling, having the ability to quickly change course is a strong attribute of the company. Unfortunately, drilling a well in Egypt isn't like doing it in the United States. We have a lot of red tape to clear with the Government Oil Company and to get agreement from our partner and contract drilling rigs. If we can make a discovery it will be worth it.

My son is back in school, first grade and now full-time. His new teacher seems nice, and a couple of my co-workers kids are also in his class. He has the usual classroom stuff, but he also gets to walk to different areas of the campus for a computer class, Egyptian culture class, and gym, which early in the year, is swimming. My son really likes to go swimming, and sometimes after school we swim at the school or on weekends we go to the Katameya Country Club. It's nice getting to the country club in the desert hills above Cairo. It's a mini vacation from the smog, trash, and noise of the city.

My position in the company is now Geologic Manager, and with that "manager" part comes personnel issues—hiring, assignments, promotions, and the like. This is not fun but I try to help people when I can. It's clear the Egyptian nationals treat me differently now with my new title.

One awkward problem is now that we have internet at the company, the company tracks internet activity and will flag any attempts to open non-work related sites. We have actually had a bit of trouble with people downloading music and movies at work. As the year 1999 progressed from summer into fall, a blur of activities occur. It is hard to explain how the high activity at work, the strain of living in a different culture, the variety of family and social activities and at least three trips out of Egypt per year for company families—makes for the crazy blur.

The Solar Eclipse

Tamir found a small crack in the water line of the AC unit. He didn't have what he needed to fix it, but will come back tomorrow morning explaining that because of the sun it was not good to be outside. My wife says, "Oh you mean the eclipse. Are you going to watch it?" He replies, "No, it is too dangerous to be outside during the eclipse; your eyes might get hurt." Sarah, the maid, says the local TV news was telling everyone to stay inside and that, along with the Y2K speculations, this was causing people to be a little hysterical over the fear of some major chaos.

Sarah asks if she can go early so she too could be home before the eclipse starts. As she's leaving, she tells me to pray about it. At about 1:00 p.m. the "call to prayer" blares from the mosque nearby. On TV they are showing men praying inside a mosque and a live eclipse shot on the inset screen. The Egyptian Petroleum Company tells all its workers they can go home at noon. The company front door security guards tell everyone to be careful when they leave the building.

Egypt experiences a partial eclipse and it casts a strange dim light outside. The streets are eerily deserted on the drive home from work.

In Egypt, once new fields are established in a concession, the Egyptian Petroleum Company requires the operator to set up a joint venture company, which employs hundreds of Egyptian nationals to every expatriate who is approved to be in the organization. These organizations are sometimes chaotic or difficult to understand as the Egyptians in the JV are employees of the Egyptian Petroleum Company. Egyptian government employees have their own projects and agendas. If you embarrass someone with Egyptian connections you can find your work permit is not approved when it is time for renewal—even some time after the incident. Paying attention to the politics and respect for the local culture of the host country is important. The company has our own office, from which some exploration concessions are operated. The requirement is to employ nine Egyptians for every expatriate brought into the country—that is why the Egypt office has a large staff.

I'll never forget that one August day during our meeting with the visiting company executives, we hear a loud popping explosion sound outside like a car back firing and then some commotion. Looking out the window, we see smoke in the street and people running. It seems like an attack at first, but later we learn that the power box on the street corner has shorted and is arcing and smoking. The company has had the power go out almost every day this summer, but not like this. Security guards and tea boys are running around with fire extinguishers, which add greatly to the smoke when applied, but do nothing to stop the electrical arc from the city power grid box.

"Electric" Willy Maustafa appears on his scooter, marches over in his jeans, ball cap, and flip flops, to the city box, reaches in with pliers and pulls out a main circuit killing the fire. Our hero.

One of the Egyptian geologists in my group lost his brother. I tell him, "Take time off for the funeral—take what you need and don't worry about it." I asked if we could send flowers and the answer is no—they don't do that here. The company will pay for an ad in the paper. I say ok while thinking, I am not sure if the ad is to announce the funeral or to describe the life of his brother.

We are working out in Gold's Gym during lunch when I spot a film crew. I answer a few questions about fitness and how I exercise regularly. Last question: "Could you live without exercise in your life?" I said yes, but it would be of less quality without it. Some of the guys at work said they saw us on TV, so my interview was broadcast all over the Arab world, however I never saw the show.

The guy's softball team starts the season strong, winning more often than not at the Victory College fields. We lost five good players from last year, so it is a surprise for us to be doing well. The company women decided to have their own team this season.

My wife joins the team, so she is playing again after a ten year layoff. My son likes going to softball games and playing around the little park with the other kids—and McDonald's has a window there. When the lights are right, you can see the dust hanging in the air.

Work is very busy in November as we prepare for early December reviews and our 2000 budget plan. However, that does not stop the "Risk Police" from visiting Egypt. Three company guys, including the Technology VP and a risk assessment consultant, arrive for three days of reviews of all aspects of our exploration prospects.

End of the Year Push

In November we have a meeting at the EGPC's offices to review the proposed Desert oil Concession with the Exploration Vice Chairman, It has taken some time to get to this point to get a project approved.

We are following the steps we are supposed to follow with many meetings and delays. As an example of this, after we are done with our exploration presentations, Bob Woods is ready to present some results and proposed work for one of our developments (with the Egypt Joint Venture Company) ...but the VC doesn't want to see the ten minute presentation because he wants more of the Egyptian team to present. Specifically, he asks for our new Egyptian national exploration manager, Abraham to be present. It is pushed off to another time.

We also host a joint Regional study meeting promoted to all the companies working in Egypt—about fifty people attend. We make the most of our technical presentation and I talk about the business side of the study group. It goes well and now the trick will be following up with the attendees to make sure they actually join the study group. This joint study group brings fees to the consultants but also to our company (small net from future sales) and that will reduce our cost—hopefully to zero for sponsoring it. It would be a great thing for me in Egypt. It will also be good for our reputation with EGPC. In the middle of November other representatives of the company and I travel to Dubai in the United Arab Emirates (UAE) to meet with our (Non Operating) partners about the Western Desert oil property development. We land in the UAE in the evening at what looks like a huge modern airport. Our cab looks like new too, and the city seems well laid-out and clean, like a nice US city. I feel like I've gone from Cairo to San Diego.

Because we landed at 1:00 a.m., we take it easy the next day, hitting the City Center Mall adjacent to the hotel and hooking up with fellow company guys for dinner. We visit a really great seafood place along the ocean. Tomorrow, we get down to business.

In a nutshell the operator moves too slowly for us, we always have to push requests to drill more wells, do more work overs, and so forth. It's even worse now, as our competitor is merging with another company and has little money to spend. The idea of meeting in Dubai is to get away and try to build some partner cooperation.

After an afternoon of meetings, we take a nice dinner boat cruise in Dubai harbor. I speak with one of our partners, Bill Ringo and his wife; it turns out, they worked for the same company I did in San

Francisco, small world. We'll see how successful these meetings are. Back home; I'm looking forward to reading my son his book: *Harry Potter and the Sorcerer's Stone* by J.K. Rowling. Apparently it's becoming quite popular in its native England and spreading in the US. My son is ready to celebrate finishing me reading to him all 309 pages. It's quite the accomplishment, so to celebrate, we're going bowling.

Things are getting hectic around the office, with the reviews for executives due in early December for the 2000 budget. We are working like crazy to get displays ready. We're going to present everything in PowerPoint using a special projector. The stress to prepare and keep up with daily duties is getting to us. It feels odd working late—even till 10:00 p.m. on some nights—for the December review. The traditional yearly review is also a chance for senior management to stop off in the Czech Republic for a pheasant hunt. Thanks to cramming on a historic level the review goes great. Everyone is happy with the 1999 results, and we expect them to approve our 2000 budget. We celebrate with a special dinner for all of us expatriates and our spouses.

This season we joined the dart league. Eight couples go to someone's house for a tournament once a month. My wife and I are lucky enough to win some points in the double elimination tournament. We also watch my son play soccer this fall, which is his first time to play. His team of six and seven year olds are fun to watch.

A consulting company from Australia sends people in again. They are working with me to do the Western Desert regional study with gravity and magnetic data plus a Jurassic regional study and special studies for other Concessions. These are private studies for the company, except the regional, which is an Egypt area study that five other companies have agreed to join with us to do.

Ringing in Y2K Stateside

The end of the year is busy, but we get some down time, too. Right after the reviews I get to schedule the Christina boat to cruise the Nile. Although some people back out, it's nice to relax with a cold drink and motor along the Nile in an old yacht to reduce the stress. We have a celebration dinner party the next night organized by Charlie's secretary—she delivers on pressure to ensure the shrimp are big. The locals get a laugh out of watching us smoke shiska, apple tobacco, in big water pipes with a glowing charcoal chuck in the bowl.

We hold out first meeting of the Egypt Area Regional Study (EARS), a partnership including five other large oil companies that operate in Egypt; no oil company has ever organized and promoted an area study like this.

Some bull sessions that started on the Christina Cruise bear fruit. James Adams and I started talking about trying to climb the pyramids again. We thought Friday, December 10th would be a good time. Usually the time to try the climb is 2:00-3:00 a.m. when the guards are sleeping. Our plan was to take advantage of Ramadan. Right after sunset the Iftar evening meal happens. Muslims fast all day, so they drop what they are doing to have this meal as soon as the cannon fires.

We run across the desert just after dark and make it to the big pyramid undetected. We climb to the top of Cheops, approximately 140 meters, in twenty minutes—just in time for the start of the sound and light show we thought started later. Instead of invisible in the darkness, we're lit up.

We start down, but every few moments we're forced to stop and lie still due to the light show flooding the back of the pyramids. The guards have started to move around and we can see them from above—at times just the red dot glow of their cigarettes. I hope they don't see us. We wait for them to move on before resuming our climb down, practically holding our breath.

Finally, we're near the ground. We hit the sand and sprint back to the street to catch a cab back to the Mena House, where our families are eating dinner. I had called my wife to let her know the descent was going slowly—it took an hour and a half to get down what had taken only twenty minutes to climb.

James and I are charged up by our spy-like nighttime escapade, and I'm sure we are grinning like Cheshire cats as we meet our family and friends at the Indian restaurant.

I don't feel like we're really getting into the Christmas spirit until my son gets to be part of a Christmas play James and his wife put on with the kids. They're doing *The Night Before Christmas*, and my son, along with some of the younger ones, gets to be a reindeer. It's fun to celebrate our holiday even here in Egypt.

We're headed out on December 15th, and there's—as always—a lot to do before we leave, especially me at work. We'll be gone three weeks. I really don't want to be in Egypt for Y2K just in case the world's financial or operating software really does propel us into chaos. Better to be on our home turf if it all just stops working.

As we head to the airport at 5:30 a.m. Wednesday, I find myself reflecting—this assignment has been more challenging than I expected it to be—harder on me at work and on my wife and my son, too. Hopefully we'll get some good R&R in Texas.

We try to make up for it a bit by hitting Disney World in Florida. Our first day at the Magic Kingdom is drizzly, but we make a brief stop at Epcot. We visit the Animal Kingdom and the Magic Kingdom with my Mom who popped over from Okeechobee—we stay at the Wilderness Lodge. We have my birthday dinner at Ohana, but my poor son is asleep on the floor from jetlag when the candle cupcake arrives—something he caused to happen by telling them it was my birthday.

We enjoy more time in Florida eating true American food, golfing, and spending time on the beach—all therapeutic—before heading to Houston and later Dallas. Santa visits us in Florida, but as we're seeing family and friends, it feels like Christmas goes on a while as we travel.

Finally on January 4, 2000 (I note that the world systems did not crash) we're boarding British Air for London. It's a mad scramble to get ready to leave. We're limited to ten bags and have to keep the weight reasonable. After a quick nap in a day room at the airport we jump on our connecting flight and we're off to Cairo—back "home."

The Year 2000 in Egypt

We are recovering from jetlag in early January when Egypt ramps up Ramadan, and the people that we employ expect a little something extra for the holiday. The gardener, the garbage man, the maid, and the boab all expect a little bonus and they are all very grateful. I only see the gardener, Gouma, when his monthly fee is due, but I see his assistant every morning—at least Gouma says thank you for the extra for Ramadan. The boab, who lives across the street, doesn't do much for us but keep an eye on things and rinse off the cars most mornings. It's funny that they probably see us as rich Westerners, and by employing their services like this, I suppose we are living on a different social level than we'd be in the States.

Other than Ramadan ending, we're settling back into life in Egypt. One kid who the teachers said was friendly with my son—didn't return to his class. My son seems to be taking it just fine. That is life as an expat kid; kids come and go at school. We start drilling an exploration well in the desert and I work to get the regional study moving, but overall I think we're all just glad to get back to normalcy after a mad dash in November and December and then vacation time.

Near the end of January, my son and I take on a new challenge— my wife flies to London to meet her mom, leaving us alone. My son and I stay in Maadi…and do fine. I take him to school in the morning, and I'm lucky to have help from the families of his friends. Two of the nights he goes to a friend's house. We make a "Welcome to Cairo" sign for my wife and Granny (her Mom), who will be staying with us until we all go on a safari trip to Kenya and Tanzania in March. That may be a bit of a stretch, but we'll work it out.

With Granny, we tour the City of the Dead. Old mosques now sit among a vast sea of Muslim graves, mainly from the Mamluk-style and built around 1200 A.D. We even climb the Minaret Towers with their convex stair steps dating back thousands of years.

I'm busy with performance reviews for the national employees working for me. Sixteen people now report to me, so this is a considerable task. I also learn that we suddenly have a scheduled review for our CEO February 20th, but my wife and I have already scheduled a visit to Luxor and Aswan at that time. I decide not to cancel our trip. Wednesday February 16th, I get off work and we head for the 7:00 p.m. flight down the Nile River to Luxor, the modern site of ancient Thebes. I've heard Luxor called the world's largest open air museum, and with the Valley of the Kings and the Valley of the Queens in the West Bank Necropolis right across the Nile, it is an amazing archeological wonder. The ruins of the temples at Karnak and Luxor actually stand within the modern city. Luxor served as the Egyptian capital during the New Kingdom.

Our guide Mokee meets us at the airport and we ride together to the Luxor Hotel on Crocodile Island. We drive to the Valley of Kings in the morning to see Ramses III, Siptah, and Thot Mosis III's tombs. Later we visit the Hatshepsut Temple—site of the 1997 Luxor massacre—and then cross the river for a walk through the Karnak Temple grounds. It's a very extensive tour, but my wife and I are eating it up.

Back in the hotel, we cool off at the pool and then eat dinner at a small British-run place before we take a walk through the Luxor Temple that night—they keep the lights on late, and it's magnificent. We're up early the next morning with breakfast by 5:00 a.m. and to the ticket booth for Nefratari's Tomb by 6:00 a.m. They sell a limited number of tickets and it is completely worth it the colors are brilliant and the entire site is in excellent condition. It is said the air rushed out when they cracked open the tomb.

We have a guide for the afternoon—a young girl from the town. The tourist trick is holding a baby goat for photos (we take some). We visit Sennofer the Gardener and Rekhmire the Worker's Moriager tombs. The Gardener's had beautiful paintings of plants and his wife, and the Moriager tomb showed the different people that worked for him—builders, food distributors, textile makers, and so forth.

That evening we fly on to Aswan and spend the night in the Cataract Hotel overlooking a fantastic river scene. Below us we can see the surprisingly clear waters of the Nile, many boats, ruins on an island and the desert in the distance. Aswan is located just north of the dam. In ancient times it was the southern border town of ancient Egypt, and since the Egyptians oriented on the life-giving Nile, the common convention was that Egypt opened or began here. Many of the stones for the statues, obelisks, and shrines of Egypt came from the granite of this area.

We visit the Nubia Museum and enjoy the tourist trappings all that day. The next day we hop another quick flight to Abu Simbel for a tour of the monument before heading back to Cairo via Aswan by that evening, much delayed thanks to Egypt Air's penchant for juggling Luxor and Aswan flights. It seemed no sooner did we hit the tarmac though I had to head for the office to catch up.

The day after we get back, we have company reviews all day with the visiting CEO. With reserves and profits up, oil prices rising, and the Cairo office's recent string of discoveries, the reviews go well. Our hard work is yielding results and those speak for themselves. The thing is, growth is fun.

Bonus

We wrap up February with a geology field trip. I enjoy the barely describable beauty of the remote hills, mountains and open deserts we visit. We drive down the Gulf of Suez road the first today, then make our way south the second—off-roading after lunch. Our final day we face a question to drive for Cairo where we knew for sure we could make it back before dark...or see one more rock outcrops. Our guide says it's only a forty-five minute drive.

That forty-five minutes turns into two hours and we park a hill away from a small valley that is very interesting. It's bounded to the west by dark basement rock cliffs running north to south, small hills on either side with volcanic intrusions and lava flow exposures. The ground of the valley is actually damp, we find, and it houses a tiny oasis of a few palm trees and a hand-dug well located at the head of the valley.

We look for arrowheads or other evidence of ancient civilization—this seems like an ideal place for one—without finding anything. The view back to the east of the desert, sloping away with varied colors and terrain and the Esh Melika range is striking.

We start driving at 1:30 p.m. and don't hit pavement until 2:30 p.m. I earn my stripes by taking over the driving, tackling the Ian Sukna road all the way to Cairo—in the dark. It's a dangerous and windy road where trucks drive with no lights and pass on the curves. The danger of slow-moving vehicles with no lights, cars or trucks broken down by the side of the road—hopefully off to the side—or any number of other hazards can be just out of sight in the foreign

Egyptian darkness. I hadn't touched a beer earlier, but as we pull into Cairo without dying, I'm greatly relieved and pop a top for a night cap.

Early in March I get a chance to visit my son's school; his teacher asks parents to be involved. She invites me to come by first thing in the morning to talk to the kids about the oil business. I bring rocks, an oil sample in a plastic pyramid, some large colorful maps, my laptop and an image projector. I give the kids a ten to fifteen minute story while they sit on the floor, then answer questions I know they'll have: How do you find oil and move it, did the dinosaurs make the oil and what makes oil and petroleum products. I'm impressed that they listen to my talk and even ask good questions at the end. It's a special moment to be part of. A couple weeks later I get a giant thank you card from the kids. I explained oil is made in part from many microscopic organisms/bugs that accumulate at the bottom of the ancient ocean. Several of the kids drew bugs on the card.

At work, I feel like I'm a big part of the Cairo office, but I'm still not sure how much they appreciate the work I do. Geophysicists have to make the structure map to show everyone else where to drill. I feel like my regional study, reservoir analysis, and other things have brought good value to the company, time will tell.

I get a chance to find out—our VP Vince says that he'll have bonus checks for us at our expatriate staff meeting. Last year the Cairo office did not make bonus, but I got a small amount for the Ivory Coast project. This year we made all five key financial goals: production volumes, lease income, lifting costs, exploration reserve additions and finding cost. The oil price increase in late 1999 helped our earnings a lot.

As a professional staff member, I expect a bonus of twenty to thirty percent of my salary. I take a look inside the letter he gives me and see a check for about forty percent of my salary. Wow!

We work hard, yet I appreciate the chance for the bigger payoffs, which didn't exist for me at my last company. I can't wait to tell my wife that the long hours and awkward living conditions here in Egypt are paying off.

On the heels of my bonus comes a big day for my regional study work. We present the Phase I results to the partnership in the Egypt

Area Regional Study. The presentation is good and the displays are impressive. Everyone is happy, especially with some of the new ideas that are developing. We're still negotiating the agreements with different partner company lawyers and others to get agreements signed, so we're holding onto the digital dataset until we get the signatures.

We celebrate my son's birthday with a Pokémon themed party at Bandar Bowling Alley. I feel happy to be able to both work hard for our family and be a part of family life.

We've got six first-graders at the party going crazy on two different lanes, and it's a blast to watch them run and drop the ball, do the dead apple thing between the legs, then see them help each other and lay on the floor to watch the ball roll slowly down the lane. The boys are going crazy when the power goes out. They start running wild across all the lanes to the other end of the alley. They only manage to sit still for a while when my wife and Granny serve cake—but it's a messy scene as we forgot forks. My son says it's his best birthday ever.

The Allards on Safari

My wife and her mom planned a great trip for us to Kenya and Tanzania, and I work hard to get my desk cleared off at work before we get away. We leave home at about 10:00 p.m. on March 16th—we manage some sleep. We arrive in Nairobi at 6:30 a.m. and meet our tour representative Fatima at the airport to review our plan. We depart about 7:00 a.m. with our driver Everest in our green square Toyota Land Cruiser with a hole cut in the roof and an extendible canopy hard top for animal viewing.

We plan to stay one night in Amboseli, Kenya, drive into Tanzania and stay at Lake Manyara, then go onto the great Serengeti Plains for two nights. We're going to do a lot of driving, but big game sightings keep it interesting. Traveling the open bush looking for animals then finding large animals is exciting.

We see so much. It's hard to describe. The highlights follow. We see a leopard in a tree with a fresh kill. A hippo lunging, a giant rhino rubbing. We watch elephants tussle, lions padding toward the shade, and Amboseli Maasai jumping, dancing, and chanting. Gazelle head-butt

191

each other and water buffalo threaten to ram our car with flared nostrils. We see pink flamingos flaring brightly against a dust storm in Lake Nabuwad. A baby rhino checks out the world while we watch, a lion eyes us from a perch in a tree, and hippos don't feel a bit self-conscious about taking a mud bath right in front of us. We see an old black giraffe defying the relentless push of father time and watch topi run, crown cranes fly, impala jump, and my son gets his first ride on a giant tortoise. A giant beetle jumps into our car and an ostrich runs in circles around our car. Our travels take us south from Nairobi through the countryside, off the main dirt road through a village and into the bush. Mount Kilimanjaro looms in the distance—Everest our driver grew up at the feet of it. After crossing a dry lake bed we see zebras and elephant herds, hippos and warthogs and many other animals and birds.

We see Maasai hunters walking along with their long legs, and at Everest's suggestion we visit their village. The chief asks for money to let us enter telling us it's for the school; we pay knowing they need it. They pen their animals in the center of the village and huts surround the perimeter. Their huts have walls of sticks smeared with cow dung—I guess you use what you have—but the songs and the dancing are by far the best. They are a tall people, and after the girls and women sing, the boys and men sing and do their jump dance. We all chant along. During their Lion Dance they produce an eerie drumming sound that really stays with me,

We arrive later at the Serena Amboseli Lodge, and my son and I take a swim before dinner. After dinner we come out of the main lodge to see a full-sized hippo grazing in the grass just over the lodge wall in plain view of the perimeter lights. I'm glad for the wall and the lights as we shut down for the night.

The next day my son and I rest while my wife and her mom go out on an early morning game drive and Mount Kilimanjaro photo op. Later that day we cross into Tanzania where we switch cars and meet a new driver, Martin, who should be with us for the remainder of the trip. We drive a paved road to Arusha and have lunch at Mesa Luna. Approaching Lake Manyara we turn off the main road onto a very bumpy, dusty, dirt road. At the end of the day we drive up a steep road going up the geologic rift shoulder, and stop for an overlook of Lake

Manyara and the rift valley. We spend the night at the Lake Manyara Serena Lodge perched on top of the cliff.

We drive by the Ngorogoro Crater for an overlook and on to Oldavi Gorge the next day, which is the site of the Leakey man discovery. We drive west onto the memorable Serengeti Plains, recent rains have made the open grass lands green. We drive by thousands of animals covering the plains in every direction. Most are wildebeest and zebra, with some gazelle. Martin says the zebra and wildebeest work together to watch for predators and move safely. Zebras can see very well, and wildebeest can smell very well. We pass by rounded granite rock outcrops sticking out of the grasslands—Kojopes. The next day, we take another game drive and see a pride of lions. Later we see a leopard dragging his kill—a reed buck—into his tree. After lunch at Seronera we drive on to hippo hole where we watch the hippos for about half an hour. At one point one large hippo close to us snorts and lunges at Martin and me. I've read that more people die from hippo attacks than lions. Martin doesn't panic and make noises waving his arms. The hippo doesn't charge—he just heads back into the river; whew. We would love to see a cheetah but no luck so far. We leave the Serengeti Serena Lodge on a mini-quest. Martin asks another driver who'd heard about one on the back side of some roadside hills. We check it out, but no cheetah. We do see a lion pride of a few females and one old male with a big slash across his nose. Later, we arrive at the Ngorogoro Crater Lodge. We do an afternoon game drive and we see a mama rhino and her baby, flamingos, and a pride of lions that have just eaten. We go out at dusk and see some Maasai herding their animals out of the crater for the evening to the serenade of their cowbells.

We have a long drive back to Nairobi. We drive away at 7:00 a.m., and in the lush green area around the corner from the hotel, we suddenly come upon a full-sized, long tusked elephant. We bump down the hills until we have to stop for the bathroom at Kabatu. It's an unplanned stop, but it's the best place for a long ways. I slip across the street and make a trade: a company hat, an old watch, and $5 for a couple of wood carvings. We stop just across the border at a big wood carving shop and buy some wooden masks and animals.

We finally arrive at the Nairobi Hilton—Nairobi is a big city but is well laid out with a few green areas—that night we eat at the Carnivore for dinner, it's fantastic. Immediately on walking in we see a huge grill pit with racks filled with skewers of meat roasting. The smoke and smells pour out and make me even hungrier. We take our seats and begin a feast.

The meal is a meat fest—every few minutes a different server comes by with some variety of meat on a skewer and serves some directly onto everyone's plate. There's the ordinary chicken of course, but also sausage, then crocodile, zebra, waterbuck, and more...and more. Finally we raise the little flag on our table to signal we're finished—we surrender. The next day, Thursday, we go north to visit some prehistoric sites on the way to Lion Hill National Park. The Kariandusi site is loaded with artifacts right in their excavated pits, along a trail and across a hill overlooking a mine and lake—all with the rift valley as a backdrop. Next stop is Hyrex Hill, which has a nice little museum showing the area and information about prehistoric to stone aged man. Louis and Mary Leakey excavated both sites during the many years they spent in the area.

After we arrive at Lion Hill Lodge at Lake Nakuru National Park, we take a game drive around the lake and see a big rhino rubbing himself—and his massive horn—on a tree. We're taking a couple of photos by the lake side when up rolls a massive dust storm, sending us fleeing for the car.

The area is very dry right now. We see dead water buffalo and a few flamingos. My wife isn't feeling well so we head back. At the lodge she lies down and decides to skip dinner. We bring her back some food, but she just picks at it—I hope she isn't coming down with anything serious. A big show at the lodge builds up to about twelve people singing and drumming till about 10:00 or 11:00 p.m., making an early night all but impossible.

I wake up at 4:00 a.m. thinking about work for the first time in a week despite the late hour—soon it will be time to go back to the Cairo chaos. A different driver gets us back to Nairobi where we visit the Kenya National Museum before lunch and take the 4:00 p.m. flight to M'Bosa on the east coast. Our tour guide and Thomas our driver take us to the beautiful White Sands Resort Seaside where we watch the sun set from our balcony. Thankfully, my wife seems fully recovered.

Saturday we take in M'Bosa, including the Bamburi Nature Trail, which is nice. My son gets to sit on a giant tortoise and feed another; we also see some snakes and crocks. Everyone is trying to sell us wood carvings—it's a huge trade in M'Bosa—but our guide tells us to hold out for better prices. We end up buying many from a company that employs about three thousand workers at about half price from the street offers.

The next day I take an early run. Later, down on the water my son and I rent a jet ski. Wow, it's fast! We have fun doing figure eights and jumping waves.

Later all four of us take a flat-topped boat with a glass bottom for a snorkeling trip. We get to snorkel at two different places anchored near the barrier reef. The fish are brilliantly colored and beautiful—parrot fish, angel fish, and striking bright red/orange starfish. Our guide picks them up so we can hold them before putting them back.

Unfortunately my son and I apparently haven't loaded up with enough sunscreen and we're already starting to flare up. Making matters worse, back in Nairobi we accidentally leave my son's Gameboy and all three games in its bag hanging on the back of his dinner chair—it's gone. No sign of it. To his credit, in spite of losing the games and the progress he made in each game, he handles it like a champ—even with the looming flight from Nairobi to Cairo.

We're back early enough for me to dart to the office for a while to begin catching up. Welcome back. It's time to work hard... and get ready for our next adventure.

Chapter 14
Full Speed Expats

May 2000

I am flying back to Cairo after my first visit to the little continent Australia. It is a lot of flying for only a one week visit. I departed Cairo on Singapore airlines on the afternoon of April 24th and fly legs of five, six and seven hours to Dubai, Singapore, and Sydney. I arrive in Sydney on the evening of the 25th. After a night at a hotel on the harbor shore, I catch a short hop in the morning to Canberra, the capitol of Australia, where I meet Ted Kordiff. We have workshop meetings over the next few days with his team of specialists concerning the regional study of Egypt.

Australia seems very similar to America, at least until people talk—especially compared to Egypt. I enjoy staying in Sydney for a night—I planned it this way—to catch some sleep and to see Sydney harbor. On my early morning run before flying to Canberra, I get some great views of the harbor, the Opera House and bridge.

The Australian capital Canberra is a planned community—it's beautiful, with wide streets, buildings spaced far apart, and a small downtown set amid rolling hills. The leaves are turning—late April is fall in Australia. I enjoy the brilliant yellow and orange colors, fresh air and morning chill. The shocking difference from dirty, ancient Cairo to beautiful and metropolitan Sydney and the capitol city Canberra hits me most on my morning runs. Jogging along the lakeside path by my hotel, I see other joggers, cyclists, and walkers out just to enjoy the sun's rays clearing the morning mist over the lake as they crest the foothills. It's seems utopian.

The work is important, but we manage some play as well, from dinner out to a round of golf at the Royal Canberra Golf Club. The code phrase was that Ron Weller and I left the office after lunch to attend a "meeting with Dr. Green." Ha. It's a beautiful course and I see my first kangaroos. Later that night we hit a casino and I actually win some money at blackjack and we hoisted several drinks in celebration.

I'm in sad shape when the hotel's phone jingles me wake me at 8:00 a.m. "Are you ready to go?" Ted asks. I've completely forgotten.

"I'm quick on the draw even sleep deprived and maybe a little hung-over, yet in five minutes I'm ready and down stairs. We take a two-hour drive—which I pretty much sleep through—to Thredboe Ski Area. There's no snow, but the hiking and scenery are great.

It's another six hundred meters to the top of Mount Krackenbow, which we skip, but we do about a ten kilometer hike down to the tree line. We see some Brumbies, Australian wild horses, high up in the scrub trees. Ted says he's never actually seen them before—only the evidence they've been there. On the drive back we stop for an overlook across the big lake in the valley, which Ted mentions inspired the poem *The Man from Snowy River*.

The next day, the guys take me wine shopping. We pick up some Shiraz, something Australia is famous for. We also buy a couple of bottles from Penfolds, and Wynn's Coonawarra Estate Cabernet. Wynn's is Oz's oldest established winery started in 1891. It is known for a thin red layer of rich soil (terra rossa) on the Coonawarra Estate key to these grapes; a layer of granite wash from the basement rocks in the area. Monday is consumed with meetings but Monday night we have a big dinner party with the entire staff—I'm the only outsider but they make me feel welcome. We're out late, and Tuesday starts early with a trip to the airport. I'm exhausted after our meetings but have a lot of hours of flight ahead of me.

We depart Tuesday afternoon and arrive in Cairo about 6:00 a.m. on Wednesday, May 3rd—that's a long day considering over twenty-four hours of air time is involved. Another day or two there would have been useful, but I have to be back in Cairo today. My wife plans to leave May 4th for Ireland. She has planned for this bike trip with several other ladies, including her sister, for some time. She leaves at 4:20 a.m. tomorrow morning.

It seems we are always looking forward to and planning a trip to another country. Our life is so hectic at times, but we find time to enjoy the things we do.

Cairo Bachelors

My son and I are on our own for eight days. My wife walks me through the daily schedule before she heads out—my son is taking some medication three times a day to get rid of an amoeba and allergy medicine as well. Also, I make his lunch——and walk him to school. I'm a little surprised that he only needs to keep a journal rather than do lots of homework, yet it's a real chore to get him to write in it most days. Other days, he writes very interesting accounts of his thoughts and the day—like when he and I cut off my mustache.

Mary Woods is kind enough to pick my son up after school, and he plays with her two kids until I can pick him up after work. We do really well together and have some great talks. One was interesting and left me introspective. "Daddy, what do you wish for?" My son asks. I had to tell him, "I'm not sure anymore. What do you wish for?" He said, "That Pokémon are real and a million dollars."

One thing I have been working to get together for the Regional Study is a structure map of the entire Western Desert. Since this is a huge area, the map is made by merging together maps made by different people in different work groups. We even hire a contractor to map areas where we had some seismic data and no map; actually this Egyptian fellow works for us on nights and weekends and during the day he works for Egypt National Oil Company in one of the Joint Venture companies.

We are in Wadi Digla, a canyon on the edge of town for a cookout with a couple other families. The kids run around in the open area. A friend Bob and I take my son and our dog Greta on a hike across and up the other side of the canyon to a cave we spotted from below. We make it up to the other side of the cave and check it out with a flashlight; no treasure was discovered.

The next day my son and I are looking at his collection of "owies" when he says, "I wonder why when Mommy kisses by boo-boos they don't hurt anymore. I miss Mommy. When you were gone Dad, I missed you." My wife finally comes back to rescue us on Saturday, May 13th—just in time. She's back with gifts and stories to tell, so happy she got to have an adventure with her sister.

199

Big Meetings

I've been managing to play a little golf this spring and I have won some cash while playing with three or four groups of guys the last couple of times. That will slow down as we prepare for the next Sr. Mgmt. company review in a couple of weeks. This spring my son and I have been playing baseball. My son is playing without a batting tee for the first time, playing coach-pitch instead—the coaches pitch to their own team. We had an unexpected change in adult volunteers who help coach my son's baseball team. So now I am a baseball coach. I pitch to the kids and have a lot of fun with them, but it's a difficult way to gain a greater opportunity to be more a part of my son's life. I am working a lot of hours to prepare for the next decision points review at work. It isn't unusual for me to see midnight at work, especially as the summer heat is here and the power is beginning to fluctuate due to the increased drain from air conditioners across Cairo. When we lose power at work, our computers are powered by their UPS backups, but those run out in a couple of hours if no power returns.

We decide it's time to switch on the generator—but that requires first shutting off about fifteen air conditioners in the building. Past experience shows the generator can't handle the entire building load, but it's enough to keep all the computers going as we push to get things ready for our next review. Now this is a sweatshop. At 6:00 p.m. we switch back to normal power—I hope it stays on and the AC can get the temperature in the building down.

Time out for some fun. The Cairo expat social group puts on a Roaring 20s dance at an American Embassy residence. What an interesting mix of folks including the American Ambassador to Egypt, Daniel Kurtzer.

Our Sr. Mgmt. arrives in time for us to work Saturday and Sunday on more reviews and to propose more wells for approval to drill—to add production because the existing producers are always on decline from their initial oil rate. As a growth company you are constantly trying to grow production to higher rates; but base level decline is always there. After the Execs return from appointments on Sunday with Egyptian government officials and partners I review my regional study. There's a lot to say, especially with the new structure maps covering large regional areas of the Western Desert. The consulting group leader Ted flew in yesterday and he presents with me. We present a variety of basic information from the regional study's products. It's well received and even generates some discussion. The point of this study is to put our known discoveries and prospects in context of the subsurface trends. The best part would be if we see new play ideas from all the work. Tuesday we meet at the Naadi Sofitel Hotel with over thirty people from the EARS—the Egypt Area Regional Study—participating companies. The EARS partnership presentation is over a year and a half in the making. It'll be nice to finally get high quality leading-edge products completed—with little help from partners.

The expert advisors, my partners, lighten the mood by donning giant "ears" at one point in the meeting—getting a few laughs. Our Spanish partners ask why more geochemistry wasn't done. We discuss that as beyond the scope of this study. Other than that everyone is pleased with the products and impressed with the quality. We receive compliments from the major company partners and a glowing letter from the Italians. Vince even thanks me for such a great study, which means a lot to me professionally. Honestly, I'm just happy that it's done.

My wife and I host a dinner party for several company people from the partnership Tuesday night at our house. We are celebrating the end of EARS. We toast "cheers for EARS" with wine and a fajita dinner.

Germany

About a week later we leave for Germany. My wife is packed for the whole summer, and my son is ready to go see family and get new toys from the States. I will only be gone for a few days in Germany; then the family flies on to the States while I return to Cairo.

When we land in Frankfurt, I realize it is finally time to slow down and smell the roses. These days it seems hard to find time to slow down. I guess with our travels we play hard as well as work hard. We rent a car and drive east from Frankfurt through thick, green forest and rolling hills. We take the scenic back roads through little towns along the river to arrive at the medieval walled city, Rothenburg Ob der Tauber. We find our way into the narrow back streets to our hotel, Reichs Kuchenmeister while enjoying the quaint cobblestone streets and ancient buildings all around us.

A medieval wall about twenty feet tall still rings the entire town. It has walkways along the top, which we of course have to check out before having dinner at a café in the town hall square. The next day we take in the criminal museums with their torture items included, and shop in some Christmas specialty stores and other fascinating little places. Then it's time to get back in the car for a drive through the countryside to the Hornburg Castle just south of Mosbach where we stay the night.

The castle, originally built in the tenth century, sits high on a hill looking down to the water and the river valley with its vineyards. The restaurant has a commanding view of the countryside and very good food. We get a chance to tour the castle, see the tiny chapel, the towers, and of course visit the dungeon—complete with a skeleton.

Saturday we drive across the valley and over the river to Gutenberg Castle, then north through hilly back roads east of Heidelberg to arrive at a very nice resort hotel just south of Frankfurt some friends recommended, the Kempinski Hotel Gravenbrunch. This marks the end of our romp through the hill country of Germany—tomorrow we must part ways. Making it even worse, tomorrow is Father's Day.

We arrive at the airport and they walk me to my gate—my flight back to Cairo leaves before their Houston flight. We spend the time talking about the first thing we want to do when we get to the States. My son is talking about some toy and my wife explains the reason we can't get it right away, to, which he replies, "You always have the advantage."

I hate leaving my family, but I enjoy who my son is becoming. My wife tells me to work hard so we can play more when we get back together—I doubt that will be a problem.

Grand Slam of Egyptian Golf

There's a lot to do at work to keep me busy. We had hoped to take another guys' trip this summer, to Cypress or Malta, but we're just too busy. On top of the usual stuff we are evaluating a property offered by the other Egyptian oil company of the government, GPC.

My Australian consultants are in town to review the Jurassic study just completed and Paul to follow up after the EARS study. I take them to dinner in Cairo to celebrate the end of the Jurassic study. We eat dinner overlooking the Nile and watching the people come out in mass as the sun—and heat—go down. I do get to play golf with Ron at Katameya to pay him back for taking me out in Canberra back in April, then later with a few other friends. It's important to get an early tee time in the summer. I actually get to play three days in a row—a "grand slam" of golf for me. All the intense work of the last few weeks balances out as I cram in as much golf as I can, juxtaposed with working late (sometimes till 10:00 p.m.) to clear my in-box in preparation to leave for the States.

As I hop on the plane, I'm wondering why I kill myself so many nights to get things caught up at work—there's a lot I could have let slide but it is just me to juggle what I can with the time I have. I'll be doing some work while I'm "on vacation" in Houston anyway. Now it's time to enjoy the flight to Frankfurt and then the USA.

Working Stateside

I work in the Houston office from July 19-21, while we stay in a hotel right across the street. I take my son with me to visit the office and drop off some regional study copies.

It's fun to take in some of the diversions here, like the Ringling Brothers Circus and an Astros game. We catch some movies—including my son's dream—the Pokémon Movie. I catch up with an old college friend. My son gets some bike riding time—it's hard. We love seeing him ride, but we didn't get him a bike in Egypt because it's not safe for him to ride there due to small roads and bad drivers.

203

I have to drive from our condo on Lake Conroe to the office to review the Egypt Regional Study Review for several folks, but that all goes well. We see some concerts while on home leave: Steely Dan at the Woodlands then later Jethro Tull in Erie and AC/DC in Cleveland. The AC/DC show with my brothers Steve and Mike and Steve's wife Judy was a special adventure. On the late night drive home from Cleveland to Erie, the interstate came to a complete stop—from a wreck we guess—it was weird getting out of our car and standing around on the highway with people from the other cars.

My wife and I try to take in as much culture or fun as we can while we're here. It's fun to get to see family and reconnect, but I wish there was more time to do more special fun things that my son would like.

The lakeside north of the Houston condo is paying off in that family has come to see us—the difference from last year is pretty stark. We blew through a lot of money and added a ton of stress by hopscotching around last year, so sitting tight in our nice little condo seems like a great idea by contrast.

We wrap up our stay with some golf for me—and more shopping for my wife. I have to hit a convention on buying and selling oil and gas properties, where our company executive is the lunch speaker.

Back at the condo packing is in full swing. I take some stuff like our bikes back to the U-Haul storage unit where we keep our summer stuff while we're in Cairo. We all stop by our old house, which stirs so many memories and still seems like home even though it is rented out.

We leave the next morning, taking off early before anyone is on the lake. The water is like glass and the image of sunrise over the lake triggers my memories of splashing in the cool water. Soon we're at the airport unloading baggage.

And then it's time to panic. I can't find my wallet. After a frantic search, we figure that my wife packed it in my shorts. It should be in one of our bags. I have my passport and a money clip, so I should be all right.

Our bags start popping out in Cairo after we clear customs. The good news is the customs guy doesn't search our bags and is happy to register our video camera; the bad news is that two of our sixteen bags don't arrive. The worse news is that one of them is the bag with my shorts and wallet in it. The other is our cooler of frozen meat. We can't get the quality of meat here in Cairo we're used to in the US so we spent some serious money while in Houston on items that stayed in Albertson's deep freezer until we picked it up on our way to the airport. If these items don't show…

I talk with the baggage people and they tell me our luggage will arrive on a flight twenty-four hours late—midnight tomorrow. It's a bit of a relief; we all hope the meat is still good.

We drag ourselves to our house and to the welcome of flowers the maid left. My son is so happy to be back he actually kisses the carpet.

Getting back is better than adjusting to being back; jetlag hits us all hard, and all differently. Our home is a crazy mess of boxes and suitcases, and awake people at all hours of the day and night. I stay up the next night to get our bags and find my wallet, but I'm up until 3:00 a.m. sorting through the partially thawed meat. Most of it can be put in the freezer but a few pieces will be left out to cook soon.

I go back to work on Sunday, forcing me into a semblance of normalcy. My son's school will follow a week later—we'll all be back to normal.

World Traveling

Soon after our return from the USA we have visitors—friends of my San Francisco brother; Nell and her friend Desmond. They began a world tour in June. Desmond teaches English in Germany and Nell works at the Gap in San Francisco—until she takes about a four month leave to travel the world. They have been to Scandinavia, Russia, China, and Thailand when they show up at our house. They're very nice—we do some tourist stuff with them.

It's fun having non-oil wing-it type people around, we all get along well with them, including my son. The driver I asked to pick them up in the car, Sahaa, really takes a liking to them; even taking them to the train station in Maadi, and then riding the train with them to Cairo to ensure they're able to make their connection to Luxor. Everything's in Arabic so it's very confusing. They don't really know when they'll be back to get some of the gear they leave at our house.

They may get more adventure than they bargained for down south. They made the trip to Luxor and Aswan and then to Dahab for scuba diving, but the real story is fire. While staying in a grass-roofed hut in Dahab, a fire sweeps through and burned down six huts including theirs. Their money and passports are in a safe, but they lose everything else—glasses, contacts, clothes, and souvenirs. The fire strikes at 3:00 a.m. and people throw their things clear of the fire. When they come back after sunrise they find the police have swept everything up. Their things saved from the fire are gone.

They return to stay with us a night, then travel on to Ireland, apparently undeterred. I really admire their attitudes and wish them well. Desmond will be teaching in Spain, which we hope to visit one day.

It's maddening to be busy at work with all the operations and to have the timing change on short notice for a full day review for our executives; a roller coaster. Kidding aside, it is still fun to be part of the high activity levels and growth.

I'm still dizzy it seems when I wake up in Bali, Indonesia, for the international AAPG, American Association of Petroleum Geologists Convention Conference. The company covered my expenses and I paid for my wife and son's trips. After a tension packed few days and hectic late nights, it's bewildering to wake up in such a beautiful exotic location.

We stay at the Nikko Bali Resort and Spa on the southern resort area of the island near where the convention is. I confirmed late, so we couldn't get a hotel within walking distance of the conference. The Nikko is amazing, built along a steep tall cliff with no other hotels nearby. Our room is located in a landscaped area on the top of the cliff, but to get to the pool and beach level, you walk to a tower and then take an elevator fifteen floors down.

Bali is a good size island that would take all day to drive across. It boasts an active volcano located in the east central area, which is covered in clouds most of the time. The island population is about three million and has grown in recent years with the growth of tourist. Outside of the developed areas you can see lush thick jungle. In fact, the traffic around Denpasar has outgrown the small road system.

The former Dutch West Indies now Indonesia and Malaysia is mostly Muslim, however Bali is over ninety percent Hindu. This religion, out of India, is more passive than Muslim and allows drinking of alcohol yet strict Hindus are vegetarians. We'll see if I can find a burger.

My wife and my son are looking forward to relaxing around the hotel and the beach, I am too, but strangely I'm also looking forward to the convention. It's a great place to pick up ideas and I love the immersion into new technology. I had to sell this trip to my bosses, for, which I wrote an effective memo named "Bali Why," and I took grief from the engineers who call "boondoggle," so I have to have something to show for the trip. I wrote a report on the many presentations and technical ideas I heard about. A few thousand attendees show—much less than the 40,000 that the AAPG might pull in for a US convention. I see several people I know from my former employer and my consultant friends in from Australia. I meet and befriend quite a few more.

My wife and my son live it up for the two and a half days I'm at the convention, but I break away Thursday for some golf at the Bali Handara Golf Course—which actually sits inside an old volcanic crater. Another crazy one to put on the list of exotic locations I've played. Getting to play golf is even better because of the ride out of town and up the mountain through terraced rice fields lined with tall palm trees. I see some young girls taking a lunch break from the rice harvest behind a temple on the edge of a small town and wish I had my camera. I tell my driver to take the scenic route, so he shows me where he's from. The course is high on the hills and beautiful—all well worth the trip.

The next day we lounge around and my wife and I go snorkeling. The three of us toured Hindu temples where we had to keep an eye on the monkeys—who will snatch food and other things. It ends all too soon, and we're traveling back to Cairo. The constant hopping of large numbers of time zones is catching up to us—I feel like I'm floating in space. Cairo is eight hours ahead of Houston, and Kuala Lumpur—which we traveled through to and from Bali—is seven hours ahead of Cairo.

The New Egypt Exploration Manager

The week of November 19th, my life in Egypt changes. It happens right after a meeting in Vince's office with two other guys. As I am on the way out the door he asks me to stay a moment—to talk to me about taking on the job of Egypt Exploration Manager. "David," he said, "Would you like the job?" My mind drifts through all the aspects. I'd have new responsibilities since many of the nationals and expatriates both report to that position. It will probably cost me some sleepless nights and it will mean being in Egypt at least two more years. I'll be handling more managerial work and less technical, and I need to make sure I can still run a computer workstation to make maps in case I have to change jobs someday.

"I'll do it," I tell him.

With that the hectic craziness starts again as our executive leaders and a board member will be here in early December for the annual Egypt Plan Reviews. We work like crazy right up until they fly in. The whole first day they seem distracted. We find out why the next day; they were busy closing a half billion dollar deal. No wonder, my mind wouldn't be on reviews either. This may be the last time I give detailed technical presentations during meetings like this because as the exploration manager my role will change a bit. I could say that I feel a sense of nostalgia…but I'd be lying. I'm looking forward to a change of duty. I'm particularly proud of our nationals, their reviews fall on Ramadan. They haven't eaten all day and they don't complain, even when our sessions run a few hours after dark.

Change of Guard

The year is winding down and with my own change come some others. A couple of families that have been here for three years or more will be moving on. I'll be taking Charlie Gibson's position. We have a luncheon at work and a dinner to celebrate their time in Egypt.

One of our Nationals sums up a great opinion: "It is so nice to have Ramadan and Christmas holidays coincide because everyone is happy." We have a few parties and other things to celebrate as we get ready for the holiday; but its full steam ahead at work from the time Sr. Management leave until my wife, my son, and I leave for our vacation to Italy on December 27th.

It's even more "fun" because during this time, I do my job and Charlie's, after he leaves December 7th. On December 12th Vince calls a closed door meeting to tell management and people involved that the company was holding negotiations to buy a competitor's interest in their Western Desert properties. We are not even supposed to tell our wives because rumors may affect negotiations, also insider stock trading rules violations are a possibility.

On December 18th, we have an open house for Christmas and we have a good turn-out. Several of the exploration geology group of nationals go in together to buy me a lovely gift, a papyrus with Happy Birthday on it and a little silver plate engraved with "From the Egypt Exploration Team, Congratulations, December 18, 2000." Turns out this is the first time nationals have been invited to an expatriate's house for a celebration.

When Vince leaves on December 22nd, he puts me "in charge" of the Egypt Region. I'm not used to the idea of sitting in as VP. Honestly things are pretty quiet as we go through the daily rituals. The biggest tension is taking a call from the CEO, which can get dicey after we update him on new wells drilling and production test volumes. And then he may ask, "What else is going on?" He wants to know how various deals are going—for which we have to wait on Government approval. Some of these proposals have been waiting for six to eight months and it is hard to understand why these things take so long.

We did have one meeting on December 24th at 10:30 a.m. Vince's assistant has to do some fast talking for us to avoid the Government oil company's suggestion of meeting on December 25th at 9:00 a.m. with the Vice Chairman of EGPC to try and push through a development plan and Cost recovery items.

Christmas in Cairo is nice. Santa manages to find our house. It's a bit strange working on December 24th and 25th, but I get out early each day.

Nevertheless, I'm relieved when Bob Woods returns from vacationing in Kenya to take over for me—I'm out of here. Time to head to Italy, Rome, Florence, and skiing in Courmayeur in the shadow of Mount Blanc.

Chapter 15
Peaks and Valleys of Our World

December 27, 2000

W e rang in the new year in 1999 in the States just in case the
world systems crashed from Y2K—ha.—but this year we opt
for something more exotic. As soon as I can escape from work, we fly
to Rome, Italy. We could have chosen anywhere in the world, but the
amazing sights of Rome and Florence have been calling to us. We
arrive in Rome on the afternoon of December 27th and are blown
away at the beautiful city. Our hotel overlooks the ruins of the Forum,
the former center of power for one of the greatest empires the world
has ever known. The temperature is cool with occasional showers,
which are an enjoyable change from dusty, warm Cairo.

The very first thing we do is walk around old Rome to see the
Forum, the Coliseum, and then the Vatican. We climbed the dome of
St. Peter's Cathedral, take a tour of the Vatican Museum, and stare in
awe at the Sistine Chapel. Our legs get a good workout as we walk
almost everywhere, looking into countless little shops, across piazzas,
and at the beautiful scenery. Everywhere our eyes turn are beautiful
interesting sites that words don't really describe well—you just plain
have to visit.

We take the train to Florence on December 30th, which is a nice
way to watch the countryside roll by and play games on the table—we
paid for first class. Florence's cathedrals are amazing and the massive
Duomo impresses even my son with its white inlay stone exterior. Our
little trooper does a terrific job putting up with his museum crazed
parents. We see Michelangelo's David as well as paintings he did, not to
mention Leonardo da Vinci and too many other Italian painters of
religious art and icons to count—some over eight hundred years old. It
is also fun to note my son recently has enjoyed the cartoon Mutant Ninja
Turtles who go by the same names: Michelangelo, Donatello etc. Ha!

We rang in the New Year at Paolt Restaurant with a gourmet dinner starting at 9:30 and a toast at midnight. As we began walking back to the hotel we approach a scene of chaos near the Uffizi Museum square. A big crowd has gathered and is shooting off fireworks; broken glass and drunken people are everywhere. My wife and I are quite concerned, the shortest path back to the hotel is through this square. I shift my wallet to my front pocket, pick up my son, and we decide to walk through the chaos.

We make it safely on the other side of the crowd and finally to our hotel room door. I reach for my wallet only to discover it's gone—I've been pickpocketed. I recall getting bumped in the crowd once and was separated from my wife for a few seconds, that's when it happened. I only had three hundred dollars in cash in it, but I must cancel all the credit cards. That is a lot of hassle and I will really miss the pictures of my son I had in there.

I report the theft to the police in the morning, but this is of course is a waste of two hours. I have my money clip and ATM card, so our trip will continue with no problem. If the young couple we hosted in Egypt earlier in the year can lose everything to a fire, we can certainly go on minus a few credit cards.

We leave the hotel and board the train—changing a couple of times through Milan and other places, and cross into the mountains. Due to a rain damaged track we have to switch to a bus for the last leg, but our trip goes on and we begin to see snow drifts piled high.

We are all impressed with the Italian Alps, as well as our room at the Grand Hotel Royal Golf—a junior suite with a couch, a huge bed, an amazing view of the mountains, with full service and Italian style dinners included. It had better be nice for $580 US per night. Many wealthy Italians are staying here on the holiday break, strolling by in front of our hotel and filling the specialty shops; I never saw so many furs walking around in one place. Snow is everywhere; deep on the ground when we arrive and it just keeps snowing. We have to ride a gondola from town across a gorge to the ski area. We pass the time waiting for the gondola by throwing snowballs at each other: everyone versus dad. We hit the slopes the first day despite some near whiteout conditions.

My son showed a lot of skill the last time we went skiing and just keeps getting better. He learns to turn back and forth and go pretty fast, and he even takes his wipeouts well. One of our skiing sessions end when he falls forward and one of his skis flops up and hits him on the head. No concussion or brain damage; he just wants to go home. He's okay by the time we get some pizza for lunch, but my wife and I quietly wonder, which home he means—our hotel, Cairo, or back in the USA. We both wonder if our rambling expatriate life is good for him sometimes.

I try some ski runs by myself at the end of each day, but they are tough. My family rides the chair for the beginner slopes, and I take a run from high up on the mountain. The powder is as deep as I have ever experienced—up to my pockets. With poor visibility and deep snow, I end up off the side of the trail in a deep ravine and have to start crawling through snow up to my chest to get out. I can see skiers going by above but they don't see me. Finally I drag myself out and ski down. The tough trails are not so well marked in Europe as what I am used to in the Rockies. The second run I try by myself doesn't go much better. I am almost down when clouds suddenly descend from the temporarily clear sky and my visibility goes to just a few feet. The normal exhilaration gets replaced by some survival adrenaline, yet I manage to feel my way down.

The final day we are to ski, we opted to just go sledding. We rent one and have lots of fun and even see a couple of small avalanches up high on the slope of the nearest mountain. The Alps here are very steep and imposing, and if the weather had been better we could have taken a series of gondolas up to an overview of Mount Blanc and across to the French border. Maybe next time.

We leave early the next morning—5:30 a.m., and between a minivan taxi, bus and train rides all day we arrive back in Rome in the late afternoon, 5:30 p.m. We take a scenic route from Milan to the West Coast catching a glimpse of the leaning Tower of Pisa. It hasn't fallen for hundreds of years and doesn't as we drive by either. The scenery as we travel along the coast with its many small towns and villages, is a pleasant way to travel and medicine for nerves long frazzled by work.

Back in Rome we find something for my son—Burger King. We also walk an old path from the Spanish Steps by Trevi Fountain to the Pantheon, one of the best preserved Roman structures. My wife spots a cozy hotel we had considered for our trip and inside she spotted Rick Steves—a Euro travel show host we are familiar with—must be a good place to stay if he is there. We note it for future reference, because if at all possible we will be back.

We wrap up our trip to Rome by mailing some postcards and packing our bags. It has been an amazing two weeks, but it will be good to get back to our Cairo "home."

Resuming "Normal" Life

Back at home things are in good order. My son has a few days before school starts. At work my new office is ready—new paint, new carpet and new design. My entire building is actually getting new carpet and in a way it is "my" building, since I am the highest level guy here as Exploration Manager. It's an odd feeling to say the least.

Sr. Management fly in to close an important acquisition and as usual their arrival time and length of stay is up in the air until the last second. They visit some very important people like the finance minister, petroleum Minister, and even the Prime Minister of Egypt while they are here. In order to feel better about all the new investment the new deal would bring, the company really wants to reach an agreement with Egypt to extend some of the producing leases in order to justify increased investment here. However, to get something in writing in Egypt is a chore. People in this part of the world may say what you want to hear, but signing a letter of intent or similar makes people here nervous to put their name on the line and take a risk. Our CEO Alex knows how to play. He along with Vince and our Chairman were made to wait around sitting on the couch outside the EGPC leader's office, for hours. Our Chairman gets tired and leaves. They finally get in the meeting and EGPC asks, "Why did he go to the plane?" They were thinking he had a commercial flight.

Alex says, "You don't understand that is a company plane and when it is time to go he will leave me. If he leaves me I can promise you some things: Last night on television we talked about how fast we could increase our investments in Egypt, if you do not confirm the deal we can slow down spending in Egypt. If you want to be responsible for that then I will walk out that door and I will not come back."

Later on back at the office Alex mentions that the two key letters were signed, then he jumps on a plane back to the States. They apparently fly through the night and arrive for work the next day. By Friday, the company holds a phone conference "board meeting" to approve the purchase of a competitor's Egyptian assets for $410 million. The news goes public the next day and the big ordeal is finally over.

Or so I think. Knowing Egyptian culture they may have a long memory of this and in the future we may find some people stalling government approvals or taking even longer than usual when we need to meet—let's hope not. If we grow things in Egypt the local people benefit. Now that the show is over things get back on track.

One bright spot is that as my son and I are working on his first pinewood derby car for Cub Scouts, he tells me that he wants to be a geologist like me when he grows up. I wake up the next morning thinking about how special that is. I have questioned myself and the impact on my family of living an expatriate lifestyle, but it appears ok at this moment.

What is a Petroleum Geologist?

I was the Geologic Manager and am now Exploration Manager for the Egypt office. Although I have a tad more responsibility the focus is the same. We work as a team to find new oil and gas fields. Geologists deal with rocks: How the earth layers were laid down bent and faulted through millions of years, what rocks the oil was cooked out of, what rocks have space these days and at what depth to drill for reservoirs. Also, how to predict what size the possible oil and/or gas field may be and to qualify the risks of each new drilling project.

The key to this is to make maps of layers underground. We use rock samples and electrical and nuclear measurements (logs) from existing wells while considering the geologic history. Most oil and gas basins of the world have existing wells—places drilled by previous operators that had an idea. Whether they found oil or not, the results and some data are usually available from that spot to help put the puzzle together. This geology data is put together with our "brother's," the geophysicists who use seismic data (sound reflections from the earth) to map layers and complete the picture where we have no wells.

Together we present a map, an interpretation of a "prospect" or proposed drilling location. We also work with engineers who portray the economics of each investment opportunity including the drilling and completion cost and possible cash flow from hydrocarbon volumes. So as geoscientists we use some science, art, creativity, business sense and a little salesmanship. A perfect mix for me.

We have to live with some risk because most wildcats (nine out of ten exploration wells) fail to find anything of value. Our typical Egypt Western Desert wells are drilled 8000-12,000 feet—depending on the specifics of each—and cost $1 to $2 million each. Oh yes, a risky but dynamic business.

We also monitor current activity (our drilling wells plus what competitors are doing) and contribute the geology to make operational well decisions—to try and complete a well or plug if it is a dry hole. Ever present is the next growth thing; to keep working on maps and studies to come up with new places and to drill or evaluate new deals from the government or other companies.

Just as I'm getting on top of things, Vince decides that I need to go to Houston for the company corporate planning meeting. 2001 is a critical year for the company, as two billion in new acquisitions in the last eighteen months have set the bar pretty high.

I do get to decompress a bit by playing a company golf tournament the day before the conference.

I am part of the Egypt presentation late on the first day. At the end of day one we discuss: "We have to reach the next level..." We have to continue the production growth in the company's base properties, but what new areas to do is the question. The company has historically not entered new countries very often. They have proceeded cautiously for that type of growth, and have added nothing internationally in the past four years for me. If we get to move out of Egypt, I do not know where we may go next. I have no experience to easily fit into the Gulf of Mexico Region, so I expect to stay on the international trail.

Switzerland Ski Trip

Back "home in Cairo" I am coaching my sons Little League team, the Ball Blasters. It is coach pitch again and I get lots of help from assistant coaches. It's a lot of fun and the kids are developing skills. Our thoughts are all turning toward a ski trip we have been planning with friends who have kids my son's age who also like to ski. A few other families decide to come too.

We fly into Zürich on the same flight as some Cairo friends who are going to a different ski area then take a train ride up into the Swiss Alps. It's a lot of fun traveling as a group and enjoying the Swiss meals together in Zurich. I order Rachlette, which is a cheese and potato array that you heat portions of in a small oven on the table.

We arrive in Zermatt the afternoon of March 3rd and everyone splits to their own places to stay. Our apartment is up on the hillside House Roger. The town is picturesque, sitting in a small mountain valley with the Matterhorn looming up the slope. No cars are allowed on the small winding streets, only small golf-cart like taxis and horse-drawn carriages.

Our friends are avid skiers being from Colorado and Wyoming, so they lead the charge for adult skiing; we arrange for a ski instructor for the kids. Roger the instructor has his hands full, but the kids—especially my son—show a lot of improvement. He is able to ski down an intermediate slope very well. The first two days we have new snow and the adult ski crew find incredible fresh powder in the "Off Pieste" trails, some places more than knee deep. This is some of the best skiing I have done in years. We ski five days of fun with group happy hours and dinners with the other families.

Then "disaster" strikes—food poisoning. I haven't been sick while traveling since Turkey in 1988, but this hits hard and fast and wipes out a day of skiing for me. I live through it and am grateful that my son and wife don't get it. No one else has any problems with the food or injuries on the slopes, which is great. Even the kids survive their instruction and testing of new limits. Everyone has sore muscles by the time we are done, but it's a good kind of sore. We will definitely try to come back.

Western Desert Trip

Back in 1999 we went on a desert camping trip—that was two years ago and for various reasons we have not gone camping very often or been far out in the Western Desert since. However friends are organizing another trip so we decide to join in. We have a long weekend for Easter so we leave Cairo at 7:00 a.m. with friends and our trip guide Magdee in his old Toyota Land Cruiser. His helpers are in another vehicle that serves as supply car and chow wagon. We will be off-road four-wheeling and camping for four nights. Our first day plan was to drive on pavement all the way through Alamein and Matruh along the Mediterranean coast and then south to Siwa Oasis—near the Libyan border. With all the friends and extended connections it's a seven-car caravan.

Our lunch stop the first day gets us off to a good start—a beautiful beach stop with a small hillside cave once the headquarters for Rommel during WWII. We drive throughout the day, finally dropping through the arid mesas into Siwa as the sun's last rays illuminate the rock cliffs. It's nothing short of amazing we have made it this far, as we had to stop about fifteen times for various reasons—and each time we did the kids scattered across the sands.

We make camp overlooking a small town and the next morning we are enjoying market day in Siwa. When we meet for lunch Magdee gives us some bad news—a khamseen, a sandstorm, has kicked up out in the Great Sand Sea and it's not safe to go in that direction. Instead we find a protected mesa outside the town and circle the cars up just as the sun is going down. With the wind up and sand blowing you can taste sand on your teeth.

Morning dawns clear and we roll out with a plan to cover the 400 km to Bahariya over the next two days. We cross the wide open spaces on a small one-lane military road that has dunes blown over it in places. It's disappointing to miss the great sand sea outside Siwa, but we get some off road time and sand dunes anyway.

We pull into Bahariya and find a cool pool in which to go for a swim—a natural spring. After lowering tire pressure to grip the loose sands and off we go. We have fun crossing the dunes before making camp and the next morning my son wakes to find the Easter Bunny has visited our tent. The kids have a great time hunting in the sand dunes for Easter eggs. We have some good off road wanderings on the way to Bahariya Oasis. We arrive that afternoon stopping just outside of town in an interesting area of low volcanic rock hills at the edge of the oasis greenery.

The kids have fun building with rocks in the sand. We all have a big happy hour drinking wine and telling stories around the campfire before dinner. It's a fun day and fun night, but in the morning our group breaks up. Our guides head off into the desert for more adventure and we take off with our friends blasting non-stop back to Cairo; about a four hour drive. We are so glad to be home—especially getting our first showers in four days.

How about the shortest international trip I ever took. Total elapsed time from my door in Cairo and the return is forty-five hours. From Cairo to Amsterdam, The Hague, Amsterdam, Paris, and back home. Our company and a major were in a joint study to evaluate the large property being offered for bid by the Egyptian government. We have a workshop in Hague, Netherlands. My co-worker and I need to attend the one day review/workshop. The meeting goes from 2:00 p.m. until 10:00 p.m. We focus on the main field area and look at costs, geology, and remaining reserves; we fly back to Cairo the next day.

Troubles at Home and Abroad

After the desert trip, it's an all-out push to get ready for our May 2001 meetings. We have internal reviews for Sr. Management and board members, which is hard enough; we also host a group of stock analysts in Cairo for reviews of our companies operations at the same time.

When our executives come to visit the Egypt team plans things like special lunches and dinners and generally throws out the red carpet—

especially with board members en route. In this case—to celebrate the step change new acquisition, we plan a big ceremonial dinner at the Citadel, an ancient fortress now called Mohamed Ali's mosque, it overlooks all of Cairo. We have a place for the Egyptian Prime Minister, Petroleum Minister, Finance Minister, Cairo Governor, and all the top EGPC guys—and none of them come. They all claim a last minute trip to Libya, which is rather insulting since this event has been planned for months. Simply put, this seems like some politics to intentionally slight our VIPs for reasons unclear to us—not directly involved in the recent negotiations with the government.

With that circus behind us I turn my attention to important things—like life. I'm coaching my son's team again, and while sometimes we coaches agree to play with three outs retiring the team, most of the time we just let all the kids bat. It's such a change from the USA where parents throw fits over little league games and push their eight-year-olds to be competitors. It's also interesting because we have four girls on the team and they're good, better than some of the boys.

It's a joy watching my son grow up. His second grade class writes a sequel to the original story of Willy Wonka and the Chocolate Factory and perform a fun play—Willy Wonka 2. My son gets the lead of Charlie Bucket who endeavors to pick his successor to run the factory. The class builds a nice stage with big props. My son does a great job and is really alive in the role.

We also have fun working together on my son's Cub Scout pinewood derby car, his purple, green and blue Gengar car—named after a Pokémon character places well—putting my son in the finals. He wins a race in the finals before getting eliminated, but it was a blast to see.

Another sign of the times is spring 2001. The Dow Jones Industry Average is now at 9,780 after breaking 11,000 last year, and the NASDAQ is down to 1,780 after touching 5,000 last year. Talk of the town is the technology stocks downturn, also known as the "Dot Com" bust. There was incredible value attributed to some technology companies who had no significant hard assets. People who invested too heavily in technology lost the majority of their value. Ouch!

Time rolls on, temps are rising, summer is coming, and families are talking about "home leave" plans as the last days of school run out. My family is away to Texas as usual and I'll be bacheloring it again for a while.

Packing and departure goes well, but then trouble strikes in Texas. The leftovers of a tropical storm are headed inland and it's bad. Friday, June 8th all of Houston starts to flood. It's bad enough we're hearing about it in Egypt and I can't stand it that I'm here, so far away and unable to help. It's the worst flooding Houston has had in a century. Water is up to the cab on semi-trucks, downtown is flooded, and as many as twenty people die—and my family is right there.

It's a couple of nervous days before I can get ahold of my wife. When I finally do, I learn that they had escaped to Lake Conroe and are safe.

To help take my mind off of it, we learn that the company CEO is coming back. There are some key issues yet to resolve. EGPC still has not approved the new development lease (which brings significant cost recovery cash back to our company) or pushed the oil lease extension, and they're still deducting huge amounts from our gas production cash flow due to a minor (less than half a percent) gas line meter reading problem. Egypt is having serious cash flow problems. Oil production is down twenty-five percent from two years ago. Our top guys meet at the Petroleum Minister's office with all the EGPC vice chairmen and the minister's top aides, but not the oil Minister. The EGPC chairman opens the meeting by saying nothing is approved and gas cash deductions will continue.

Alex looks him in the eye and says, "Then this meeting is over" and walks out. We're withholding hundreds of millions of dollars, contingent on EGPC approving the resolution of our issues. To hold our line; rigs will stop drilling and seismic crews may stop—all effective July 1st if we don't get what we need.

The deadline approaches and then passes with them doing little, as we expected. In fact it takes a solid month of sticking to our guns and working with them before we get the signature agreement with EGPC on what will be done. In the end we sweeten the terms a bit to get it done.

Diversion to Israel & Vacation

For years I have heard that crossing the border from Egypt to Israel is like going from Mexico into the USA—night and day. Randy Jordon and I decide to drive over on Friday morning and return on Saturday just to get a good steak, beer, and do something different.

Starting with the border it is obvious things are different on the other side. The Egypt side is the usual slow waiting process, but the Israel side is full of sharp-looking young border guards—mostly women—running the check point. They quiz Randy on our hotel plans and he passes through and waits while they question me repeatedly over a stamp in my passport from the Syrian embassy. It is from a geology trip that I didn't get to make. Finally we are allowed through, but they don't put an Israel stamp in my passport. Instead they stamp a loose piece of paper when I explain that I work in the area and may have to visit neighboring countries for geology business. Others have told us to do this as it should make crossing into other Arab countries easier. It must be tough living in Israel; surrounded by peoples that want to kill you—no wonder they are edgy people.

We take a taxi into Elat and it does look nice. Some very fancy hotels line the water and reddish mountains ring the town. We find our restaurant and start on some Argentinian beef and two foot tall beer glasses.

We hit a club after dinner, and we notice the Israelis are a bit tense. It's a much more Western country than the Arab countries around it. We head back early with me driving and Randy in the back seat eating peanuts. Okay...

I start ticking down the days until I can get out of here and join my wife and my son. I start putting in some crazy hours to get caught up before I leave—as usual, but I have good things to look forward to.

The plan is that I'll fly to Spain for the Festival de San Fermin, the Running of the Bulls, and then some golf before flying back to Cairo and then to the States. Bob Woods and I fly into Spain and meet the fellows. We meet Cal Winters and his buddies from Wisconsin, pile into a rented RV and drive about seven hours across Spain to Pamplona, a town in the foothills of the Pyrenees Mountains famous for the Running of the Bulls. For years these guys have conducted man-trips, revolving around drinking, called "Penske Tour" events—tracked by newsletters, points and talk of awards.

We pull in at 2:00 a.m. and see a sea of people down every street. We park the RV and walk in on foot, grab some sangria, and before I know it, we're sitting on a fence overlooking a sea of people dancing, it's 6:00 a.m. We decide to go get our running shoes. Walking towards the runner's start area we come across Max Miller one of our crew who was very drunk and said, "Follow me if you want to run."

We slipped under the barricade and lost Max in a crowd of thousands of runners. Bob and I manage to stay together still in "check it out" mode, not necessarily thinking of running today and planning for tomorrow. Yet fate must have decreed it because after weaving through the sea of runners to the front, the police locked arm-in-arm across the front and push us back into the crowd when we try to get out—the time to run is at hand. We eye the slippery cobblestone street in front of us and start thinking of what we've gotten ourselves into. A Canadian hockey player next to us is very funny yelling out to the crowd, "Gentlemen, keep your elbows up and run like hell."

Suddenly it's time, and we take off running. We make the first turn and I slip going up the hill—but I have some leather gloves on. I bounce up off the street before I get trampled, not by the bulls but by people—and make the rest of the run. We are in the front of the pack way ahead of the bulls. However by the time we cover the mile and a half course, as we turn into the stadium—which is filling with people, we are just seconds ahead of the bulls. The herd of bulls is coming, you can hear them thundering as the sea of runners parts before them.

Once the running herd of bulls arrives in the stadium, they move them out; they are the actual fighting bulls. They run some other bulls into the arena to provide some fun for the runners still milling around on the floor and the fans in the stands. A big black bull delights the crowd by tossing some runners, but they keep him distracted so he can't gore and trample the people he knocks down. I'm very glad to now be in the safety of the seats, my heart still hammering in my chest and suffering a strange sleep-deprived, death-avoiding euphoria.

After the team does some searching we find Max that afternoon. He has stitches on his face, a tale of a bull running injury and passing out in a park. He's now officially "Pamplona Max." At the right moment in our travels in the RV I make a passionate reading to the group from Ernest Hemmingway's novel *The Sun Also Rises*: "The fiesta was really started. It kept up day and night for seven days. The dancing kept up, the drinking kept up, and the noise went on. The things that happened could only have happened during a fiesta. Everything became quite unreal finally and it seemed as though nothing could have any consequences. It seemed out of place to think of consequences during the fiesta. All during the fiesta you had the feeling even when it was quiet, that you had to shout any remark to make it heard. It was the same feeling about any action. It was a fiesta and it went on for seven days."

We catch the bull fight that night and it is indeed quite the spectacle—the bull fighting and the crowds as well. Bands play, colors abound and sangria flows. The matadors have style and charisma, each a little different as they play the crowd and work the bull down to the killing point. You can see the blood even from our stands high up and I am amazed that this is still a spectator sport in our politically correct modern world.

We play golf that afternoon—with a minimum # beers required to avoid stroke penalty in the competition. The next day we travel about half way back to Barcelona for go-cart racing at Zaragoza and more golf. In the morning we barely make our flight back to Cairo while the rest of the guys head down the coast for more fun. What an incredible experience it's been.

Before I leave, I work two days till about 10:00 p.m. each night before packing hurriedly as usual. I fly out at 6:30 a.m. for the US. After a few days in Houston we fly to Denver and rent a car to drive up near Granby to the King Mountain Dude Ranch for a few days of fun, horses, hiking, fishing, and swimming. We weren't sure this was a good choice until we got up there and the ambiance of the rolling foothills and hanging around a horse ranch started to soak in. Not only is it an amazing place, there are some boys my son's age for him to play with. The boys love the horses, crafts, counselor girls and game room too.

My son isn't too sure about horses, but he grows more comfortable by the end of the week, and my wife and I both become much better riders on some nice adult rides through mountain meadows with our wranglers.

The next day, we ride down to the Colorado River for a rafting trip; too little time on the water but it is fun anyway. Just to see the old cabins along the river from mining days, a couple rapids and a riverside lunch stop is worth it to me.

That night, someone brings in a karaoke machine—which at first I think is going to be lame ends up being a lot of fun. I actually get prodded into singing and find out I can actually sing. The best part is when my son and his new friends join me to sing "Secret Agent Man"—the first song I ever learned on guitar.

A Death in the Family

It's been a wonderful time away in Houston with vacation time in Colorado, however like the last three years, we stayed busy enough that time seems to have flown by. We return to Cairo with a new family member, Scruffy (a West Highland Terrier) who travels well in a carry-on bag under the seat. His first meeting with our large German Shepherd girl Greta goes okay after she initially growls—Scruffy gets excited and chases Greta around trying to play. That night he gets into the kennel in my son's room with Greta on the floor by our bed.

The next day I get a call from my wife who was awakened from a nap in the living room to hear Greta take a few rough last breaths...and then that was it. "I think she's dead Dave," my wife calls to tell me.

My son and his friend Michael have come to our house to play— they help me bury Greta. She had over thirteen good years. We dig a big hole in the yard and carry her out. My son brings his keyboard out and we have a little ceremony for a very good dog. I'm happy we have Scruffy around, as his puppy antics don't leave much time for my son to mourn the loss of such a good friend. He starts school soon after with a new teacher, Mr. Warren, his first male teacher. He knows some kids in his new class, which is good.

New World Order

When I get back to work the acquisition deal for more Egypt property, which closed in April, boosts our expatriate count from twenty-three to forty-six staff. Things have changed in our little community in Egypt. More changes come as well within the government oil company. Hopefully the new EGPC chairman will try to get things done; the company seems to be on a new page and moving forward again.

Then things really change, it's September 11th. We happen to be in my bosses' office in Egypt as US. morning news reports start to come in that a plane has just hit the World Trade Towers in New York City—no, an update, two planes. We immediately realize it is not an accident but terrorism—I won't work late tonight. At home we stay up late glued to CNN. A major act of terrorism has struck at home in the US and we learn thousands of people have lost their lives in this incredible tragedy.

Here in Egypt, we watch a drop in the American stock market and its effect on the company—and we watch our backs. Security measures increase in many ways, including at my son's school—and companies are dusting off security plans. Tension here is always just under a simmer because of Israeli-Palestinian conflict to say nothing of everyday terrorism threats. I've heard some in this region saying that America got what it deserved, but these are typically uneducated people who believe propaganda. Our Egyptian staff is ashamed of the bad people who would do this under the name of Islam.

I have to fly to London to present our Egypt Regional Study paper together with Ted our consultant from Australia on September 17th; I'm nervous about flying and being away from my family so soon after the attack. I arrive on schedule and the conference proceeds normally over a couple days. When I prepare to fly out security out of Heathrow is crazy, everyone waits outside the airport in makeshift tents. Free sandwiches and drinks are provided and flights are hours behind as they walk in one planeload of people at a time to check-in and go. I am okay with tighter security measures, however it makes me happy to get home.

Time passes and nothing happens to us in Egypt. Just in case, there's no trick-or-treating this Halloween, just a big festival inside the school. One point of normality for us is sports, which for now continue after being shut down for a few weeks. My son's soccer team, where he's turning into quite the goalie, and the company men's and women's softball teams resume play. As temperatures drop in the fall, so do tensions that the terrorism will spread and affect us. There are things going on in the world however. The U.S. led coalition, including England and others began bombing Taliban military targets in Afghanistan on October 7th after they refuse to turn over Bin Laden. We are on holiday in Sharm at the Hyatt for Egypt Holiday—Military Day on October 6th, the day bombing starts. The US Ambassador to Egypt (Daniel Kurtzer) was staying there as well so we felt somewhat safe. Sunday night we have "NFL football on one channel and the war on the other" as someone put it, "The War on Terrorism" had begun. Spearheaded by the USA with other countries joined in, the efforts would drag on for who knows how long.

South Africa

The tension has been ratcheted up on all of us; still we are looking forward to an end-of-the-year trip to South Africa. The Company executives leave after the year-end reviews and we fly out of Cairo on December 13th. Despite school getting out and our own Christmas decorations up at the house, it doesn't seem like it's almost Christmas. With it being summer weather in the southern hemisphere this time of year I wonder what South Africans do for Christmas traditions.

We fly into Dubai and then to Johannesburg before connecting to a flight to Port Elizabeth, where we are staying initially on the east coast. We rent a car and I have to drive on the wrong side of the road—British-style, but we make it to our hotel safely. A beautiful beach, brand new shopping, a restaurant and entertainment complex and the Boardwalk is all right next door. The weather feels like Southern California and it's clean and green.

The next morning, we drive about a hundred kilometers northwest through Grahamstown to Addo Elephant Park. We see a herd of elephants at the park headquarters then take a dirt road to some of the remote parts of the park—we even have to stop at one point to allow an elephant to cross the road ahead of us. Everyone enjoys these up close encounters with the gentle giants, but then it's time to head back to the hotel—and the beach. The next day we begin our travels south, which eventually will lead us to Cape Town. Today we are on a beautiful 150 kilometer drive along a coastal route with gorgeous scenery; we arrive at Storms River Park. We watch the big surf crashing on the rocky coast, enjoy seeing the large number of dolphins playing in the surf and hike the Otter Trail to a waterfall. The restaurant is cozy and we enjoy the good food and the short hike to the suspension bridge across the Storm River. I brave the cool ocean water for a swim. The sunset is beautiful. We decide despite the elephants this is the highlight so far.

We check out and cruise over four hundred kilometers—too far— to get to the little village of Arniston with its small white stucco houses with their heavy thatched roofs. We love the colorful little fishing boats in the cove and the clean hotel with a plain front lawn dominated by the small beachfront fishing community. We eat a great dinner for my birthday.

In the morning we take a short hop to the lighthouse and Cape Agulhas, the southern-most land of the African continent where the Indian and Atlantic Oceans meet. It's actually further south than the more prominent and more famous Cape Hope. Then we're back in the car on our way to Paarl—another four hundred kilometer drive. We stop along the way to check out little shops. My son wants to look out over the cliff before we leave one stop and we're glad we did; we catch a whale sticking his tail up in the air. He's a bit late from the normal migration timing out of here so it's a treat to see this straggler.

We arrive in the late afternoon skirting the northeast edge of Cape Town before arriving in Paarl in the rolling foothills of wine country. Lanquedoc Bed and Breakfast and olive farm where we stayed is so scenic—large white cottages, manicured lawns, horses and vineyards. A steep granite peaked mountain ridge forms the skyline to the east—

what a place. While in the area we visit Cape Town and its Toys R Us then meet up with our friends for lunch at a winery called Joostenburg. We take the back roads there. The food and wine are incredible, the scenery restful and the sunsets inspiring.

Time has flown by and it's almost time to leave—good vacations go by so fast. We drive into Cape Town and end up shopping and eating and even catching a movie—*Monsters Inc.*, since I can't talk my son into seeing *The Lord of the Rings*. We somehow manage to fit all our purchases—including twenty two bottles of wine.—into our luggage and the next day we start back for Cairo. What a great trip and fitting way to end the year—good food, great scenery and fine wine.

Santa manages to find us again for Christmas—we keep trying to shake him, but he's a smart old guy. Unfortunately, since I'm in charge of the Egypt Region—scary thought—I have to go in for a few hours on Christmas Day. Later we eat a dinner of ham from South Africa. The year plays itself out with me fielding calls from the CEO every day. With New Year's Eve falling on a work night and no one planning anything we have a few people over to ring in the New Year. It's fun to welcome it with wine from South Africa (actually lots of wine) and our friends from Egypt all gathered here in Cairo. Let's hope 2002 is as blessed a time.

Chapter 16
Our Last Days in Egypt

January, 2002

T he game has definitely changed since my company increased the Egypt investments. Plenty of involvement with Sr. Management to make sure we grow this thing right. The week after the reviews I'm off to Perth, Australia, as part of a company team to review their exploration prospects. I was asked to participate to provide a different view and input to the team process.

I arrive just in time for Australian Day—their version of Independence Day. The Perth riverfront near my hotel is filled with people—apparently about a million—to see a spectacular fireworks show.

It's interesting that Australian Day is celebrating the arrival of the First Fleet in Sydney Cove in 1788 and the day the British declared their sovereignty over the eastern seaboard. Apparently in recent years the aboriginal peoples are more of an issue and to be politically correct, one must be sensitive to their rights as native Australians. The Australia Day fireworks narrative is laced with comments about the ancient heritage of Australia and how they are one united peoples.

I get to catch the final round of the Johnnie Walker Classic golf tournament, a European PGA event. Seeing pro golfers in person is fun. A friend who used to work in Cairo asks if I want to go out on his sailboat with him and his family and friends, so I grab a cab to Free Mantle where I find Paul Miller and his boat at a yacht club dock. We spend a fantastic day on the water and sail across the bay to an island where we have a picnic on the beach.

I pull out my cell phone and call my brother in California from the boat—it's just amazing that I can dial his number with a cell phone while riding on a sailboat off the coast of Western Australia.

Back in Egypt our next trip is off road—back to the White Desert along with a few other families. Our desert trip last year was to Siwa Oasis; but we have not been back to this magical White Desert since our original visit in 1999. It's a long weekend off work in honor of the Barium Feast, which occurs seventy days after the end of Ramadan. Four families all in white Toyota Land Cruisers join our guides on the trek.

We camp the first night outside the Bahariya Oasis and arrive at our camp site the following day at dusk after a pit stop at Crystal Mountain, a rock outcrop fascinating to geologists and kids who want to find black star crystals.

As we are setting up camp, the kids take off to run around and climb the unusual looking white chalk rock mounds that protrude out of the tan sand as small mounds or towers through the area. Suddenly we hear a scream, it's my son. He's running back from the rocks screaming at the top of his lungs.

He throws himself into my arms, his face covered in blood. I can't understand what he's trying to tell me through the tears but I can immediately tell that he has fallen from cuts on his face along with his knee and hand. Is his nose broken? He may have a concussion; I can see a knot rising on his forehead already.

A crowd of concerned adults and kids gathers around the blanket where my wife and I try to treat his injuries. Bob sets up our tent while we take care of him. Our initial scary thoughts are if this is a serious medical situation we are out in the desert hours from Cairo and will have to start driving immediately—thank God his nose isn't broken. He had fallen forward on his face; Ouch! Scalp wounds bleed a lot, but it doesn't look like he has a concussion either. In a few hours with bandages in place he is back up and we carry on.

That afternoon, we decide to drive out onto some big sand dunes for a picnic lunch and cover some interesting terrain in the White Desert. However, no sooner do we park the cars and start setting up our tarp when the wind begins to pick up. We adults begin to exchange nervous glances and Bob yells; "khamseen!" Fifteen minutes later lunch is canceled and we are driving back to the main camp—just ahead of a sandstorm. Visibility isn't too bad and we make it back to camp without trouble. Our tent has blown over but I tie it down and secure all our stuff. We hunker down to wait out the intense winds and sand storm.

By dusk the wind is calm and we try to have some fun. My son spent the afternoon playing with his Game Boy in our car. He finally emerges as Jim pulls out his guitar and plays a couple tunes. We all take turns singing the "Sand in Your Eyes Blues" around the campfire.

Back-to-Back Trips

My son and I work for weeks on the ramps for a skateboarding party for his birthday—the day finally arrives with ten boys coming over. Scooters, skateboards, skates and kids and no one gets hurt, I'm amazed.

Before any of the sleepover boys are awake I am gone—headed to Houston for an American Association of Petroleum Geologists (AAPG) convention where I will co-chair a session for E&P activities in north Africa and Eurasia, with a guy I met in Egypt who works for a major company. This trip has been months in the making and the best part is I am able to skip up to Erie, Pennsylvania and see some family. It makes for a brutal travel day though.

Tuesday is the big day, and I get to the convention center early for the speakers breakfast. First in our session is a talk on the petroleum potential of Egypt, then Doug Eller presents the paper he wrote with Jake and me as co-authors about the Western Nile Delta Tertiary Play, the session goes well. We have fun with it and stay on schedule. This morning's session with about 200 attendees, is one of seven different rooms in session at the same time. This is a big convention involving tens of thousands of people.

I get to see people I know from college and other companies and then it's off to a Rockets game where they beat Seattle. Overall, a very successful trip.

Insanity—I'm only back for a day before we fly out of Cairo on a spring break ski vacation with a couple of other families in the Alps. The first night we drive to the scenic little town of Annecy for an overnight at Allobroges Hotel. The next day we drive through Alberville (site of 1992 Winter Olympics) and on up to Courchevel, France at an elevation of 1,850 meters (just over 6000 ft.); which seems low by Colorado standards, but we are surrounded by large snow covered mountains here in the Alps.

Our hotel is Les Chaltes du Forum, sitting in a nice little ski town with cobblestone streets, wooden buildings and a big ski area. My son has turned into quite a good skier, especially when he switches to a better instructor the second day (he got stuck in a beginner class the first day) and handles a steep bumpy run with me without a problem. We try to get him snowboarding lessons too, but there aren't enough kids to hold the class.

We have a blast skiing, including a steep black run that goes straight down the mountain face. Some of the guys and I go out in some deep powder in bad conditions—almost no visibility and get a real rush, but most of it is pretty normal stuff.

Some of the best fun we have is actually in the shopping mall in the center of town where some mountain climber guys set up a rock climbing wall, an adventure rope net, suspension bridge climbing trek and a giant rope swing off a third floor balcony where you swing across the mall's entire atrium. The kids climb to the top of the rock wall and do the giant swing. Joey lets out a funny Tarzan yell as he swings. My son and I do the rope climb suspended high above the people walking below. They could never do something like this in the States for fear of lawsuits. The ropes and sledding we get to do as families makes it an even more enjoyable trip; we all have a blast being away from Egypt for a while.

We are back in time to ramp up for the next technical review for Sr. Mgmt. and surprisingly we actually make sure to be done with our reviews in time for our softball game. Alex attends the game and cheers us on. Since the Egypt property acquisition, things seem to be "going up and to the right (like a chart of oil production growth through time!).

We spend Easter at the Red Sea in Sharm on the south end of the Sinai Peninsula for some pool time and snorkeling. My son straps on a mask this time and sees the colorful reef. We have a great little break with the other families we know, but there are more topless women than I can ever remember seeing here before—many of them should not be!

Oil & Culture

Back at work in Cairo, I decide to get the guest flats basement cleaned out—finally. They're moving all the rock core samples out and laborers are carrying the trash outside and burning it in a barrel—but then we get a call that there's a fire. Well, yes, we think—in the barrel. But it isn't in the barrel—it's pouring out of the basement. Glenn and I rush down to find that the workers, rather than carrying all the trash all the way outside to the barrel, had decided to begin burning it right there in the basement. Amazing!

The rest of spring is uneventful, working hard to keep drilling oil and gas wells to increase production, playing softball and golf and carrying on in the swing of life here in Egypt. A special golf story is Randy "Toad" Jordon and Dave "Bitch" Allard defeating Cal Randall and his partner in the "Mena House Challenge" golf match to even the series at 2-2. I shoot my best ever at Katameya, an 84.

The MaSalama Party is for the families moving out. It is a nice evening setup outside on the lawn with catered food. After our leader presents the official Co. going away gifts, people get up and present roast material—there are some hilarious roast efforts.

An offshore wildcat deep water well in the Western Mediterranean Concession is finally complete—it should have been done by year end 2001, but we had a few setbacks for repairs. It was drilled in 1,000 meters of water. The rig actually stays in position by computer-operated thrusters rather than anchors.

The pressure is on geosciences not to make a mistake, as the gross cost will be about $15 million for the thirty-day project. The cost of operating in deep water is just on another level. We want not only a good prospect but to not have well control problems. Thursday, April 25th, we start to see log pay, and that night Jake and I stay up late watching the main pay section being drilled.

By Friday we know we have a keeper—we see enough pay thickness to know we have a significant discovery. By the following Monday, we're presenting logs in a videoconference to our executives in Houston. We have to kick everyone not on the project out of the room and do another presentation at 1:00 a.m. Cairo time, to a full room in Houston and we receive a standing ovation. Considering this is a discovery and the first deep water exploration well in company history, our Chairman is quoted as saying, "This is the most significant well in our forty-seven year history."

We continue to have trouble with the Egyptian side of the equation, however. We get the runaround from EGPC on some concessions, and finally we drive to EGAS—the gas side of things—to present a prospect to the Egypt VP. We need Egyptian approval on all new business spending to get paid back in cost recovery through production. However, this day he's very positive and agrees to send a letter of approval of the drilling project.

Later on the phone we hear, "Oh, we never received your fax." So my co-worker tells him, "I have your secretary on the line, and she confirms that you received it at 1:45 p.m." We caught him cold. Reluctantly he approves, sends the letter on and we get final approval to drill.

The longer we're here, the more apparent it is that some Arabs feel differently about lying than we do in Western business. We noticed some prefer to tell us what we want to hear and avoid a face-to-face confrontation to keep things positive. But it has at least as much to do with a culture that's averse to doing anything that might lead to a mistake that might jeopardize their position—even when it's in the best interest of their company or country to approve.

However with our offshore discovery, the company decides to drill another well right away—and three more deep-water wells by the end of the year. The total cost of the five wells will be about $70 million. We need to drill now before the deep water rig is gone to the next project for another company.

As summer closes in, we head to Paris for a family fun getaway. We visit Paris Disney and tour some Paris sights, including the city sites by fat tire bike. We have a lot of fun, but then it's time for us to part—me back to Cairo, the family to the States for the summer.

The office is bachelor town for a while. I play some golf and endure another round of reviews with senior management. However, by July 19th, I am flying to Houston myself; after a guy's golf trip to

Malaga, Spain, with 3 of the usual suspect fellows! We stay near Mirabella on the Costa del Sol and have a great time.

After a few days of golf, drinking, and little sleep, the return trip is far from uneventful. We miss our connection and have to spend a night in Madrid. We toured the city by day and found four Irish pubs that night.

Flying along the North African coast the next day, the Egypt Air plane suddenly takes a hard right and down—the pilot said we are picking up stranded passengers in Tunisia. We thought we were hijacked. It turned out to be a brief stop to load a few smelly folks on and we beat it back to Cairo—apparently they had been stranded a couple of days.

I'll miss Bob Woods, a kindred spirit geologist and good friend. He and his family are moving to Canada, but they will do well. How long will we be here ourselves? I don't know—maybe another year. I guess we will see what the future brings.

R&R is Always Too Short

The end of the year is winding around, and December is the busiest time of year for us at work. We're trying to wrap things up and achieve our goals and review our proposed plan for next year, so we're gathering results from the last year and making our plan requests for next year. These reviews take so much time to prepare, then the actual reviews take up three entire days, during which time not much else gets done.

However, we get to celebrate their end with a golf tourney—JV Hellions against the HQ Lodge. The Lodge pulled out a victory, although it's hotly contested. It's all tied up until our man rams a long putt in to take the win, but due to some concern he may have played the wrong ball coming up the fairway to 18, emails begin to fly back and forth right up until it's time for us to depart for winter break.

By Wednesday, December 18th, we're ready to leave Cairo. The family and I depart Cairo on British Air to arrive London about noon; survive Heathrow hell, arrive at the Crown Royal Hotel, take a taxi to the Tube, and on to Westminster. Christmas season evenings in

London are nice; we ride the London Eye Ferris wheel near the Thames River. We even get to see a theatre production by Ben Elton, We Will Rock you. Great show—my son gives it four of five stars.

Christmas with family in the States is a huge improvement over celebrating by ourselves in Egypt, and it's been about five years since I've been to Midland to see familiar people and places. Most of my wife's family shows, and it's a restful week of Christmas cheer.

My son and I fly to Florida while my wife makes a detour to Dallas to see her sister Beverly for a few days. Our flight has to put down in San Antonio instead of Houston, and after delays, we don't land in Florida until about 3:00 a.m. We can't check in to our hotel until some other people check out. After a few hours of sleep, my son and I hit the Magic Kingdom as planned—he's been a trooper though this.

We have a great time and put in a full day, seeing the night parade on the way out. We hit a big rainstorm on the way to my mom's in time for New Year's Eve, where we have to wake up Grandma. We pick up my wife at the airport and enjoy relaxing in Okeechobee for a few days before heading back to Houston so I can take a Landmark ZMap Course. I want to keep up my skills in case I need to make a map on the job or even work as a geologist again someday instead of a paper-pushing manager.

Slogging through the first quarter is easier because we're looking forward to a ski trip to Austria. We go to Saalbach, Austria, about an hour and a half drive from Salzburg in February. Another company family organized the trip—our new ski buddies. Three other families join us on the trip. It's fun hanging out with such a big group. I learned of a Mozart Dinner Concert in Salzburg. The concert is in St. Peter's Abbey, which was built in 803 AD and the vocalists are excellent.

The skiing is great, and my son finally gets to try snowboarding—he gets me to learn with him. We hire a private tutor, a young girl—snowboarding is hard just like they said it would be. We start on the bunny slope and fall on our butts a lot, but we learn the basics that morning and then fool around that afternoon ourselves. I wanted to go skiing the next day, but my son talks me into snowboarding with him another day. I'm glad we do because on day two we both start to get a feel for it. That afternoon we move off the bunny slope to a regular slope and get better at making our turns back and forth. It is fun, and we both have a good sense of accomplishment. Interestingly from that point forward; my son remained a snowboarder and I remained a skier.

The following day we celebrate my wife's birthday with a sleigh ride in the country. Teams of two huge work horses pulled each of the two sleighs with about fourteen people each to the ranch for a warming drink. We sleigh back to town for a nice dinner with amazing deserts, including my wife's desert with a giant sparkler burning while family and friends sang happy birthday. It's been a really fun trip.

We're back for just a couple of days before I have to fly to London for business. We enjoyed some culture, had an all-day meeting and I managed to catch the British Imperial War Museum before flying out for another late arrival in Cairo. Sunday Vince Keller calls me to talk about a few issues and then asks me to come by his office before or after lunch. I show up around 11:00 a.m. wondering what is up.

"I'll cut to the chase," Vince says quickly. "You've been selected to be the Exploration Manager for our new region Apache North Sea in the Aberdeen, Scotland office. I have asked that you get a promotion and raise out of the deal. Your new boss James Brooks is flying out of Houston this afternoon. Here is his cell phone number so you can give him a call."

The talk with my new boss goes well, and this is a great opportunity for me. I called the CEO to get his thoughts on this new job: He says I should hire the best people, no matter where they're from.

He finishes, "I'm pleased you will take the job. I think you're one of the best 'explorationists' in the company." The tone changes: "Now—don't screw it up." He finishes, half kidding—maybe.

So I put together a proposed schedule that allows my son to finish fourth grade in CAC, allows a reasonable transition from my Cairo job, and enables me to not miss all of the family-type events. I email a one-page summary to James and call him to discuss it. I'm in an interesting spot: the US could attack Iraq any day, and I don't want to be away from my family when/if that happens, and I don't want to uproot our son from his school until the summer break.

On the other hand, I need to get off to a fast start on the new job. Vince tells me, "If you need to drop Egypt and run, don't worry about it." I lay awake a few nights wondering what to do.

Scotland Bound

On March 5, 2003, I depart for Aberdeen, Scotland—only my wife and our Egypt Management know why I'm really going. Everyone else thinks I'm going to do prospect risk assessments. It's an odd office— an open area layout and no one has a proper office. Everyone works at desks with low walls separating them. It seems strange.

I tour the housing options. They call Aberdeen the "Granite City" because grey granite stone is used for most buildings. That first weekend, I take a drive by Stonehaven to visit the Dunnotter Castle on the coast. They built Dunnotter in the 1600s after William Wallace sacked the old structure.

Word gets out that I'll be moving, so James has a town-hall style meeting to introduce me to the office. I have to tell Vince back in Egypt about it because word will surely spread. He paves the way at the office, so I call my wife and ask her to speak to my son so he doesn't hear it from friends first. He cries for a while because he'll miss his friends but then brightens up when he hears how nice it will be.

I'm back in Cairo and things are moving fast, however here in Cairo it's strange being a lame duck. The US doesn't respect my plans, I guess, because on March 20th together with the UK allied forces attack Iraq. The Arab world is very upset, and to be safe the Cairo American School is closed on Thursday. At work we're open but are welcome to stay with our families, which many people do. Protests are flaring up all over the Arab world, and I delay my departure to Scotland while we hunker down—no baseball games, no distractions. We all just sort of hold our breath and wait to see what will happen.

In downtown Cairo the police use water cannons to break up protestors marching towards the US embassy. Here in Maadi things stay quiet and school cautiously opens Sunday. I head back to Scotland on March 26th for a couple weeks stay to get sorted—as they say here.

March 29th is an interesting day. I'm invited to go to a rugby match in Edinburgh, along with a couple other exploration managers. Scotland wins the game, which I found fascinating to watch as it's very similar to American football—big boys and no pads!.

At home, we get things ready and try to spend some time with friends. My son performs in a fourth and fifth grade musical in his suit. He looks so sharp.

We fly out together for Scotland by the middle of April to look for a house and for my family to see Aberdeen. We look at several communities located along the Dee River: Cults Milltimbre, Peter Cutter, and Banchory. We take a pass on the Lil' America style Westhill neighborhood built in the 60s or 70s after big oil was discovered in the North Sea. We settle on country living; in Drumoak—and what a place it is.

Manse Steading built in the early 1800s was the stables at the old Minister's estate, now it's a rambling six bedroom with wooden floors and lots of windows and doors. A lawn surrounds our place and the huge trees all around give it a scenic quality. There's a duck pond nearby, and it's only a few hundred yards to the Dee River. My wife and my son fly back to Cairo and I stay on to work—it's chaos trying to hire people and get the office set up. I head back to Cairo to wrap things up making it in time for my son's baseball game on Friday. The whole month of May is jam packed—saying goodbye to all our friends, some we've known since 1998. My wife departs on a bike trip to the Netherlands with her sister and some other lady friends, so my son and I are on our own for a week, it's a good time for us to relate. I'm more flexible with work now and can walk him to school and meet at 3:00 p.m. when he gets out. I help coach his baseball team and he comes with me to a final few softball games. I've really enjoyed being my son's baseball coach—maybe even more than he liked playing; although his teammates voted him an all-star player. It's fitting we have our goodbye party outdoors. We both feel sad to be leaving so many friends from the life we've made here. It's hard to believe it's been five years of life in Egypt.

We're lucky to be moving to the North Sea, and we are actually looking forward to the change. The oil industry, and the stock analysts in particular are watching to see if the company can be successful in the harsh North Sea environment. The Egypt exploration group has a special going away party for me; a special long lunch on a Nile cruise boat. It's an interesting feeling to know that the mystique of being "Mr. Dave," advocate of the nationals, will not come with me out of the third world. These are good people and I have enjoyed getting to know them and their culture.

It's time to bid goodbye to the desert, the pharaohs and their pyramids, and say hello to the misty green hills of Scotland.

Chapter 17
Oil's Journey to Scotland

Spring, 2003

This past year has involved some major changes for us, most notably that we moved to our new North Sea Operating Region based out of Aberdeen, Scotland. Along the way I have to remember to look breathlessly at everything along the trail…the old world we are leaving and the new vistas of Scotland.

From March through June I have been going back and forth between my family in Cairo and my new job in Aberdeen. The North Sea office opened in February and my new VP says, "You better get here or I will hire your team for you."

I arrive just in time for the first North Sea reviews with our CEO—what luck. For exploration we scramble to pull together a review of our progress and plans. I show a good overview of the organization we need, what deals we have looked at, and what we have done so far on the offshore oil field we bought from another company. We are still in a grace period—sort of—I heard that we have until next year to get our staff together and firing on all cylinders… no pressure.

I also get the opportunity to go offshore to visit the field together with the others who have made the trip from Houston HQ for the reviews in Scotland. We fly offshore about 100 miles to the Field in a giant helicopter even though we would normally—in order to work offshore—be required to take three days of training for safety and survival. We get that waived for this special trip where we will not stay overnight. Even so, we do go through a safety review before we put on our survival suits, which are heavy-duty dry suits with locator beacons and air breathing packs. If you land in the cold North Sea water, you lose mobility in minutes and drown without the suit.

We stop briefly at Alpha and Bravo platforms before taking a tour of Delta platform. We have had shut downs almost weekly since we took over the field, one after another mechanical problems. When the field shuts down the cash flow stops. The platforms are tied together with oil pipelines, which tie to the export line to shore. Any significant pressure disruption in the system on one platform shuts down the whole field. I spent time on an offshore drilling rig in China, but I have never been on a production platform. The Field facilities and huge platforms were originally put in service 100 miles offshore in the 1970s. Some pipeline equipment, pumping and processing devices have been added and replaced over the years as the technology has evolved. The maze of pipes and large machines on the different levels of the platform is impressive. From the railing I can see other platforms in the distance—beyond that just water.

When we get back from offshore the CFO wants to play some golf so I have to take one for the team. We go out to Newmachar in the hills near Aberdeen. We managed to play nine holes and endure a brief rain but have a good time.

With the reviews completed, I have a little exploration team dinner, then it's time to fly back to Cairo; possibly for the last time. Our address where we have lived since 1999 looks so empty with all of our stuff packed. With things wrapping up, we organize a farewell party for my son. Friends from his class, his Cub Scouts den, and a few other kids make up a group of twelve boys to meet at our house and then go on a felucca ride—the ancient style wooden sailboat out on the Nile River—piloted by an Egyptian guy in galabiya robes. I hope my son has good closure with his friends and is ready to begin a new adventure.

The last days in Cairo are hectic and go like this: the day after school ends in Cairo is the most unique send off—a "Rock and Roll Felucca Party" in boats on the Nile River. I sat in with the "One Night Stand" band earlier in the year, but the fellows think of a proper send-off. We bring our guitars, they have battery-powered amps, and Kevin Cole brings cases of beer. We lash two feluccas together to fit everyone, about 30 people, and we jam into the night.

The next night is a farewell dinner for my wife and, hosted by our VP, Vince. The next day is my last round of golf at Katameya. I stayed out of the rock and sand hazards lining many fairways and shot an 84; one of my better rounds of the past two years. The next day, June 14th, we fly out on KLM through Amsterdam and find ourselves in Aberdeen to start a new life.

Full of Scots

Hello Scotland. Our house is not ready yet (sound familiar?) So we live in the Spires Apartments while we wait a couple weeks to get into the house. I have to leave my family in the apartment for a couple of days to go on a field trip. The Exploration team, led by University of Aberdeen professors, travel north of Aberdeen to the Morey Firth area to see the rocks. Jurassic and some Devonian rocks are exposed in creek beds and seaside outcrops. It's a brilliant, scenic drive through the rolling open hills and up the rugged coastline in the occasional moments of sun, but mostly cloudy with some drizzling rain. One day we past the old location of a former gold rush town (the buildings are all gone now).

We manage to have some fun buying things to use in the new house, but most of my wife and son's time is boring while I am busy at work. We move into our rental house in Drumoak in late June. A couple days later, they leave for Texas. I will follow in a couple of weeks—very busy at work.

The culture of the office and working in the UK is very different than Egypt and a bit difficult to describe, but I imagine like most things I will get used to it. Working with the Government Oil Company in the UK, the regulators of industry, involves many new rules to learn and new people to work with.

Our home shipment arrives July 10th, and it takes all day with just me and the three movers to get the stuff in the house. Partly because the old steading house is down a narrow lane off the main road that goes under the old railway bridge the Queen had dismantled to dissuade folks from taking the train out to the summer palace—Balmoral. So you see the fellows have to offload the big truck into a smaller truck to run down to the house, one small load at a time. I am running around directing where things go the best I can—I sure miss my wife right now. The movers are great and they work late to get everything in the house on that first day. We also find a few damaged items, which is surprising considering where we came from. One of the movers, Tich said, "Bonne house you've got here."

I meet some new friends to play golf with, and one summer night we finish at 10:30 p.m. They say that during the peak summer light you can play until midnight. Imagine that—a full eighteen holes after a long day of work.

In July, I make a few trips to the party trail of Aberdeen with some fellow employees, downtown Union Street is a crazy place. Almost every night I see a lot of people having fun after a few drinks but do not see any rough Scots looking for a fight that I have heard about over the years.

Summer Vacation

If we had known about my transfer to Scotland prior to planning our home leave this summer, we may have done it differently. However, we have family reunions set up—in Boston and my side in Colorado. We will miss a record warm and sunny Scottish summer. We have been enjoying sunny days with little rain, almost drought conditions for here. The water levels are so low this year that the salmon can't swim upstream to spawn and many are dying in the harbor.

I leave Aberdeen in July to join the family in Boston, Massachusetts. It's fun to see old town Boston, taking a duck tour (an amphibious vehicle from World War II) and doing some whale watching. I was actually born in Massachusetts but have never been to Boston before.

My son and I go to Six Flags over New England in Springfield and spend about nine hours in the park riding roller coasters, one of his current fascinations. We drive through the Berkshire Hills to Lenox where my folks met and to Pittsfield where I find the house where I lived my first few years.

It's interesting for me to drive around Pittsfield and show my son where I am from; I hope it is interesting to him. We also visit my cousin and his family and stay for dinner. We drive to Cape Cod and play putt putt golf and swim while the ladies are in Canada doing genealogy research. We see Plymouth Rock then meet up and spend two nights in New Hampshire among the scenic lakes.

We detour to Houston for a few days of errands and medical checkups. I pop into the HQ. When the founder sees me, he says, "Are you here to quit?" When I tell him no, he says, "Well, come over here and give me a hug." We are getting to be a large company, but it still has a family feel.

Then it is off to Colorado for my family reunion. It has taken a year planning to get us all together, and it is great to see everyone in Buena Vista. We enjoy five great nights with a campfire every night, rent ATVs, ride bikes, enjoy some hot springs, and check out a mountain ghost town—but mostly we just enjoy being together. Friends from Egypt visit for a night. Our families got to know each other when Bob Woods and I worked for the company in Cairo. The kids have grown since we last saw them, but their daughter and my son having been in class together in Egypt, have a link that is hard to explain to most people—they were expat kids in a 3rd world country, which creates unique bonds and shields.

Vacation is over—it's time to push, pack, and get everything ready for another trip to our overseas home.

We have a minor snag when the Federal Express package containing our UK visas and my work permit is sent on to Scotland, despite the fact that I asked them to hold it for me in Houston. It gets solved. The courier with our documents flies from Aberdeen all the way back to Houston. He gets off his flight and down to our check in area about one hour before our flight is to leave. We make the handoff, with only moments to spare.

A New Life in the UK

We touch down in Aberdeen about midday and have to race to the school for orientation. We missed the morning orientation but the receptionist shows us around the nice little school, which is built in an old manor house. There are only about three hundred and fifty students total, including preschool—12th grade. It's a small, tightknit group, which will be different from Cairo.

My son actually misses his first day of school with a bout of croup and we stay up all night with him doing breathing treatments. The next day we are trying to get over jet lag as we launch ourselves into the UK healthcare system. My wife has trouble getting him an appointment, but she finally manages to talk them into one. We have to see a general practitioner before we can go see a specialist, which my son needs, and we learn no UK health care professional is allowed to continue giving my son the allergy shots he has been on for a year. They do not believe in that medication here, and we have to throw away a year's supply of allergy medication. We see firsthand how frustrating this type of healthcare system can be.

We decide to buy a car while we are here; a blue Honda CRV about a year old for 14,000 pounds sterling....yes it is right side drive.

It's not all work and no play—I win my first golf tournament. It's a great day of sun, plenty of wind gusts and spots of rain. I knew that I played well, an 83 at Kimney, but I am still surprised when I receive a nicely engraved silver whiskey flask as the first place trophy.

I get to play more golf as we settle in, and I even get to fly back to Cairo in October to play the Pharaohs Cup, which the Iraqi war delayed from April. Team USA plays with honor against Team World in a thirty-two man a side Ryder Cup format—we come up one point short. I am just glad to get to see some friends from Cairo, feels like a touring golf pro for a minute and even a greater sense of closure from our Egypt days.

Even my son is breaking new ground; he spends a week away from home for the first time ever on a school trip. It is a strange feeling around the house all week with him gone, but I am very proud of how grown-up he is becoming.

We drive to the Highland Games at Bramar west of Aberdeen on a bright sunny September day. We see all the activities and leave early, but we see the Queen's motorcade driving to the games—I wave, and through the tinted glass, I'm sure we get a royal greeting. Later, we find out Prime Minister Tony Blair was there too—the local crowd booed him due to the war situation.

The Executives arrive in Aberdeen to review our field performance well by well and plan some goals for 2004. The plan will be for field production to remain steady, do some workovers, and perform some repairs to get production up. It is interesting to see how the engineers work through all the production data curves to understand what each well in each field is capable of producing in order to project the company cash flow.

I travel to the AAPG (American Association of Petroleum Geologists) International meeting in Barcelona, Spain, where I see many fellow employees—and a Carlos Santana concert; he puts on a great show and adds some political commentary in Spanish—which I don't ever learn the details of. I make that trip as I was committed to give a talk about the structural styles of Egyptian Western Desert long before the transfer to Scotland.

By late October we have our exploration team in place: a petrophysicist (ties the rock data to electric well log data), two technicians, our group secretary, my "PA" (personal assistant—hope I don't get spoiled because she is sharp), three geophysicists, and two geologists.

The next day I attend a mid-day church service downtown at the old Kirk of St. Nicholas in honor of "Oilmen Remembrance"—for those that died in the North Sea oil business. Out front afterwards one of my co-workers points out a guy he knew who survived the Piper Alpha disaster by jumping off the platform. This was back in 1988, and 167 people died. Sixty-one survivors braved freezing waters to escape the explosion that's been the industry's worst incident for loss of life. It's a sobering reminder of how critical it is to do our jobs right—more than company profits and bonuses hang in the margin. From the office we need to plan things well and identify risks, but the people in the "oil field" run the operation with all the high-risk that comes with our business.

Our North Sea operations folks spend many days of November through early December doing workshops for the offshore guys, trying to show them that we intend to spend money and grow, that we need people to bring ideas forward and work with a sense of urgency. Mike, who works for us and has worked in this area of the North Sea for his entire career, tells a great story about how they tore the rig off Echo. It had to be removed so the giant jack-up rig we leased can fit over the top of the platform and drill several new wells faster and with more muscle to reach out father from the platform. A great story of the workshop came when one guy explained, "We used to hide spare parts to keep things going because the former operator was not spending enough to keep adequate spare parts around the platforms."

Things at home are coming together too—we settle down and find a church more quickly than I thought, and my son is already getting involved in his new school. He plays trombone in his first school concert, what a special moment.

I played a December round of golf with Shaun Renson at Montrose; original construction was 1562. It's a "dreak"—a dreary day—but I end up with the best Stableford score of 37 on the back 9. We have to really look to find someplace to get food and drink after the Saturday round. I am amazed that here in the UK many stores close early and miss some prime sale times such as right after work or on weekdays.

A UK-Thai Christmas

Christmas is coming soon. The end of the year is winding down and the North Sea Company Christmas party is December 12th at the Ardoe House. About 170 people show, and everyone is dressed very nicely. Our VP decides to wear a kilt, which is common for a few Scotsman, but the American is the talk of the evening. The 18th is the Christmas lunch, another local tradition. James Brooks is gone, so I'm sitting in as managing director—and under my watch—yikes, we leave about noon (as planned) on a bus into town for the Copthorn Hotel. Nobody plans to drive themselves home—the "Christmas Lunch," common for Aberdeen based companies involves plenty of drinking.

Over the meal I get up and propose some toasts: A goodbye to a transferee, another's fortieth birthday and a Merry Christmas to all. Apparently people know it's my birthday because they add a fourth toast for me. The truly funny part is that my VP told my secretary, before he left, that I was turning fifty and she believed him; in spite of that event being a few years away. She got me a cake and candle with a fifty on it—good for a few laughs. After dinner, the karaoke machine and DJ set up in the bar and we had a great time. Yes, I did sing.

It looks like it's going to be a white Christmas—by dinner on Sunday December 21st, it's all white outside and by the next morning we have three or four inches. I pull my son up the hill by our house a few times on his snowboard so he can make a few runs, and we run the sled a few times. Before you know it, it's Christmas Eve. We go to church at Banchory and then have a great dinner at home. I start Christmas day with an early morning run, and I can see the lights popping on in houses with little kids. By the time I'm back my son is ready to get up and open presents. It's a good morning together, and later on we go to dinner with a few other families at a friend's house—a very nice day.

The next day, we pile into a plane and head to Thailand, where we will catch a little sun and enjoy the remaining vacation time for 2003. We need to sun up for our first winter in Aberdeen, and we arrange to visit at the same time as Kevin Cole's family; their son was my son's best friend in Cairo so this should be a blast. After flying overnight, we land in Bangkok and catch a prop plane for the hour and a half flight to Koh Samui, a beautiful little island that welcomes us with thatched roofed huts and no walls; at the airport.

The drive across the island isn't impressive—some scruffy little towns—but the Santiburi Dusit Hotel looks very nice. We check in, and suddenly I see familiar faces—the Coles walk by. Our villa is set in a row of villas with an ocean view. "Welcome to the Allards to Santiburi" is carved into a big fruit to greet us.

That night after some pool and beach time we join our friends for a poolside seafood buffet and a fire-dance show, where boys and girls wear native costumes and show us their local dances. The next day we are joined by another co-worker's family and we all enjoy a Thailand tourist day, riding elephants and crocodile watching before a big group dinner at the You and Me Restaurant—great name, right? We decide to not pay the $300 each for the New Year's Eve party provided by the hotel, instead we set up another dinner on the beach. We shoot some fireworks off down at the beach—and we survive a few hectic moments as several people shoot fireworks in various directions.

We spend New Year's Day taking a sunny boat ride to another island Kah Pa Naa, which is beautiful. My wife and I do some more snorkeling while our son stays in the boat, a little tired from his late night.

The next day we spend our last island day at the Meridian hotel on the other side of the island, for some water sports. The sunset behind the tiny islands, with their limestone cliffs, is memorable. We dine that night high up on the cliffs above the Meridian at the Royal Thai Restaurant. The Thai dancer's performance included the, apparently famous Bird Dance. In Buddhist mythology of Southeast Asia, it stems from the lover Kinnaris, depicted as a half-bird, half-woman creature.

We bid our friends good-bye the following day and fly business class all the way home. I arrive at the office at 10:30 a.m. Monday morning while my family crashes at home. Maybe we cut this a little too close...

New Season

I used to get over jet lag easier than I do now, it seems—maybe due to getting older. After we get back from Thailand, I struggle to work through it and get sharp. It takes a week for me to feel like a human being again—just in time as we prepare for a January Egypt operations review.

It's not as bad preparing for this senior management visits these days, as we are a growing company that went from making income of $100 million the year I joined (1997) up to making $1.1 billion in 2003. The company has managed twenty percent growth per year over the past twelve years. Okay, some of that recent income increase is the price of oil going up, but we are an acquisitions and drilling company, our stock price reflects daily production and our reserves in the ground. It's fun to be part of a growth company. It's the company's fiftieth anniversary this year, so the normally stressful meeting approaches with a sense that we're actually going somewhere.

We work hard to prepare for our reviews and the night before, Our CEO cancels the trip. Heavy snow begins to accumulate in Aberdeen and the company plane stops in Dublin on January 26th. The executives have to get back to Houston for a quarterly earnings call on January 29th, and they're not sure they can get out of Aberdeen due to the storm—so they turn around and head back to Houston. We present our stuff to our VP James instead, since we worked so hard to prepare it. Pulling together reviews for senior management sounds like a waste of time, but some good things happen in the process: a) building a summary clarifies the many accomplishments of the past months, which I seem to miss running so fast day-to-day; and b) ideas and recommendations drop out of the process.

My wife and I take up a 'well-head' equipment company's offer to attend their Robbie Burns supper on the yacht Britannia, in Edinburgh. They hired a night on the former royal family's yacht for the festivities around Scotland's favorite poet son, Robert Burns. His "Ode to the Haggis" is a famous poem about the infamous Scottish dish; typically recited when the oatmeal-and-entrails filled sheep's stomach are served in honor of his birthday at "Burn's Suppers." His other most famous writing is a New Year's Eve favorite, Auld Lang Syne. My wife and I enjoy an evening on a yacht that has entertained government leaders in ports all over the world. We feel pretty special – even though the boat is docked and no longer in service!

Early in February we get logs on our first company-drilled North Sea well. We used a giant jack-up rig to straddle the platform and drill quickly. The rig was late coming to us from the other operator and then it was stuck in port for about a month due to high seas and wind. High seas could easily roll over the top heavy giant drilling rig while anchors up and sailing, so they wait for a calm spell to move in. Production from the Field is up, we're knocking costs down and we plan to drill twenty-two field wells this year.

I fly to London for a meeting in the Geologic Society of Great Britain's Burlington House. It's a classic old building where hangs the first geologic map of England made in the early 1800s by William 'Strata' Smith. He's known as the "Father of English Geology" for creating the "map that changed the world." Craig Davis and I are there to meet a couple guys from another oil company to try and make a deal by joining forces on their oil lease located near our Field.

A few days later, we get out on a family trip to explore our Scottish countryside—the Highlands. With snow on the ground and more expected, we take off for a drive to Aviemore, a popular winter sports town in the Cairngorm Mountains. By the time we drive over the first set of hills into the open treeless hills around Leight Ski Area it's snowing and blowing. We make it down into the Spey River valley and then on into Aviemore safely by early afternoon enjoying the white-blanketed countryside. We'll definitely have to come back in the summer to enjoy some hill walking.

The snow keeps coming and we hunker down in our little two-bedroom renter which accepts pets, so our white Westie, Scruffy, makes the trip with us. All this snow would have made for great skiing the next day…if the road to the ski area was open. We stay in town and walk to a great sledding hill near the Hilton hotel and put my son's sled and snow board to good use.

Real Life

My son graduates from Webelos to Boy Scouts. He's a big boy now and I'm happy to share some things with him. We go on our first camping adventure with Troop 248 to the King's Cliff shooting range to fire shotguns, pellet rifles, learn some archery—and the basics of fly fishing. It's a chilly night but jokes and skits around the campfire help keep our minds off it.

Spring is a joy here in Scotland, everything turns green—which is shocking still after five years in Egypt. Before that I lived in Texas so this type of season change is really nice. Also, it's warming up a little.

It is incredible how rapidly the amount of light per day changes in Aberdeen. The December low point light span is 8:30 a.m. till 3:30 p.m., and by April we are back to light from about 7:00 a.m. to 6:00 p.m.—about two and a half minutes per day of change. It takes some time getting used to the dark misty rains almost every day, but you just have to stay active and get out. As my friend said, "There is no such thing as bad weather only bad clothes."

I get a special invite to play a golf tournament with a seismic company who hosted an event on the private course at Balmoral,

Queen Elizabeth's summer castle. It's a special opportunity, as they allow only eight charity functions a year on the grounds, and the only others who get to play there are friends of the royals. In fact, as we're coming down the sixth hole, we have to stop play to let the Queen and the Duke walk their Corgi dogs through. Now that's something you don't see every day.

I have my game on and our team ends up one putt away from winning. A few days later I play well and land on the day one leaderboard in the Aberdeen Oilman's Golf Tournament at Gleneagles. I fall back in the pack on day two—maybe due to a few too many adult beverages Friday night. This is a weekend away with a black tie dinner Saturday night, a special event; especially since my wife joins me.

In June the company flies me out to Florida for a leadership course. I've always wondered if I have leadership skills and this course uses feedback from my peers and bosses at work to formulate conclusions about me. Besides the Meyers-Briggs and FIROB personality assessments, there is feedback from the other managers in the course, plus the Campbell Leadership Index. Both indicate I have some leadership skills. This will help me decide if I want to push on with management or stay focused on the technical side for my career.

I pop over to Houston for a few meetings and a doctor's visit, then back to Florida, where I pick up my Mom so we can fly back to Scotland together. One minor hiccup—her new passport is missing. A mad scramble in Miami for a one-day passport re-issue and we're on our way. I arrange things so I can fly with her and it's a good thing— the journey turns into a marathon with storm delays in Washington and an extra night's stay, bringing us into Aberdeen a day later than expected. I gave her my business-class seat, which was great—until they gave her too much wine with dinner and they brought me up from the back to sit with her. Oh, Mom.

It is fun doing tourist things with her including flying into London. I had to meet my boss there—where we watch rain take out any play that day at Wimbledon but have a nice lunch with some industry folks. My family, now including my sister Sue, enjoy the London Eye Ferris wheel and we see the play *Chitty Chitty Bang Bang* that night. The next day we see Buckingham Palace before heading back to Aberdeen.

Later we drive across North Scotland to see Elgin, Inverness, and Dornoch castles. We stay the night at Dornoch Castle Hotel. The next day, we see Loch Ness—but no Nessie—before driving home. My brother Bill makes the trip to Scotland too. This is the first time my family has come to visit us overseas. Egypt was a bit more difficult; although my wife's mom, sister and niece made it there.

One day we drive to Stonehaven to go on a bird boat trip. We meet Captain Brian in the harbor and off we sail away on a delightful sunny run down the coast line to see thousands of birds along the cliffs just south from Donotter Castle. We have a delightful dinner in a pub overlooking the tiny harbor with small fishing boats stranded on the sands with the tide out. Another day we visit the old church ruins down river from our house along the River Dee originally built around 1120, likely about the time the French Templar Knights were active in the area. A flood in the early 1800s destroyed that church and they moved it up the hill at Drumoak. About that time the Manse Steading was built for the minister where we now live. Just after July 4th, my family and family visitors part Scotland—except my brother Bill.

A couple days later, I drop Bill at the airport in Dyce—very close to my office. Later from my office I hear the roar of jet engines of the KLM morning flight and walk over to the window just in time to see the blue and white plane with him in it lift into the sky and disappear into the clouds.

The last week of July I play my best golf of the summer by shooting 84 after work one day with a 10:30 p.m. finish, then an 81 in the club tourney that weekend. Playing golf as a member of a club here (Inchmarlo) is an immersion in the local culture and it is tough to win. I am trying to play faster golf too.

My Mother-in-law, Teddy Stickney, comes out later that summer to tour Scotland. We have a blast—including heading north to Wick and then touring the Orkney Islands. The trip on the ferry from John O'Grotts is easy, but fog obscures the scenery. Everyone finds the archeology fascinating. Scara Brae is a prehistoric settlement from four or five thousand years back, and near-by we see the perfectly round stone circle layout.

We take a fall break trip to Cyprus with another expat family for a solid week of fun and relaxation, staying at the fine Four Seasons resort. The scenery and heat reminded me of Egypt. We all spend time on a catamaran and of course play some golf.

As 2004 draws on, November brings another meeting with senior management—we have good news. We brought on twelve new producers before year end and will make solid profits for our North Sea region. This is a contrast to Egypt, where we continually struggled to: get things done quickly, get approval from the government and meet company objectives. Here things are evolving smoothly and it removes some stress as we present progress at each review with Sr. Mgmt.

With the job going well, everything we do seems more enjoyable, like spending time with my son for Boy Scout activities. We get to see different places in Scotland through Boy Scout outings. Usually Scouting is an all-male event however these days we see some female adult leaders and we add moms to adapt to the small expat community in Scotland. On one outing my wife and another mom have to come to join us for a campout at Haddo House because we're short on dads.

Deck the Scottish Halls

The rundown to the end of the year is a busy time for me with family and work. The Petroleum Exploration Society of Great Britain (PESGB) is the premier UK organization for petroleum business and they have an annual three day meeting that thousands attend. I'm a keynote speaker in the opening morning session—right after the Petroleum Minister for Great Britain. No pressure though, right? I walk out to see about five hundred people in the auditorium—but I know that this session is broadcast to all the other rooms in the exhibition center. I take a deep breath...and get through it smoothly—I think. At the end there are a few questions. One guy asks, "How do you think the locals feel now considering the way your American company has improved the Field you guys bought?" "Well," I say, "We were are at a crossroads, the field needed a lot of investment and the company that sold it had other larger world-wide projects to focus on." Bullet dodged, I get off the stage before I can hang myself with an ill-advised comment.

The dark days of December are upon us with mid-afternooon sunsets. I don't sing karaoke at the Christmas lunch this year and head home early for my birthday. We enjoy hosting a party at our house and we have a nice turn-out of folks, including many from work.

Christmas is white and low key just hanging out at the house together, but we have a fun family trip planned—meeting up with Egypt friends at our old ski haunt, Saalbach, Austria. We spend a couple days in Salzburg and then New Year's Day move to the slopes.

My son wants to focus on snowboarding, so he takes some lessons with a private teacher, but does well keeping up with his friends on their skis. We have fun hanging out with the other four families we knew from our Egypt days. We are a crew when we go out to a restaurant with so many kids and adults. Our room is a bit noisy—right by the elevator—and we hear late at night; very festive Russians on holiday for the Orthodox Christmas.

Our first full year in Scotland has been good to us—good progress at work, lots of time with family and some great exploration of our new surroundings. Getting to end one year and begin another with our friends in Austria is just the icing on the cake, but compared to life in the third world we're enjoying the UK immensely. We ring out the old year and in with the new with high expectations for the future.

The Matterhorn Mountain, Switzerland

Aberdeen Granite Houses

The Manse at Drumoak, our Landlords house

Boy Scouts, chopping wood in Scotland

Drum Castle near Aberdeen Scotland. Original from 1280.
Occupied by the Irvine family from 1323 to 1975

Bremar Games Scotland, Pipe Band Leader

Industry dinner at the Museum of Natural History, London England

Me on the 18th at Carnoustie

Thailand Jungle Tour

Thailand sunset

Chapter 18

Sooner Than Later, the Midwest

January 2005

The new year in Scotland is much like the old—work and diversions. Work is going well with production up and costs down. I take a couple of golf lessons and think that I am striking the ball better. My scores should come down, but it's golf—there is always something off. It is a difficult game to hit on all cylinders and score great.

In April our Boy Scout troop has a trip to Fordell Firs, down near Edinburgh. This campsite has some special activities, which the boys really love, like rappelling, cave tunnels and obstacle course trails. The man-made cave complex seems to be the most popular. We stay two nights and share the area with several troops of British scouts, which was memorable as the lone American Troop. Other than the morning flag ceremony the boys don't mix.

My son has to go home early, as he and another boy are both a little sick. I need to stay as an Adult leader. That evening when I ask for a show of hands only young Nathan from our American Troop wants to go to the all camp campfire the second night, so I take him. They gather all the troops and put on a good campfire with plenty of songs and skits. We play along and lead the group in the "Sticky Moose" song. I'm struck by how lucky I am to be a part of this scene. I enjoy Scouting as an adult not just for the fun events and camping but also to be able to help other boys make their way along the trail of life.

Craig Davis and I travel to Stavanger, Norway—my first time there, or Scandinavia at all for that matter. We meet with a technical data and consulting company at Olje Museum as part of our efforts to build a presentation about the value for our company to enter Norway for oil and gas business.

In May the Scout Troop hikes Bennachie Hill and camps that night at Daviot, adjacent an ancient stone circle. The boys go wild with tent-knocking-down fun, but late that night about 3:00 a.m. a couple of drunks decide to walk through our camp. Impressively, another adult leader dons his adult scout uniform, emerges from his tent and I hear as he talks them into leaving—just as I'm getting dressed to face what might be a tense situation.

In May we begin drilling an offshore wildcat well. Our first North Sea deep well, it's a Jurassic aged sand target at more than twelve thousand feet. Some other deals are finally closing, including the one that comes back from the dead, the fiasco of 2003 where our license round partnership fell apart at the last minute. After some additional discussions, we agree to "farm-in" or join the other company in the block and together we look forward to results from drilling the Polecat prospect. Our North Sea office continues to push forward with aggressive growth drilling wells to increase production in our Field.

Our Aberdeen Troop Scoutmaster is moving back to the US and I get the job. Mike had a special Court of Honor in May to hand out advancement and merit badges to the boys for their work the past few months—and to announce me as Troop 248 Scoutmaster. He also put together a great slide show, a summary of the year—it's well done. I recall the memorable events and know the positive influence adult Scout leaders have on so many boys.

With the summer upon us, it's time for me to travel home—Houston. Medical appointments for us are getting more invasive and less fun as we do stress, dermatology and colon checks. Ah, the joys of getting older. We stay at a Galleria hotel, catch an Astros game, and enjoy some good Mexican food.

I stop by the office to meet with the Gulf of Mexico Group. Summer at the Lake Conroe condo is nice but hot. I fly out to Colorado to visit my sister Sue, and my Mom, who is now living with her in Colorado. We knew it was coming; dementia is a cruel thing. I fly back to Houston just in time to pack and fly back to Scotland—and from there I will hop a flight the next morning to Ireland to play golf.

I'm tired, but as I'm sorting my bags back in Aberdeen late that night, I notice our house has a new guest—a bat, hanging on the curtains in the bedroom. By the time I catch and release the bat, I'm basically just lying down before I have to get up and fly. Even so, we make it to Ireland and meet up with a group of guys we know from Egypt at the spectacular course "Old Head"—perched on the cliffs above the Celtic Sea. I manage to shoot an exciting eighty-one, good for low man of the day. We stay at a little hotel in the quaint Kinsale Harbor and the next day fly to Dublin to play our last Irish round at the scenic Druid's Glenn.

Moments to Remember

In early July we make a presentation in London to the British Government Oil and Gas group of the Department of Trade and Industry (DTI) as part of the "23rd Round" oil and gas license application process. The lease sale process here takes time to prepare the application papers, including a proposed work program, but making a live presentation and Q&A with the decision making group is a bit nerve racking. Three of us make the presentation and we're more relaxed than the year before—considering we know several of the DTI people now—it seems to go well. The block winners will be published in a couple of months.

One summer highlight is attending the British Open, and on Friday I make it to this year's venue, the Old Course in St Andrews. It's a fine, sunny day to watch the best golfers in the world. However, one I had never seen before is here, Jack Nicklaus. It will be Jack's last British Open, and even at sixty-five he almost makes the cut. He won "The Open" three times during his career, and Scotland even published a five pound note with his image on it. I walk along a few holes while he plays with Tom Watson and Luke Donald—the crowd cheers his every move. When Jack smashes a long drive almost to the green and pauses his walk to the eighteenth green and stands on the Swilcan Bridge to wave goodbye, I am there. This is a special moment I will always remember. Oh by the way, I make it back on Sunday to see Tiger win it.

My family is back in the UK, and everything is right in my world again. I get an invite to play in a partner companies Commercial Group's golf tournament at Cruden Bay where we enjoy a nine-hole warm up and then lunch before the eighteen-hole tournament on the main course. It's a fine seaside course with a challenging layout; especially tough today with a gusting wind.

I simply play the best round of my life—eagle on four on my way to a seventy-eight. It's good enough for a tournament win. I get a trophy, golf bag and my name engraved on the big trophy that sits in their office lobby.

Summer camp is a typical summer adventure for most Boy Scout Troops. Aberdeen Troop 248's adventure has a twist—we have a long way to go to get there. We travel by car from Aberdeen to Newcastle, drive onto a car ferry, sail overnight to the Netherlands and then drive to Boy Scout Camp Freedom in Germany. It's a fantastic week for boys and adults alike; the staff does a great job at teaching and entertaining.

Our tents are green canvas types on wooden platforms just like I used as a boy at summer camp in Mississippi. The difference is the staff who are an outgoing bunch of characters full of funny skits, songs and daily character portraits. It was an up-lifting experience for me to be involved with.

Some of the great memories include: the morning flag ceremony, camp fires, water activities, lashing wood for our camp entrance, helping boys with tasks, the echoes of many voices in the mess hall, and the remote site order of the arrow induction ceremony. Camp Freedom is celebrating its fiftieth anniversary and has support from the US military who have had bases in Germany since WWII.

Pay dirt

The first deep North Sea well we drill, an exploration wildcat targeting the Jurassic at 12,500 feet just east of our Field is a discovery. This is on a farm-out block we drilled to earn into and this success after months of negotiation is exciting. We found pay earlier this summer and decided to drill a sidetrack down dip from the discovery to verify how large the field might be. The production test was only 1,100 BOPD due to the low permeability at the sidetrack location and the small volume of associated gas, meaning a development may not have enough rate or recover enough from the reserves in place to be economically attractive. We considered a second sidetrack to prove enough volume but after meeting with the partners we decide not to spend another six million pounds to drill a second sidetrack at this time. It's a tough call but the right call. We really needed some additional sub-surface study to verify the best next place to drill. Excessive up-front costs can really hurt project economics.

We're excited to find oil on two other discoveries during the year. Shallow oil in the Tertiary aged sand and the third discovery operated by another company, is a Jurassic oil sand discovery. The downdip sidetrack there found water far offshore in the Outer Moray Firth, Central North Sea. So we have three oil discoveries with no assurance that any of the three are large enough to make money. The North Sea is tough for exploration. The thought is that all the large easy to see structures and big fields have been found back in the 60s and 70s. However another company popped into a huge oil field in 2001— estimates as high as a billion barrels of recoverable oil, this excited the industry onto a hot "new play"—the Jurassic oil sands.

Industry competitors do work together at times. I attend my first UK offshore operation association meeting of Exploration Managers to discuss ways to work better together for oil and gas concerns and influence the government in a productive, positive manner.

People I work with co-authored a paper that was accepted for presentation at the International AAPG conference in Paris, France. The other guys/lead authors were not available so I give the paper. At a conference like this, speakers have about a 25 minute slot and display Power Point slides as we speak. It was a very technical story about new seismic applications for our Field area. We tell a great story about the seismic process, trap types drilled and the positive results including oil production going up. I think it goes well. With the pressure of giving a talk is over, I take the train into downtown Paris and tour the Louvre—fabulous.

I finally take the three day North Sea offshore survival course, in order to be able to go offshore to our Field overnight and talk to the guys about what we are drilling and how we are growing. The survival class is filled with a very interesting cross section of local people, most of whom are training to be offshore workers. The class teachers have a heavy local accent; but I follow along. We have fun learning about water safety, wet/dry suits, breathing apparatus, helicopters and fire safety.

The rest of the year seems to rush by. The Boy Scout troop has a cool camp out at Haddo House and build a tower and catapults, actually a trebuchet with logs lashed together by rope. It was a scene out in front of the old mansion, several catapults competing for the longest launch.

Back in Drumoak, one misty morning I get a speeding ticket, and a few weeks later have to go to the Stonehaven courthouse where I sit through twelve cases before I'm called up in front of the grand ol' lady judge. Yes, they are wearing robes. I have my say but still got nearly the maximum fine for both speeding and a "thin tread" tire—five points and 240 Pounds.

My boss, James C., one day suggests we should farm-out some of our prospects to get some of that "big money that is flying around the North Sea these days." Raymond Lodge and I go to the Prospect Fair in London and we promote our block; a deep, expensive-to-drill prospect that looks risky but could be big. I introduce Raymond, who speaks at the "Prospects To Go" session and we generate a lot of interest for our deal. Later that day I am on a six person independent company panel discussion on what we look for in a deal and what makes them go.

It's another Scottish Christmas and we welcome another New Year on foreign soil. It's a full life, but we wonder how much longer we'll be in Aberdeen. Believe it or not we've been here nearly three years. People come and go and most of my son's best friends have moved or will move away next year. This is one downside of being an expat kid; you make friends and the next year they may be gone. It creates a type of shield defense mechanism in the child. Expat kids relate to each other in a way that others cannot. We want to get back to the States in order for my son to experience high school in the US before he graduates. We have friends and associates, but we have not made any really close friends, so it's safe to say we have our eyes focused down the road—it might be time to go.

One Well Away

My purpose seems blurred after flying all night from Houston and has me thinking. We do not know where we will live after Aberdeen.

On the road reflection; I estimate I have eclipsed a million air miles. Time slides on, listen close and look breathlessly or you will miss it.

During a January review in Aberdeen we explain that in 2005 we drilled fifteen Field development wells increasing field production and booked good oil volumes. Outside our field we drilled six wildcat wells and had two discoveries, both of which will probably make money—but more drilling is needed to be sure. While showing our CEO maps of the discoveries I say, "I would like to do better."

Alex Gordon replies, "Allard, you're one well away from being a hero."

The Reservoir Engineer Manager says, "Dave, you are a hero, tell him about Egypt and what you did there." It is great to be a part of new discoveries and be appreciated although in the CEO's comment I detected a plea for a better next well.

In February we return to Zermatt, Switzerland, to ski in the shadow of the Matterhorn with a few other company families. It's a fun time, with my son rocking the snow board. It's ironic: after a winter with no snow in Scotland, we return from our ski trip to snow for four straight days at our home.

I continue on as Scout Master for my son's troop, which is fun— we return to Fordell Firs April 2nd. This year, in addition to the caves we do a high zip line too. As usual there are many UK Scouts in for the weekend, which means over two hundred Scouts gathered around the flags for the morning ceremony. My wife joins us in camp the second night and I think she enjoys it—except she has different ideas on how closely the boys cooking should be managed by the adults. Things get interesting for the older boys when a big group of girls set up camp right next to ours on Saturday. British scouting is co-ed. There is a bit of interaction, but nothing goes on late as far as I can tell.

It's just another day in the life in Aberdeen when I get a phone call from James, C. my boss, calling from the USA. "Dave, you should think about being Exploration Manager for the Central US; you would live in Tulsa, Oklahoma," he tells me. Wow, I'm in shock. Not long ago I had a talk with the vice president of HR about getting us back to the States, which I thought might be for next year. To hear about it right now really surprises me. "You should call Randy Bering to discuss it," he says. Randy is the Central Vice President.

I make the call and it sounds good—it's a lateral move, not a promotion, but it will be a good opportunity to learn the company's domestic business—which is key for my career and utility to the company. Tulsa sounds like a nice place to live, four hundred thousand people with middle American values. The last three guys in that job went on to become vice presidents.

I go home and talk to my family about it. "What would you guys think of moving to the United States, Tulsa, Oklahoma?" I ask them. My son seems excited about moving to the United States. "Not Texas?" my wife asks. We're all ready to move, but it's still a shock.

After discussing it, we all agree: it's the right thing to do. I call Randy back. "I'll take the job," I tell him. He's skeptical at first. "Maybe you need to make a trip here before you decide," he suggests. "Randy, after Cairo, this will be no problem." The stage is set for another chapter of our lives.

A couple days late, I depart on an Exploration Mangers field trip— to Iceland. Organized through the UK Oil Operators Association (UKOOA), a good group of my peers from other companies will be there to exchange ideas. Landing at Reykjavik is like setting foot on the moon. I see a geothermal power station, volcanoes and geysers; what a fascinating landscape.

I call the CEO from Iceland and tell him I'll take the job. He's pleased. We have a decent conversation about it. He says that it's good experience for my development and adds, "If that goes well, after that maybe you can run something." I have that to think about as I look out my cabin window across a stark, barren landscape with mountains in the distance. It stays light almost to midnight that time of year in Iceland.

New Adventures, Painful Loss

Word is leaking out, so James announces the news of my transfer on Tuesday at the office in Aberdeen.

Late in May I fly to Tulsa to meet people at the office, including my new boss and to look for a house. We get together for breakfast on Monday morning—Memorial Day—and talk a long time. He is willing to try some new exploration plays if I find them, in addition to the large number of exploitation wells typically drilled in the Central Region each year. As I drive through town looking at houses and neighborhoods, I see that Tulsa is a nice town and seems like an easy place to live.

I'm there for a quarterly review with Sr. Mgmt., which is very different than what I've been used to. The reviews begin—one fifteen minute review after another. I get a feeling for what is going on. This USA lower 48 oil and gas is a high volume, tight margin business.

My wife flies in that evening and we look at houses together Thursday. We make an offer on a house on Friday with a deal agreed upon before we leave town. Back in Aberdeen it's a hectic push for me at work and end of school year exams for my son. We're also closing on the new house in Oklahoma, selling our old one in Houston, which we rented out the entire time we lived overseas and are considering selling the Lake Conroe condo as well.

Troop 248 has a lot going on too, with our end of the school year Court of Honor where we hand out numerous merit badges and rank advancements. My son reaches Star rank. We celebrate our activities of the 2005-2006 campaign, for which I enjoyed presenting a PowerPoint slide show. It is fun to remember all the things we did as a Troop. I play an Allman Brothers instrumental song while the slides roll, which is better than me talking. We say goodbye to those who are leaving and exchange a lot of thank-yous to all the people who make Scouts possible. For me, it's an honor to give something back to Scouting—not just spending time with my son but helping other boys, too.

Saturday June 10th, I have a message to call my sister, and Sue says, "Dave, our little brother Michael is dead." What a shock. He had recently sent a thank-you card for the fortieth birthday gift we gave him, saying he had stopped using drugs. He had not been drunk in three years.

I'm numb as I finish talking to Sue and later as I get home and tell my wife and son, it's a hard day. The next morning I wake up and say out loud, "Why did you have to go?"

My wife's Mom, Teddy, and brother Scott Stickney and his kids fly in for a planned one week visit to Aberdeen on June 17th — the last visitors we'll have before we leave Scotland. It's actually good to have some visitors as we cope with our loss. My wife and son stay in Aberdeen, but I fly to the States for Mike's funeral.

I can't help but think, as I fly in to PA, that I had thought about visiting Erie when I was in the US last month to check out Tulsa. I didn't, and now I wonder if it would have changed anything if I had. Family members are coming in from all over gathering for this sad occasion. Well over a hundred people show up for the memorial in Erie; which is touching to know Mike had a positive influence on so many including friends, family, neighbors, people from school and work. I see people from Erie that I haven't seen in years. The next day, I fly back to Aberdeen, where preparations are well under way for the move. My wife is sorting what to pack, sell, give or throw away. One Saturday we have a UK "boot" (trunk) sale where we sell a few things for low prices before ending up giving a lot of it away.

In July we take our home leave vacation with my family heading to Tulsa to get things sorted—including closing on our new home. I fly to Houston for some doctors' appointments and to check on the sale of our old home there. I fly to Colorado to spend some time with my Mother. It's hard—she knows who I am, but her conversation is very scattered due to Alzheimer's. She looks a lot older, but we still walk the dog around my sister's neighborhood in the foothills of the Rockies. It's difficult to see her talk about something real one moment and then go on to an illusion. I can tell she's glad to see me, however.

In Tulsa we sort some things out at the new house, swim in our pool and finish out the last of our summer home leave. It's hot here but I think we're going to like it.

With break over, we fly back to Aberdeen to see to the move. As we sit out by our tree fort in the yard one night burning old junk wood, my wife, son, dog Scruffy and I have a nice time and wish we had done this more during our stay at Manse Steading in Drumoak. That said, we also are thankful for the outdoor beauty of Scotland, the bike rides to Banchory, sledding down our hill, times on the river, and my countless early morning runs. We'll miss being able to walk up the hill for dinner at our local pub the Irving Arms, and the friendly "hello" from old George. We've made good memories here.

Inside the house seems chaotic, but my wife has done this before and has a plan. My son and I have our Boy Scout summer camp soon, so that stuff has to stay out, and while she gets the house ready we depart for Germany. Those going on the trip meet at the school, pile into cars and we set out to Newcastle. We arrive and drive our cars up on the ferry for the overnight trip across the North Sea. In the morning we drive off the ferry into the Netherlands and soon are burning up the German autobahn and arrive in camp Freedom.

Due to a shortage of instructors, Troop 248's adult leadership supplies some help with teaching fishing, swimming, and camp inspections. I enjoy teaching the morning class of swimming merit badge along with my fellow instructor—a young camp staff member. Some new activities at camp this year include: launching model rockets in a field under the theme of "Space—the Final Frontier" and a Viking stick tossing game called "koob." Everyone has a blast, and my son especially loves the archery—plus he earns merit badges in swimming, camping, and leatherworking. The biggest event for him however is going through the Order of the Arrow ordeal (a subset of Boy Scouts for "honored campers" that the Troop votes you in for). I'm very proud of him for sticking to the all-day work detail and camping overnight alone in the woods.

The whole week creates so many memories but soon it's over, and our five-car caravan pulls away from camp. This is likely the last time we'll likely see any of the other campers again—most of whom live in Germany these days but hail from all over the USA.

Tulsa Bound

By the time my son and I return from Germany, the house is empty and my wife and our dog Scruffy have moved into the Treetops Hilton. I have to stay on a couple of days to get my family and our dog Scruffy on their flight. Just in time, however, due to a new bomb threat from liquid carry-ons, British Air bans carry-ons. I think quickly and get the whole trip transferred to KLM through Amsterdam.

My last day in the UK is August 10th. After I leave the Exploration Manager business with my replacement, I drive into the hills to Balliter to participate in the Highland Games. It's an overcast cool day, and drizzling—perfect Scottish weather. My local co-worker gets me signed up for our main event, the Scottish Hill run. I run the hill strongly but run out of gas on the return to the stadium just missing the chance to earn a "fiver," as a top group finisher. No I did not wear a kilt but some did. That night is a going away party for James our VP who is moving back to Houston. I get an honorable mention too; in fact they asked me to sing (acapella in front of the whole office—no thanks). With a few hours' sleep, a hangover, a sore back from the hill run and a light heart I depart for the next chapter of our lives.

I land in "Green Country," what they call north-east Oklahoma where Tulsa is located, where it is hot. Well it is August, what do you expect. Having spent time in Scotland, one can forget what hot weather is like. We beat the heat by staying indoors or in our swimming pool and for that first weekend we acclimate just fine.

The interesting thing is that while we're excited about our nice nearly new home in the USA, it's doesn't feel right somehow. We don't know anyone and there's no sense of adventure like we've had in our overseas posts. Maybe this is the reverse culture shock some people talk about.

The house is full of boxes and will be for the foreseeable future. The air shipment is taking too long, and some of the stuff we get out of storage in Houston has suffered water damage from the flood or just gone missing. It's hard to fully settle in; some part of me wonders if this is just "temporary" again, not a real place where we sink roots.

Getting started at work in the Central Region is like going back in time. I haven't worked in the lower forty-eight in over eighteen years, so the philosophy of making profit by drilling lots of low-risk, moderate flow rate wells is quite the departure. Interestingly my company made an acquisition from my former company last year, and I find myself talking about some of the same fields I worked twenty years ago. In 2006 we ended up drilling 390 operated wells, and joined many others operated by others where we have an interest. It feels funny to not wear a tie to work for the first time in eighteen years. We have a well approval meeting every Friday where one team after another parades in to the small conference room to get their proposed well work approved. It's a very different environment.

I'm acclimating and I'm doing a good job learning all the new areas we work and the large staff/players on our team. The team is 20 plus geology staff, many of who have worked in this group for more than 10 years. The geology of the OK Anadarko and E. Texas Basins is exciting and a new thing to learn. We also have the Permian Basin, which I have worked before. Starting over at any new assignment is hard work and finding the two-way street comfort zone with everyone takes time. Oh my—

After thinking I would be home most of the time on this "domestic" job; I find I am not. Following my first day of Tulsa work in August we go to Houston for three days of management meetings. In September we go to Denver for a Wyoming deal review, another day in Houston and take the company plane to the Co. ranch in Wyoming. In October we're in Austin and Golden, Colorado for college recruiting, then Denver for the Wyoming deal part two. To Pennsylvania and in November to Corpus Christi to look at an acquisition deal. The selling Co.'s owner Dwaine Moore takes us to lunch on the large and famous King Ranch where we see huge deer leaping across the road on the way in. I take one for the team, smoking a cigar in the car on the way back to Corpus with Dwaine. Then there is one more trip to Houston for a companywide portfolio risk meeting. Whew!

Normal life comes subtlety moving in, aided by rituals like Thanksgiving. We take our first road trip since getting back to the States and rent a U-Haul full of extra items we've accumulated over the years. With beds, TVs and bikes loaded we drive to Dallas where we give it all to my wife's brother. We have Thanksgiving dinner in Dallas with my wife's Mom, Teddy "Grannie" Stickney, and Scott and family before heading to Houston to check out the Lake Conroe condo. We unload more stuff in Houston that's still in storage—swimming through sentimental items—we leave what we don't want for the Salvation Army to pick up.

Christmas time is nearly upon us, but at the company Christmas party my wife and I notice we still feel like outsiders—guess this culture adjustment after eight years overseas may take a while. A few days before Christmas we drive to Midland to be with my wife's family. The time at Teddy's house has a comfortable family feel. We're back in Tulsa to ring in the New Year at home, safe from crazy drunks and bad weather.

Spring Changes

It stays cold for much of our first winter in Tulsa—I don't get to play golf till early March and shoot an 86, not bad for being rusty. At work we learn that we've beaten all our region 2006 goals for production rate, finding cost, drilling for new discoveries or reserves, rate of return, and lifting cost per barrel. Big bonuses abound. Our success is good because other regions had a rough year. As activity has steadily increased in the industry over recent years with high product prices, service costs have risen as well. Natural gas prices have dropped from over $9/MCF a year ago to about a $7/MCF range. Oil prices are now over $60/BBL and rising. The economics for drilling prospects are tricky in this dynamic environment, especially when service costs have nearly doubled for things like big drilling rigs and well completion costs.

In March I get plugged in to the US scene again by attending the North American Prospect Exposition (NAPE) in Houston. Hundreds of small booths are setup by the "sellers" to show prospects, which they want partners to share the cost, and thousands of geologists and investors walk the floor to find good opportunities. My job is to review as many deals as possible to hopefully find some good ones, get new play ideas, and make contacts. I see many old friends and former co-workers I haven't seen for years. Unfortunately, I have a couple leads but don't find any great deals. The term "Resource Play" is everywhere at the convention. People are paying big bucks for leases in numerous US basins. The hydraulic fracturing of tighter rocks has opened tighter "sealing or source rock" shale rocks to be gas targets. The shale layers in different basins are typically thick and cover large areas underground. The investor's attraction to repeatable economic drilling locations over a large play has changed the business.

For my son's fourteenth birthday we go skiing at Breckenridge and Copper Mountain, Colorado. I recall first learning to ski the big runs back in the 80s with Suzy Danger; like the "American Flyer." These days the areas also offer huge terrain parks with jumps, half pipes and grinding rails, In April, I fly to Pennsylvania to see family—including my Mom. It's good to see family and friends but Mom has gotten worse. Alzheimer's is a terrible disease. She doesn't really know who I am. It's hard, but we still talk about "David," Scotland, and Oklahoma.

I fly to Alabama for a golf trip on the Robert Trent Jones "trail"—a first-class outing put on by an oil field service company. This invitation is a great opportunity to meet others in the oil industry. They're a classy bunch of gents—higher level guys from competitors and service companies. Oh; and to play golf where the Senior Tour will be in a couple of weeks is ok too. My best round is an 83 at Ross Bridge but it could have been even better as many golfers might say as we usually think of a missed putt or two.

I also attend the company shareholder meeting for the first time since 1998. Our executives make solid presentations and our founder makes several good points and some colorful remarks during his forty-minute speech. I'm proud to work for the company and feel we're headed in the right direction. I note our US onshore group, and many other US onshore operating companies, do not adequately utilize modern seismic data in our efforts to identify more oil and gas opportunities, we just don't spend the money on it. The thought is that onshore seismic data does not have the clarity to improve maps of the formation targets that are controlled with data points from the thousands of wells drilled onshore. The advances in seismic data processing in recent years and increased computing power bring in better processing, quicker turn-around, noise reduction and different data filter versions that offer higher quality seismic data to see smaller structures and make stratigraphic interpretation. This gives the geoscience team a chance to put together new prospects. It is a typical struggle of the oil business; how much money do you spend to reduce the risk of high cost drilling.

The quarterly review comes right on the heels of the shareholder meeting for us in Tulsa; the executives have a few extra folks on the plane as they will fly on to Canada for a review. The company is good at changing things on a quarterly basis to ensure the annual results are on track. For the Central USA, we are behind on our annual oil and gas production goals, but we have enough prospect inventory to juggle a couple rigs and drill more wells to catch up. We are currently running twenty-two drilling rigs, which is a main focus for my team—to keep up with and more importantly where to drill next.

Our presentation is focused on how we are jumping on the Permian Basin properties acquired this year that we took over as operator. The Region existing ("producers") well count is now about 12,000 after a couple of large property acquisitions in the past few years. Overall this year the production engineers will make repairs or improvements to about 1600 wells and spend a total of about $280 million. 2007 drilling capital for 370 new wells is projected at over $400 Million. The company acquisition and exploitation process is amazing. Our field people in total now drive about one million miles each month. What a concept of activity. Living abroad offered its challenges but so has settling in back in the States. Each step has been what we thought was best for our family—we can only trust and pray that we've made good choices and we're going in the right direction. I believe we are and I'm eager to see what the next years bring. One thing I learned years ago; if you look over your shoulder in the "race" of life you will get passed—so keep going forward.

Chapter 19
Oil Boom

July, 2007

My family spent a week in June at Texas Archeology Field School—where they worked on an old mission. It was warm, but at least there was a swimming hole. Our new order of business is actually a new family member. My wife and my son come home with Cairn Terrier, a multi-colored dark little bundle of energy named Sami.

No sooner is the puppy home it seems, the then would-be primary care giver, my son, is off to Boy Scout summer camp. Camp Tom Hale is located southeast of McAlester, Oklahoma, in some rolling hills and has been a Boy Scout camp for one hundred years. It's the main scout camp for Oklahoma, and despite some rain, my son has a good time swimming in the lake, sailing, kayaking, rowing, more swimming, shooting shotguns, archery, crafts, mountain biking…and more swimming. About seven hundred boys are there this week with Troops from the surrounding states. I have to work so I spend the day Sunday and come back Friday night. I'm there for the Order of the Arrow "tap-out" ceremony and the festive Closing Campfire.

My summer play time comes in the form of a long weekend in Vegas when I meet up with the fellows, a reunion of the "Bull Run Boys." The highlight for me was shooting a 38-38 at the TPC Canyons course on Friday, a record round.

We have a short end of summer vacation to Hilton Head, South Carolina. On Tuesday, the day before we leave, I take the day off so my son and I can go to Southern Hills for the practice round of the PGA Championship. I think he finds it interesting to a point: like when we manage to complete our trek out to the 17th tee to see Tiger Woods.

The next day we land in Savannah, Georgia, tour the town, and enjoy a healthy, heavy lunch at Paula Dean's place before driving over to our ocean-view suite in Hilton Head. The island is a planned community with everything tucked into the trees.

Over the next couple of days we spend time swimming and riding fat-tired bikes around the neighborhoods or on the beach itself, fly a kite—and a highlight; the dolphin sunset cruise we take on an old boat out of the Marina. A storm out at sea keeps us from checking out the true ocean waters but we get to enjoy a playful pod of dolphins and a beautiful orange sunset. It's a great, much-needed vacation—even though I don't hit a single golf ball (unless you count the Legends putt-putt course, where my son had the best score!).

Back to Real Life

It's nice to have the rhythm and connections of school and work to anchor us, because otherwise we're having trouble—still—really fitting in here in Tulsa. They say Tulsa can be hard to break into socially, the longtime established locals do not go out of their way to invite new people to many things, but it seems almost boring to be here after what we've done the past several years. Reverse culture shock. We have settled into St. Patrick's Episcopal Church located near 81st and Garnett, which helps us get balance and grounding in our new community.

Regular life has resumed after our summer outings, punctuated with a quick trip my wife and I sneak off to for our September anniversary to Big Cedar Lodge in Missouri. Hawaii will have to wait. We have a very nice time with great scenery, bike rides, canoe trips and nice walks together. September takes me to the University of Oklahoma's main campus at Norman to recruit young geoscientists. During this first campus visit for my company at OU, I interview seventeen students for summer intern opportunities. That is too many for one day, but I want to get the word out in the OU geoscience department. It is a challenge to draw young talent to Tulsa. Years ago we tended to hire only experienced professional staff, but more recently, because the company has grown so much and due to industry demographics we have a tremendous talent gap between five and twenty years' experience. We must add staff straight from college and train them on the job.

Later in the month I'm off to Houston for a Management planning meeting to talk about "Resource Potential" and how to move more of these reserves from the possible or idea phase, to the corporate reserve books.

We have a good couple of days talking about how to add reserves/resource potential, retain people and attract new hires from college. Work isn't all work now and I get back to Tulsa from Houston just in time to re-pack and hop on the company plane for Wyoming for the great Deer Hunt. The next day is enjoyable on a pheasant hunt, walking the fields near the river, watching the dogs work and kick up birds. That night at the lodge, as people gather for dinner, I get drafted to the Sr. Mgmt. team for the deer hunting contest. It seems some of the top guys are missing this year so I will try to fill in. They pick me up at 5:30 am and our trio is off to the hills—in the dark. We don't see much the first morning, but driving back to the lodge for lunch we got behind an opposing team truck and as we come around the corner we see them parked and out shooting. Bang, they get a big deer in an area that my team leader had scouted. The next day I become the focus of the team when the gents realized I have never killed a deer. Growing up in PA I went on deer hunts but never got a shot. It was fun driving all over the 22,000 acre ranch. Finally that afternoon on a hill side we spot some deer. I make a clean hundred yard kill shot. He's a nice ten point buck—mid-range for this ranch, and far from the size to win the big buck contest, but it's a very special moment for me. Doc. guides me through the cleaning process as only a retired heart surgeon could.

We wrap up the hunt, and people start catching one of two company planes out. We make a pit stop in Denver and I drive up to the Colorado School of Mines in Golden for some recruiting. The students at Mines are impressive. An interesting side note about the student's caliber—of the eight guys I interviewed, six are Eagle Scouts.

Grand Canyon & Texas Trips

My family and I recently made a list of places in the world we would like to visit. One I put on the list was the Grand Canyon. The last time

283

my wife visited was her childhood and me in 1979, I hiked to the bottom with a couple college buddies.

To get there we fly from Tulsa to Vegas during my son's October school break. We catch the Cirque du Soleil Ka show the first night—and get a backstage tour, thanks to my friend Max, a fellow Spain trip pal. The Vegas route allows us to pick up a small tour plane and land right at the edge of the Grand Canyon park rather than driving all the miles in a rental. The small plane is filled with us and a Japanese tour group making us comically out of place.

Flying into the Grand Canyon area is breathtaking—as fabulous as I remember. We hike around and tour the rim, down the Kiabab Trail a short distance, enjoy the beautiful views and take in an amazing sunset. We stay the night at a hotel in the park and enjoy seeing the elk at the park grazing on the lawn in front of the lodge completely used to the park visitors. It's a fun family outing and we bookend it with seeing the magic and mystery of Penn and Teller back in Vegas. I met these guys back in the early 80s in San Francisco through my brother's circle of entertainer friends. Brother Bill is one of five guys that are Duck's Breath Mystery Theatre—an American version of a Monty Python type comedy group.

I go to Houston In November for a mix of business and pleasure—okay, mostly for fun. A Scottish friend of mine will get married soon, so he planned a golf outing and dinner for his Houston area friends. A few of his friends and relatives make the trip from the UK too.

We make the trip down to Midland for Thanksgiving and we really enjoy being within driving distance of family for holidays. With oil booming again Midland is growing, with new apartment buildings and stores going in since my last visit. It's nice to spend time with old friends in Midland.

The Perfect Ice Storm

I'm at Gore Boy's Ranch, where our Boy Scout Troop is doing a service project weekend. We're staying in the large bunk house near the lake. We just got in last night and cleared some brush today, but decide to cut our trip short and return to Tulsa that Saturday afternoon.

The boys are disappointed since this is the only "indoor" outing of the year plus the adults do all the cooking—but I have a bad feeling about this one.

We get in just ahead of the ice storm, and throughout the day the storm shows it is real—the temp is dropping. A soaking misty, steady sleet is coming down, as the temperature drops lower and lower. It does that for a day. Then comes day two—ice forms on everything as it is snowing ice pellets, which start to accumulate on the ground.

We watch as ice begins to coat absolutely everything in a layer of perfectly clear ice. Every plant, tree, branch, and power line, not to mention roads and everything else is coated with ice inches thick. It just keeps coming. Trees are drooping and, branches straining under the increasing weight. The air has a hushed, strained note…

It's the middle of the night we suddenly lose all power and everything goes off. Everything! No light is on in the house except things that have batteries and as we get up and look around we see that the whole neighborhood is dark. Branches, strained under a burden of ice have started to break. We learn later the power problem is that branches fell and took out power lines, cutting power to numerous homes and shut down the grid.

Our house has a natural gas powered stove, fireplace, and water heater, so our place is livable—barely. The temp inside the house drops quickly—we huddle around the fire place. School is of course out, and I don't go to work—we don't even *try* to get out on the ice-coated roads.

We sit tight for two and a half days—very long cold days—without power and learn that a quarter of a million people in the Tulsa area are without power. We actually get ours back pretty "early," many people are expected to have to wait many days. Power crews and medics from all over a multi-state area flood in to help people in Tulsa and Oklahoma City and their outlying areas who are without power—it's quite the testimony to the nature of people in the Midwest that they all band together to help during a time like this.

Happy New Year

Happy New Year indeed. 2007 was full of change and adjustment. By December 2007, oil prices had gone to $95 per barrel and in January 2008, oil trades over $100 per barrel. Wow, another boom seems to be here. Gas is over $9/MCF and gasoline at the pump is solidly into $3 plus. This rise is not clear in its origins or stamina, so maybe it's short lived, or maybe it's just the start.

Early in the year a few of us fly to Dallas to look at an East Texas deal with a private company. This is an interesting bit of Texas history as the company, Hunt Oil is led by Ray Hunt, who has built a substantial company. His father, H.L Hunt was one of the original Texas Oil men who built significant wealth in the growth of East Texas oil discoveries pre-World War II. A former co-worker and friend of mine Ryan Butler who now works in Dallas, takes me to the Petroleum Club downtown, which is very nice—we catch up on old times. Then, we are back in Tulsa town for the company Christmas party of all things. Yes, being January we're a little late, but the Oklahoma Ice Storm of '07 postponed the original date. We enjoy the Christmas flashback. February sees the Houston North American Prospect Expo—but no good deals despite some familiar faces. It also sees something else: our share appreciation stock plan pays out—very nicely to those employees that have been with the company for a while. The concept is the company stock hits the price target and doubles over a couple years' time creating billions of dollars in value for the shareholders. The payout to employees that drove that growth seems well worth it.

My son's birthday arrives in March, and the days of Pokémon and dinosaur birthdays are over—we go skiing in Colorado. We rent a nice little house in the woods in Breckenridge and get in some great skiing and boarding. Our CO friends come up Monday night, and we have a nice dinner and ski together the next day. But reunion time isn't over, turns out—we bump into some friends from Aberdeen. They're in Houston these days and their son was one of my son's pals in Aberdeen. What a great trip.

In April I travel to PA to visit family. I decide that on the way I should take a side trip to Augusta, Georgia, for the Masters. I find a ticket for $900 on the Internet for Thursday, the first day of tournament competition. It's like people have said, the ambiance of the Masters in person, walking the grounds, seeing the rolling hills, is something you do not totally appreciate from TV, even today's high definition TV. I see all the top golf pros of the day and some old heroes too: Arnold Palmer and Gary Player. The food and drinks were super cheap: sandwich $1.50, Coke $1.00—Masters logo souvenir shirts and hats, etc., that you can only buy here are not cheap. I follow players all day and when I get home a few days later and review the recording I'm surprised to see myself on the network broadcast.

Erie, PA isn't exactly on the way home from Georgia, but I fly in to visit Steve, Judy, and Mom. Bill comes to visit, and it's good. We spend a lot of time with Mom, and she's very chatty—a good change.

Spring brings some more golf for me, including some lessons with the head pro at La Fortune,—not enough for me to win a tourney at Forest Ridge the next day but enjoyable. Shortly after that comes the company Hack & Frac at Cherokee Hills, where I shoot an 81—tough course, great score. Next up is Pinehurst, North Carolina, for a guy's golfing trip. Eight guys, four days, six rounds. The golf is fine, but hanging out with a bunch of good guys is a great time. I play steadily and turn in a couple good rounds—80 and 81. For me, I have learned that when I am playing golf, I am able to block out all the other concerns of life and just play the game. It is a game of concentration but like a mini vacation walking among the green beauty of a course.

Sandwiched in between golf, we have a quarterly review for our US onshore Region based in Tulsa. We are on pace for another solid year. Prices are up, so economics look better on most of the stuff we drill. Costs are running up too, however.

Summer in the Mountains and High Oil Prices

It's now spring, 2008, and life has been good in any case. The oil and gas landscape remains volatile, with oil selling over $100 per barrel in 2008 and sadly war continuing in Iraq. We're thinking of finding a place in the mountains, a cabin or condo in Colorado so we wait patiently until school is out and then fly to Colorado Springs for a southern Colorado tour. We drive to Manitou Springs then South Fork to see places along the river, in the woods, or near a golf course. All are nice, but it's just too small of a town—too isolated.

Pagosa Springs comes next and it is built with retirement housing—lots of duplexes of the condo/townhome variety. On to Durango. The drive west towards Durango is scenic with mountain views and rolling hills. Durango itself is a scenic, old town sprawling along the river valley. Ft. Lewis College sits on top of a mesa in town, and when we go up there to take in the view we see a stage setup.

"Tonight we have a concert by the Beach Boys," our realtor tells us. We capture tickets and the three of us go. We watch Jesse Collin Young play first, then the Beach Boys start just in time for clouds to roll in. The temperature drops and rain starts. We find some shelter and think how long these guys have been playing music—and still sound good.

Over the next couple days, we tour properties in several areas. One day we drive out to Mesa Verde to see the cliff dwellings. Durango is a fine little town with a river running through it and mountains all around. The golf courses are not bad either. We selected a few finalists in our search for "our place in the mountains." In the end, we decide that early summer may be a high-price time to buy so perhaps some patience will get us a better price.

We go to the Texas Archeology Field School on the Wheeler Ranch Mr. Wheeler in the northern Texas panhandle in June. It's a first class operation with the ranch providing water and screening equipment and a closing concert by Asleep at the Wheel. The ranch owner, Wheeler Ranch Mr. Wheeler, is an archeology enthusiast and tells my wife she better bring her husband next year if my company wants to drill any more wells on his ranch.

My son has just enough time to get home and repack before he's headed to Camp John Hale in southeastern Oklahoma for a week of summer camp with the Boy Scouts. My wife drives down south with us and she enjoys seeing the camp; we leave my son with Troop 185 and take the scenic route through the Ouachita Mountains on the way back to Tulsa.

I drive back to camp on Thursday to spend the last two nights with the Troop and to pull the trailer home. My son did the outbound program for older boys all week since he no longer needs merit badges. They did a variety of things—sailing, hiking, games, and climbing. On Friday I join his group for some problem-solving games and end with a climb and a ride down the zip line. My son's glad to get home after a busy few weeks since school broke for summer.

The oil business continues to ramp up in a dramatic fashion. Since oil traded over $100 in January, the price has risen to over $130 in May, and early summer high trades over $140 per barrel. Natural gas lagged behind a bit but still comes up over $10 /MCF. Rigs are being built again, and fracking crews have more business than they can get to. Summer rolls on, and we celebrate the Fourth of July by parking and walking onto the old Jenks Bridge with thousands of others to watch the fireworks. From where we stand we can see Jenks' fireworks—Tulsa's city fireworks as well as those set off by Southern Hills Country Club. Summer time is my favorite season of the year, time for swimming, more golf, vacation trips, and long days outside. The season is fleeting and over before you know it. Soon the end of summer is upon us; almost.

Surfer Dude

As I approach my fiftieth birthday, I feel like I have lived a good interesting life, but I should do something different to celebrate the year. My friend from the Egypt days, Bob Wood had the idea to go surfing, we run with it. California is the answer. We land in San Diego on a Monday afternoon in August and drive to Encinitas, our surf headquarters. James Adams and his friend Ron arrived to join a real event. Bob has lined us up at Eli Howard's Surf School for three days—I find some golf courses near-by.

We meet at the surf school headquarters in the park on the cliff over the beach at Encinitas. Our instructors are all experienced surfers and good guys. Our class has a couple older guys like us, and several younger kids. We go over techniques on our boards on the beach then zip up our wetsuits and hit the waves.

The surf is long, steady, smallish waves perfect for popping up and catching a ride. All four of us get up and catch waves—a successful outing. It's nice just sitting on our boards out in the surf watching for "a good wave" That afternoon we tee it up at Encinitas, a nice public course on the Rolling Hills on the edge of town. We start about 3:30 and have a few small bets to discuss but in the end just focus on playing. It's a great afternoon—hot air balloons in the distance, an occasional cigar, and we all drink a couple of beers. However, in the end, I carded a 75. It's my best score ever. Wow! What a great finish as the sun sets and the marshal comes to collect the flag stick as we putt out.

That night we find a little café in town. They seat us at a table right next to a guy playing guitar music—familiar tunes but he is not singing them. Before you know it, we're singing along a bit. He encourages us, and we became part of the show. He even let me play a tune. I sang "Melissa." What a great day.

Another morning of surfing follows breakfast at Denny's—our new Encinitas tradition. Frisbee on the beach, then north toward LA to play golf at Crossings Carlsbad. Half way through the round James buys us all tall beers, but it does not throw me off. I carded one under on the front—in the zone again. We only finish seventeen holes before the marshal drives by followed by several other golfers as darkness encroaches. "The course is closed," he tells us. We ignore him and let them pass and the other guys encourage me to play the last hole—to make it official. I just miss the putt for a sandy par and close with a bogey to card a 73 (35-38.) Wow!

Thursday, we play nine holes at Torey Pines, site of Tiger Woods' 2008 one-legged victory in the US Open Championship. It's a story of sporting legend, how he played with a torn ACL and stress fractures, and now we're here, playing the same course.

Friday it's time to part ways—Bob and I cruise up the coast for an epic Highway 1 road trip while the other guys stay at the beach. We cruise along the rolling, rocky coastline on our way to Santa Cruz, where we find a free concert on the beach by Greg Rollie, former

Santana keyboard player; before heading on to Sausalito and our hotel looking over San Francisco Bay.

Saturday morning my brother Bill and his wife Margaret meets us for breakfast and we do a quick drive up into the Marin headlands, it's too foggy to see much—then on to their house. We catch a Giants game that evening but while they beat LA, Barry Bonds doesn't add any home runs to his tally.

So ends an epic summer. School will start for my son by the time I get back. It's been an interesting ride. My wife accuses me of over celebrating my birthday "year." Ok I may be guilty of that.

Grand Canyon USA, Graham 2007

Allard Brothers Mike, Steve and Mom 2003

California Surfers 2008, me on the right.

Chapter 20
The Oil Price Slide

August, 2008

My son starting tenth grade at Jenks signals the end of summer. I hope it will be another good year for him he's growing so much; now he has his first girlfriend. In other ways he's still just our son—playing computer games and doing Boy Scout activities. These days he likes the computer video game World of Warcraft—maybe too much.

We enjoy riding bikes together as a family, and my son and I finally take ours to a Tulsa urban wilderness, Turkey Mountain ("mountain" is a bit generous). Just across the river from Tulsa, it's a scenic network of trails stretched across a wooded hill. It's a great ride across the hills and back. Another summer tradition is to cruise around a lake on jet skis, at least once! We find a place at Lake Keystone to rent a couple wave runners and on Labor Day we tour most of the lake on a good fast ride.

The world seems stable; the Iraqi war seems to be winding down, and the price of oil is off its July high of $147 a barrel. My wife and I celebrate our twenty-first anniversary in September, which is testimony to this wonderful woman in my life. She handles coordinating construction of a sunroom addition to the house. The most interesting moment is when they park a boom truck in front of the house, hook up a cement truck and run the line over the top of our two story house to lay the cement foundation out back.

I am playing golf in a Petroleum Golf Invitational in Enid, Oklahoma. This is a great networking event that our Landman Manager, Jake invited me to. There are people from both large and small independent oil companies, and you never know who might bring you the next deal. I win a "closest to the pin" prize, which is more golf balls.

It's fall and I am back at the company planning meetings. We want to maintain the can-do, fast moving, family culture that has served us so well, even as we grow into a bigger company. We're responsibility-driven and incentivized for results that I think will see us through even rough economic times. Our planning session is too early in the year to realize prices and the economy are on a major slide, although we did consider a meltdown. We have seen enough economic ripples that we knew we were in some type of down cycle.

Oil drops below $100 a barrel in October; down $40 from the peak in July. We fear the price may continue a downward slide.

Celebrations of Different Kinds

I don't let oil's slide get me down, so in honor of the big five-oh coming up, I arrange an October birthday celebration trip. Most of my friends are too busy later in the year closer to my December 18th birthday, so a Halloween weekend in Las Vegas it is.

Really, it's just an excuse to get some of the guys together for golf. We hit Rio Secco the first day and Carolina Pines later. My brother Bill arrives from San Francisco and joins us for dinner in the Stratosphere on the last night. We have some fun at the tables, with Bill and his hot hand actually finishing the night up a couple hundred bucks.

Friday night is Halloween, which is a trip in Vegas. Everyone it seems is in costume—except us. The party atmosphere is thick with many extravagant costumes. I find myself beginning to question the opulent hedonistic lifestyle in Vegas…but just for a moment.

I get home in time for the election—John McCain vs. Barak Obama. McCain looked to have brought in some zip from the outspoken Sarah Palin, who overshadowed Obama's choice of Joe Biden. As the electoral votes are counted out, we have a first for our nation—an African American President. "Blue" states all over are celebrating, but I guess in time we will see what impact this has on our lives.

My son's Boy Scout Eagle project is a proposal to build a sidewalk connecting St. Patrick's Church to the Forest Hills rest home next door.

The Church Vestry approved the idea, which is a good one, and I'm very proud of him for planning to do such a meaningful project.

My wife and I host the first Tulsa Newcomer's Dart Night at our house. It was a great idea of hers to model it after the couples dart league we enjoyed in Egypt.

Also in November, at work we have the final review by Medhat Sakawy who is over from Egypt on a short-term assignment in Tulsa for eight weeks. He is a geologist who used to work for me back in Egypt. He does a nice job with his mapping project. For me it is fun as I again become Mr. Dave; the typical exchange with guys I worked with in Egypt. It is a nice perk for the Egyptian guys to make a business trip to the US.

At work we enjoy a Core Description Day at the core storage facility in Norman, Oklahoma as part of a reservoir study of the Anadarko Basin. Friday my son and I travel with Troop 185 to the Gore Boy's Ranch again for our service trip; last year our stay was cut short by the great Ice Storm of '07. We usually cut brush and burn it as our main work contribution to the ranch. The first year we went, we didn't even see the boys who live there. Mostly from broken homes, these boys are on their own with no parental support. This time, we meet a group of the boys and even played some dodge ball. The Gore boys crushed Troop 185, and then we mixed the teams up. They seem like good boys from what I can see. They've been through things our boys have only heard about and can't really even imagine. I hope our visit is of some value to these boys.

We're back just a week ahead of, wait for it...an ice storm. This one isn't as bad as last year. We have our potluck Christmas lunch at the office a few days later.

And then, finally, after much anticipation it is my actual fiftieth birthday. It's hard to believe—hard for me to grasp, though I've had plenty of time to prepare. Time really does go faster the older you get. We invite a group of people to lunch—a nice low-key event with my wife and guys I know from work. We follow up with an "open house" at our place—a few people figured out it was for my birthday not just Christmas.

Christmas day we celebrate just the three of us, and while we normally like to get together with other family, this year we just hang together. I'm totally unprepared for my present however—my wife and son surprise me with a birthday/Christmas trip to Costa Rica.

Costa Rica

After a great Christmas with my little family, we land the day after Christmas without incident in San Juan Costa Rica. We've arranged a driver through our old Lake Conroe property manager who has started up a travel business in Costa Rica. Hector picks us up from the airport and takes us to the hotel, situated in the rolling hills and small mountains of San Juan.

We settle in and take a quick tour of town before Hector takes us to a hillside restaurant overlooking the valley. We eat some great local food, and after the sun goes down, the view of the city lights in the valley is fine.

The next day, Saturday, we drive to La Fortuna. Unfortunately Hector can't take us and we get a replacement driver. He thinks a bridge is out, so we detour—no water falls and garden place. Instead, we see rolling farmland along the mountainsides before lunching at an airstrip restaurant near La Fortuna. Not quite what we planned, but beautiful anyway.

We arrive at our villa at the base of the volcano. The gardens of the grounds and layout of individual small cabins were fantastic. They reminded us of Hawaii. We take a taxi into town and have a nice dinner.

Saturday is zip line day. We take a taxi up the mountain to the adventure center. Like many interesting gadgets, the zip line concept was invented long ago—but Costa Rica made it a commercial success. The three of us are put with a big family group there to have some fun like us. We don our harnesses, helmets, and gloves, and then one by one fly down the zip lines, crossing ravines high above the jungle floor from one platform to the next. We do eight different lines to get back to the base, some as long as 800 meters. It feels like you are flying over the jungle, a truly exhilarating experience. Later, my son and I join an ATV tour that is a blast. We each drive our own machines along a route through country roads, villages, and to a couple different rivers, one of which we stop at for a swim. A rope swing off a steep rock bank ends with a release to drop in a pool below the falls.

Hector meets us Sunday morning for our drive to the town of Jaco on the coast. The roadside hamburgers are not much to crow about, but the changes in scenery are beautiful. The floral changes as we drop out of the "cloud forest" climate are amazing. A flat tire causes us to stop for a while on a country hillside. A man even comes out of his house to help Hector and we're on our way.

The Marriott Resort we check into may not be typical Costa Rica, but it has all the elements we are looking for on this part of our vacation: large pool, nice beach, spa, gym, and a golf course. A short walk away is a marina with some nice restaurants and some huge boats. To buy a villa the price range is $400k—$1 million US.

The next day, my son and I go into Jaco to the beach to meet up with a surf school. We gather with a few other beginning surfers on the beach then don our wet suits and hit the waves. My son and I are matched with Dennis, who helps us read the waves and get up. My son catches a wave and stands up soon after we get going, which is great to see. We each catch several more waves until Dennis is ready to go in, but he let us stay out by ourselves for a few more waves. Cool.

We spend the last day of 2008 in Costa Rica taking a ride to a nearby bay to meet up with a kayak/snorkeling guide for the day. Wilbur grew up here and has lived on the water all his life, kayaking, fishing, surfing and so forth.

Together with the rest of our small group, we walk down the beach and load up into kayaks—a two-man for my wife and me, with my son in his own. We paddle along the coast to another beach, where we break out the snorkeling gear, and we see a few colorful fish and starfish during our dip. After a break for fruit on the beach, we paddle back, to end a fine day trip.

We celebrate New Year's Eve with a lobster feast in town at a busy restaurant where they have set up a tent outside to handle the crowd. There's a band of roving musicians playing reggae and island music. We enjoy the dinner before returning to the resort. Around midnight the fireworks start and we take them in from the balcony as they shoot up from the marina. What a great trip. Now we have some idea why Costa Rica is so popular.

Back to Real Life...and Oil

So my birthday/Christmas trip to Costa Rica is the best present of my life, but like all good things it came to an end. Back in Tulsa, regular life resumes. My son has a chemistry final I help him study for during the Costa Rica trip. I need to get back to work to watch the global collapse of oil. The oil price rose to over $140 a barrel in June, finally hitting a record high of $147 a barrel in July, it collapsed to less than $40 a barrel in December. Natural gas is down too, and the US drilling rig count is half what it was in early 2008. These are the buzz topics of the North American Prospect Expo I attend in Houston in early February. Many Americans are happy at least with the gasoline price per gallon down from over $4 last year to less than $2 per gallon in 2009. Many people do not know there is a series of exchanges, costs and taxes between the production of oil and gas we drill for, to the refined products sold at the pump.

In the spring of 2009, the natural gas price is down between $3 and $2 at times due to cheaper Rockies gas pulling our mid-continent market price down. The boom of shale gas drilling kept US supplies up and added 40 TCFG of reserves in 2008. Also, the poor economy had caused big company shipments of LNG that were aimed at Asia or Europe to be sold to the USA market. Our natural gas price could remain soft for years. We just hope the lack of drilling does not relate to more layoffs.

February presses on and the stock market appears to be near the bottom—the DOW is at 7,500 after starting the month at 8,200. My broker and I agree to buy some stocks, mainly oil, which has been beat way down. We buy some good companies at a discount. As they say, "Buy on panic, and sell on euphoria," so we hope for the best.

I don't want it to sound all doom and gloom—obviously by buying stock we expect things to improve. Not only that, it's not all work. Brother Steve and Judy arrive in Tulsa to get ready for a big tournament in Branson and stay the week with us. Steve is the number two bass fisherman in Pennsylvania and he'll be facing off with the other state finalists on Bull Shoal's Lake, Missouri, site of the National Finals Bass Fishing Tourney. They cruise over to Branson on Tuesday to get some practice days in.

Friday I pick my other brother, Bill, up after work and we drive to Branson and find Steve and Judy in the show room. Steve had a tough day as a "rider" (number one man from each State was designated boat driver, while 2nd is a boat rider) and only caught a couple of fish during the day. He's in the lower half of the standings and he'll need to finish in the top of his region to make top six and qualify for the two pro tournaments.

Early Saturday, we're up at 5:00 am to see the boat starts. There's a PA announcer and show trailer set up by the water. Ranger providing boats, Chevy providing trucks and contestants get free room and board; this is a big deal tournament. Steve does better but ends up mid-pack, he swears. "Next time, I control my own destiny." In his defense conditions were tough and not many contestants caught their five-fish limit.

After the closing dinner, we drive to Tulsa in order to make flights Sunday morning. Bill and I reminisce back at the house in the morning after getting Steve and Judy on their flight—including some picking (going to California—for them days in 1980). We then head out, Bill to San Francisco and me to Durango to meet my wife, son, and his gal Becky (and the two dogs) at the finest condo/townhome we've ever rented. With four bedrooms, it's the perfect base for a week of snowboarding and skiing.

We all go out to dinner to celebrate my son's birthday. It's a great trip, with everyone enjoying the warm blue-skied weather—maybe too warm, as the slopes are a little soft at the base. Still, a lovely time by all...until it's time to drive back to Tulsa and we tackle all 895 miles in one stretch. Ouch! But we just keep going—down the long road.

Spring & Summer

In April I play golf for the first time in 2009, trying to prepare for a guys golf trip to Marble Falls near Austin, later in the month. Eight of us hit golf courses on Horseshoe Bay. I wait until the last round to put a good score up, when I fire off a 78.

In June I fly to San Francisco, California. The first night is an evening of song where a variety of people play a song or two, run by the keyboard player with a house band of bass, drums, and guitar. There are some great performers including my brother Bill with a version of Kansas City that kicked with the big band and me on lead guitar. My son and wife miss Bill's 60th Birthday Backyard Bash. Incredibly for San Francisco it stays clear and warm through the backyard cookout party—a stream of people come and go with live acoustic music to boot.

All good things pass; I catch a 5:00 p.m. flight to Denver to attend the AAPG (American Association of Petroleum Geologists). It's nice to attend an AAPG National Convention again; to immerse in the technology and networking.

Summer's full on now, and in June we drive to Perryton, Texas, for Texas Archeology Field School. My wife and son went to this same location last year, but I missed it. I'm glad I am going to see the place this year. It's a long, flat drive but we finally arrive at the lake-side park and set up our rented pop-up camping trailer next to my wife's Mom, Teddy.

We get set up, and then it's time for a camp dinner. Soon after dark though, something unexpected happens, Teddy tips over a chair and falls. Not good. She hurt her arm and my wife decides to take her to the local hospital where they discover it's broken.

We continue through June with my wife helping Teddy in Midland and my son and I bacheloring it. I talk Becky and my son into going with me to Oklahoma City's Frontier City amusement park to catch some rides and to see Grand Funk Railroad live in concert. Okay, mostly it's about the show—they play all the classics and put on a great show. Hearing these old songs takes me back to memories of my early 1970's childhood days in Mississippi.

I play some golf—it's 101 degrees in Tulsa, and I shoot an 81 at Emerald falls. One day a few Venture Scouts and I practice canoe skills at Lake Skiatook near Tulsa. It's our shakedown "cruise" at Zink Ranch camp to prepare for our upcoming trip to Minnesota, Boy Scouts of America high adventure base camp in the Boundary Waters Wilderness area.

June turns into July and here comes our BSA trip—fifteen hours in a fifteen passenger van from Tulsa. The boys set up a TV and Xbox on a board in the back to stay busy during the long drive. We stay in KOA cabins near Minneapolis on the way up.

We arrive at camp on a warm, sunny day and go through the check-in process with our guide, young Lucas. We plan our route, check out our gear, pack our food for the week, and find our cabin for the night. Lucas comes to our cabin and looked over our gear to make sure we had what was needed and no more. The goal is to have our personal gear for the week fit inside a space of a pickle barrel.

Late the next morning we finally get to the water and load our canoes. There are three people to a canoe, plus gear packs and three large whale bags containing our personal gear, two food bags and one green bag with cooking gear. We select the old style and heavy duty aluminum canoes that weigh about sixty-five pounds each as opposed to the lighter, more expensive (and more fragile) fiberglass ones. The packs weigh 50-70 pounds each, so the amount of stuff we load in the canoes is impressive.

After months of planning, we are off across the lake. Our route will be north to the Canadian border and out west through a river system and then back across several lakes. We'll cover over fifty miles in five days.

There are so many sights, sounds, and experiences over these five days, it's hard to write about it all. We lose the sun after day one and the call of the loons in the evening is a magical sound. Fresh fish for dinner, portages of all types, wet boots, eagles, deer, a few other people—it's an awesome experience. We sail across Jack Fish Bay, take visibility readings, sing traveling songs, read topo maps and experience the wind, rain, and waterfalls. We take in Hudson Bay, eat stale bread, get sore shoulders…and no one complains.

I'm almost sad to return to civilization and Bucky Burgers instead of floating through the wilderness, but we have to go back some time. We take in the rendezvous farewell show and see some big black bears on the way out on a long drive home. It's been an incredible adventure with a great group of guys, and I think everyone takes away a special memory. I'm proud to lead and be part of a high adventure like this.

Golf & School

Late that summer I am lucky to play some golf at Karsten Creek, home of the OSU golf team, for the company Hack & Frac contractor appreciation golf tourney. My team grabs third place, and I take home some cash from a side bet. After the tourney, I meet-up with the family and my son's girlfriend in Stillwater for a tour of Oklahoma State University. The school is larger than I thought and it has a nice feel to it. A few days later we tour the University of Oklahoma in Norman. In the end, it's good for all of us to see but my son doesn't like it as well as OSU. I guess we'll see what the future holds.

July 30th there's Aerosmith at the BOK Center in Tulsa. After so many years of their music, finally I will see what I think is one of the best American rock and roll bands of the 70s. Better yet, the opening act is ZZ Top.

As August wears on, I play some of my best golf of the year, winning the first round of match play tourney at Forest Ridge, my home course. A week later, I fire an 82 but lost on the 18th hole to another member Steve, he shot 75 with no mistakes. My son's driving himself to school since he's taking engineering and math classes at Tulsa Tech before going to Jenks in the afternoon for English, physics, and history. It's odd for him to drive away to school every morning, instead of catching the bus, but he's growing up.

Speaking of growing up, my son's Eagle Project is about to happen. We visit the site with a cement expert, to work out what work the scouts will do and what the cement guys will do.

We launch my son's big day at the church. Several boys from his Troop show up to help when we start at 9:00 a.m. We manage to find time for a pizza break and then wrap up at 2:30 p.m. After a few days of rain, the cement is poured—and it looks great. We paint the crosswalk, put up signs and finalize cleanup about a month after the project starts.

Work On

As the third quarter of 2009 closes, it's clear the economy is on the mend. Normally, during a downturn oil companies tend to make large acquisitions of new properties but though we look, people remain too proud of their assets and want too much money for them. So we were left for now with "dry powder"/cash in hand.

Things are in a state of change at the company, with Jake Langton moving to Houston to take the role of Vice President Global New Ventures to replace a former VP who unexpectedly retires. Under the old company system exploration was secondary to the regions focus on lower risk development drilling programs—making goals such as rate of return on drilling capital invested in the calendar year. This New Ventures team will focus on "organic" exploration growth in areas new to the company. Over the next three to five years we expect to acquire or lease some new acreage for growth opportunities in the US or internationally, where ever the best deals reside. Things are changing at home too as I do not see things the same as the new Central US VP. I fly to Dallas for the company management conference where all regions of the company meet to plan for the next year, hear the latest strategy and network. Some of the analysis shows the company is not a leader in its peer group. We are still working on how to grow. The next size we seek to become is tough. We are already a very large independent. It became clear at that meeting that I should look around for another company job outside of Tulsa. So it begins...

We travel to Midland, TX for Thanksgiving, a grand affair with family and friends. It's fun and we celebrate my Mother-in-law—Teddy's eightieth. She's going strong; her arm long since mended. Midland is an interesting place to visit, because we see family and our old friends. In December the company announced plans to split the West Texas—Permian Basin properties away from the Tulsa based

Central US operations and form a new Region based in Midland, TX. The company will have a hard time recruiting employees to move to Midland. I take a survey of my group. Most of us vote to stay in Tulsa, although by this time I expect I will be leaving Tulsa.

Over the past month, I've managed to line up a couple of new job options. One is Exploration Manager for Argentina, the second possibility is Exploration Manager in the new Global New Ventures Group in Houston. Talking about these new jobs is uplifting. I still have some stress to work through. It's unfortunate, but that's the breaks. At least I have options.

We have a surprise management conference in the middle of December since the economy is picking up, so I hop on a plane the day after my son's Eagle Board of Reviews. It's an amazing evening and momentous for him—I wouldn't miss it for the world. My son invited several people: Father Shelby and a few adult leaders from our Troop. After an introduction, I, the Dad, have to wait outside while my son answers questions about his Scouting career and his Eagle project. After nearly an hour, I'm called in for the last couple of fun questions—and the congratulations. I am so happy for him and he seems pleased to finish. There will be an awards ceremony sometime next year, but this closure is sweet. Congratulations my son on finishing your Eagle in fine form.

So I'm a day late getting to Houston for the conference; a gathering of about 75 people including leadership and management. Since the Texas Team is not assembled, I get to present the (W.TX) Permian Basin Technical summary. I get to show the development projects, water floods, etc. Just the stuff people think I don't care much about—but I do like all aspects of the business. True, much of my career is as an exploration guy. I deliver a solid presentation—in spite of stepping on a wad of gum, behind the podium—while I was speaking! I try to stay positive and professional as always.

Christmas '09

I fly to Erie to visit Steve, Judy, and Mom and I land with snow on the ground. I have not been there since the spring.

I get to catch up with a few old friends, which is nice, but visiting with Mom is tough. Alzheimer's is really taking its toll. She does not know who I am, and while she talks happily about various things, her speech is slurred at times. She is eating well, but she is confined to the wheel chair or bed, which is so sad to see considering just a few years ago she was swimming laps and riding her bike around her neighborhood in Florida. On Sunday afternoon, I take her to church. It was a nice little service with many songs.

Cold and snowy weather grips the nation. Delays cause me to miss my connection in Minnesota and I have to spend the night. I get up early and manage to make an earlier flight via stand-by. Big snows hit the east coast, but I manage to make it back to Tulsa for a quiet, snowy Christmas at home. We have not lived in Tulsa too many years, yet the winters seem mild—not this year. During December it stays below freezing for three weeks straight and we have nearly a foot of snow to shovel on Christmas day. A couple days after Christmas, my son and I get in some sled riding on a highway over-pass hillside.

I use some vacation time to get a final contract in place for the company to buy a couple million dollars' worth of new 3D seismic data covering our new Anadarko Basin granite wash horizontal drilling play in Oklahoma. Historically, seismic has not been a strong tool for this Region due to so much well control, so it is work to get it approved. We also recently hired a seismic interpretation expert, which helped the case to progress this part of the business. The famous quote I heard in Tulsa is, "In the mid-continent US, seismic works about .001% of the time—and that is being generous."

My wife and I spend New Year's Eve dinner at a Japanese place—my son is out with friends—thinking that just as we've made a good home here in Tulsa, I'll have to take a job elsewhere.

I don't know what place the future will hold—Buenos Aires, Houston or somewhere else? What I do know is that I have a lovely family and we'll make it just fine.

Chapter 21
Full Circle

The New Year, comes with the specter of change hanging over it. I'm looking outside of Tulsa for work with the principle focus to stay with the company. I'm under-utilized working in Tulsa and the situation is more stressful than it needs to be.

There's one person I want to talk with before my final decision, the CEO: "I need to know if the Houston based New Ventures team is for real," I say. Bringing him up to date on the situation that I have two choices. "It's for real," he tells me. "But it will probably take two or three years to ensure we have it right. First we need to put together a good team." He thinks a moment. "Honestly, I think the Argentina job would be good for you".

Argentina

January 2010 I land in Argentina to check out the possibility of taking the job here; a so called "look-see." It would be a great job for me and the money would be nice but it would be a long way to my family in Tulsa.

I start by checking out the lay of the land. The old harbor area has been renovated to a very clean, safe and cool area of town. In the old days, it was a seedy, rundown, island port area. Across the park is the sprawling city of Buenos Aires.

I walk from the Hilton to the Company office. The first person I see at the office is Ron Banks, the new Vice President and Country Manager for the Argentina office. We worked together in Egypt, I know he's a good guy and he should bring a calm hand to the region.

Buenos Aires is a big city with lots of old charm, although it seems modern at first glance. Crime is a concern for the expatriates—mostly non-violent robberies, but as the economy slows people seem to grow more desperate. I visit with folks in the office and learn there is much to do on the exploration front—I won't be bored if I come to work here.

Argentina is known for good wine and great steaks. We go to dinner with a group of about eight of us, including Ron Banks, to a steak place where they say you can cut the prime roast with a spoon; they weren't kidding.

Friday we play golf at Pilar Golf Club, located 60 kilometers north out the Pan American highway. By now I have a pretty good idea about what living and—working in Argentina would be like. Buenos Aires is a fabulous city, the people are beautiful and the culture is interesting. The office would be a good environment and I know a few other guys from our Egypt days together, so it might be kind of fun. The biggest threat for business seems to be the unions that can shut down field operations by flexing their muscle with strong arm tactics to demand "improvements" for the people.

However, while Argentina would be an interesting assignment, as the week has worn on and I take a look at some apartments, it just doesn't feel right. The "commute" back and forth from Tulsa would be long and not very frequent. My wife and I talk about it and decide that we're not okay with this adventure.

I make the first call, "Thanks, Vince, but I don't think its right for me," I tell him. He understands. I then get on the phone to tell Jake, "I'll take the New Ventures job in Houston." I make my decision on January 18th, and my first day at work in Houston will be February 15th, so I have roughly a month to get everything in place. I'll miss the Argentine steaks, but the stakes of moving to Buenos Aires are just too high. Back to Houston I go.

Full Circle

I go to work on the twelfth floor in Houston, February of 2010—the same floor where I started in 1997. I have officially come full circle with this company; from Houston—around the world and back to Houston. The first person I run into as I get off the elevator on the first day is my new boss. I think he welcomes seeing a familiar/ friendly face after being overseas for so many years. Not to mention he is under a lot of pressure to build a new organization.

"I have been kept overseas like a pet for twenty years," he jokes. "Now it is time to adjust and adapt. I have a feeling we will build something good."

I drive the yellow Mustang down to Houston in late February—a long eight hours from Tulsa punctuated by a few bursts of speed through the rolling hills of east Texas. I have settled on a routine to work in Houston and fly to Tulsa most every weekend. I am now one of three million Americans who live and work in different cities.

In my new capacity I get another flashback when a couple of us fly to California to visit an Oil Company to review a potential deal. Santa Barbara is a beautiful town by the sea and the area of my first field trip to look at rock outcrops in 1981, while on my first petroleum geologist job in the industry working in San Francisco. It would be wild to live here now and work in the oil business on the West coast but I think Houston is the only thing in the cards for me for a while.

Back and forth I go. I'm home for important stuff, my son's birthday and later that month the Eagle Court of Honor. Plenty of family members and friends show up for the day and I'm so proud of him. Troop 185 sends the most Eagles off in one day ever; five boys. In honor of our Scotland Scouting experience, we have a bagpiper play to start the ceremony. It is a memorable day to hear about each of the boy's experiences on the long road to Eagle. Only about three percent of the boys who join Boy Scouts of America make the top rank of Eagle. They're all good boys who are a pleasure to work with and I expect they will go on to lead positive and interesting lives.

March is a time to tour college campuses with my son, now a junior in high school. The Texas tour includes UT Austin, San Marcos, and then after a cruise through the beautiful Texas Hill Country, on to Houston. It is fun to see each campus, hear the great things about the school, and meet various energetic young people. Rice University is a fun tour with an alumni day going on at the same time. We finish with University of Houston. For dinner we meet up with friends from our Scotland days.

Work is a blur figuring out our new group, new mission and to find new plays to enter for the company world-wide. Craig Davis started working on the most promising New Ventures project in our North

American area before I transferred in—to explore in Alaska's Cook Inlet. We have angles to get acreage there, so we take a trip to gather information.

I fly to Anchorage from Tulsa. It is a longer flight from Tulsa or Houston to Anchorage than to London. The team meets up at the Captain Cook Hotel to plan out our meetings. We spend our time meeting with various people such as government regulatory representatives and field operations people. We came into Alaska trying to keep a "low profile," trying not to let people know we are in town because we are still trying to make deals and buy acreage. On the second day we are in town the press calls the State Department of Natural Resources and asks the Director who we planned to meet with and if he knew anything about us being in town. He says, "No comment."

So much for our "low profile." The last two days we attend an oil and gas geology workshop put on by the State of Alaska—Department of Natural Resources;—they want more investors in the state.

A Deep Water Gulf of Mexico Tragedy

April brings a sad note. The Macondo deep water well in the Gulf of Mexico drills into oil pay sands but loses control. The blowout and oil spill changes the U.S. oil business.

The deep water Horizon drilling ship explodes in fire on April 20, 2010; lives are lost and she sinks in 5,000 feet of water off the coast of Louisiana. They lose control of the new field pay zone when gas blows out and catches on fire while they are working to temporarily abandon the discovery well. Ironically the operating company officials who were there to celebrate a year with no safety incidents leave only hours before the tragedy.

The problem is the blowout preventers failed to seal the well after flow started and thousands of barrels of oil are spewing out of the ruptured pipe near the seafloor. They really do not know the exact rate. The press likes to report the number in gallons (42 gallons in an oil barrel)—and the numbers just keep coming. The well will spill over six million gallons in the first month and is still out of control despite many attempts to cap it. Oil has spread over a huge area of the Gulf and is threatening to wash ashore—which would add significantly to the disaster.

There are questions put to the operations service companies on cement job quality and concerns with the blow-out-preventer equipment. However, the operator will face covering the largest portion of the costs if the court concludes they were at fault. Being a responsible company, the operator will likely spend significantly on their own to resolve damage long before a court ruling is sorted out. The basic facts are provided here, consistent with the news and what the operator has provided in public statements. The guys operating the offshore equipment are highly trained and I expect worked hard to manage the situation. Some of the details we will never know since not all those guys survived.

The magnitude of the immediate operations response put together by the operator to control the spill and resolve issues is impressive. It is a good thing for the United States that the operator is a large integrated major oil company with the resources to support this large response operation.

By June the operator has put $32 billion aside to pay for damages. BP stock drops by fifty percent by early summer and they announce a plan to sell significant assets, up to $20B US, to help pay for damages and to avoid being taken over by another major company. The twenty-five percent working interest partner in the well claimed no responsibility because they were not the operator, but their stock drops anyway. It's dark days for the whole industry, and they're getting darker.

The U.S. government decrees a shutdown of all deep water operations country wide. Twice, regional judges strike down the ruling, but the third time, Ken Salazar of the United States Secretary of the Interior, supports the Energy Department ruling; so it sticks. Huge financial issues result with rigs under contract and many service companies shut down. The ruling is for deep water—however shallow water drilling permits are slow played too. This incident will no doubt lead to new regulations and procedures. It will change the way we do oil and gas business in the USA and potentially worldwide. This is a black-eye for the industry, and that is too bad because the industry as a whole operates very responsibly and with many safety procedures. It is just a risky business to drill into high pressure targets, and occasionally people lose control of wells, especially "wildcat" wells exploring for new fields for new energy sources.

Trinidad

In May on a flight to Trinidad we fly right over the offshore spill area and I get to see it for myself from 35,000 feet. From the air the oil slick is a brownish-orange color and it stretches for as far as the eye can see. The magnitude of the spill is shocking. I can see skim boats near the shore, three deep water drill ships, and the support vessels at the Macondo well site working to contain the spill. It's sobering.

The New Ventures team—me and two other geoscientists arrive that evening in Port O'Spain, Trinidad. Our objectives are to review the data available in the data room for the shallow water marine oil and gas lease bid round. We also plan to make a presentation about our company to both the Petroleum Ministry and to the Government of the Republic of Trinidad and Tobago oil company, Petrotrin.

Sid is from Trinidad and his father runs a shipping company that does industrial work, primarily for the oil industry. We walk off the plane and he insists we go directly to a sidewalk stand and have "doubles," a local staple that's basically corn tortillas with a spicy green meat sauce inside. We eat our snack then pick up a rental car and head into town.

The next day we arrive at the tiny data room overlooking the harbor and start sifting through the well and seismic records. Later that morning, we present our "This is our company story of what we could do in Trinidad" talk to a group of people from the Ministry of Energy. I gave a talk with examples of our company's international exploration and field development experiences, it goes really well. Morgi, the group manager, recognizes me from our days working for my last company, the International Division at the office in Houston. Wow! What a small world.

The Ministry runs the lease sale, but Petrotrin is the main government company that operates the drilling and producing wells. We visit their building far from town and meet with a few key representatives who are excited about what we could do—it's nice to be recognized as a good company.

Our hotel overlooks the harbor but even better than the view and food there is the time we have at Sid's family home where his mother, brothers, sisters, and their families visit with us and serve us a delightful meal on their porch high on the hill overlooking Port O'Spain. A couple days later, after we'd wrapped up our work, we go out on the family's fishing boat—which is about a 40 foot ocean worthy beast of a boat. We don't catch anything but it's still fun and a great chance to see the surrounding area, including an island prison, the northern coast and local rigs stacked in a harbor. It's a fun trip to another exotic locale. We head for home mission accomplished.

After returning to Houston we ramp up our evaluation efforts for Trinidad. It is difficult to explain to someone outside the oil business what we do to gather data, map, interpret, assess prospects, and put together a story of why we think we can make money here finding oil and gas to produce. In order to do that we have to understand the basic geology, then what kind of traps exist as proven in the basin or might exist as new ideas. Then we look closely at the results of wells drilled in the basin to verify our story. We then calculate the potential reserves in each prospect. After that, if we have enough volume to be excited about the potential, we involve reservoir engineers who refine the expected volumes, drilling and production equipment costs and run the economics to see what return on capital might be expected. It's quite the process and we put in a lot of expensive research before we even think about drilling somewhere.

We present our findings to the leadership team who wisely look for the presenting team—us, to show technical accuracy and some passion about what we're proposing the company do. We're interested enough to buy the bid round data package, but there are problems with the data. Back to Trinidad.

By the time we've got all the data we need, we're up against the government's bid deadline—time for some long, hard extra hours and late nights getting it done. In the end we conclude the deeper water blocks offshore are too risky for us. We are interested in the shallow water off the west coast. Well, the license round block doesn't work out. We fall short of the materiality for board approval to make a new country entry so no bid. On to the next project.

Commuter

I've gotten my commute between Houston and Tulsa worked out pretty well. I leave Houston on the Friday afternoon flight landing in Tulsa around 4:00 p.m. I fly back Sunday nights around 8:00 p.m., so my door-to-door between Houston and Tulsa is about three hours, which could be worse.

It's hard being apart from my family. My son is studying to take the ACT and the SAT college entrance exams, looking at colleges, and will work a summer job. My wife is there to help him—he'll need good test scores to get into the right school. He doesn't know what he wants to study yet, a common situation for most young men.

Our pool sits in our backyard between my wife's beautiful gardens and the tall trees. The way we have our house set up makes it feel like we have real roots. It also makes me think, "How it is my life involves a job that causes so much travel and moving?" I savor our time at the Tulsa home, knowing that one day I may wake up...and be somewhere else.

One summer trip is to Erie to visit family; my Mom and my brother Steve and his wife Judy. Mom looks about the same, even though she talks about random things, I love to listen because you hear tidbits of people and places from her life. She can't walk or talk clearly, has not said my name in many years, and is on a slow Alzheimer's decline. She is a resilient lady; Hilda Allard Hughes. On another summer trip we fly to Portland, Oregon for our nephew's wedding. The city has a different feel and has a slogan: "Let's keep Portland weird." The Portland Jazz Festival and fireworks are a great finish to our visit.

Later that summer I meet my brother Steve and his wife Judy in the Vegas heat to celebrate their twentieth anniversary—along with their friends. We saw Rush play at the MGM Grand—they played the Moving Pictures album in its entirety along with other material. We enjoy observing the variety of hedonistic people that are drawn to Vegas, and of course we rock late into the night.

I land in Anchorage, Alaska with a few co-workers to do a meet and greet of key government and others important to the oil business in this region. It is a good decision to meet with some of the officials in government regulator roles before we start operations. In addition Alaska has an environmental activist's community that runs an agenda and a Native American population that controls some of the lands. Our group has meetings with the state regulators, the press, Native Americans and other operators. I'm the manager for this new Alaska project and I am pleased to get support from my bosses to do this right; one reason I took this New Ventures job in Houston.

We get to use the company plane, which saves so much time. Flying commercial requires a connection in Seattle and typically a ten hour odyssey. I must tell you that driving your car to a small hanger and walking onto the company jet is a special treat, especially after so many years of commercial air travel. On the return trip the wind is right and we don't even have to stop for fuel. From Anchorage to Houston takes about six hours and we land in time for dinner Monday.

September welcomes the return of the Big Buck Hunt for the company. Some of us slip in a little golf on our own; but it's nice to have the hunt back after a year off. We gather in the lodge that first evening and enjoy catching up with one another—who hail from all the different company offices around the world. The first morning teams scatter across the ranch before dawn. Our deer hunting team of four are riding in the car at 5:30 a.m. – in the dark, out to the field. Stan our company security man says, "I have never hunted deer before, only people." Clearly he has some military experience. We don't take a shot the first day, but on day two our hunt team leader takes us to a secret canyon he knows about. We take two deer from there that day. While we are cleaning the first kill, Stan walks back into the canyon and boom, he kills a monster mule deer that later we learned scored 161 Boone and Crockett. Suddenly we are in the game. The big buck hunt is a team game and the two best deer scores from each team are the team score. That afternoon I shoot a deer hiding in the hillside brush from 228 yards away. In spite of my heart racing, I only needed one shot. It is a big deer with a large rack that scores 141. We still don't win but I enjoy driving around the big open range scouting for game. We fly back to Houston Sunday. It is odd that sometimes I think I should just be home instead. It's a weird feeling to decide what to do at times with this darn commuter life from Tulsa to work in Houston, causing me to miss out on some family time. My son will finish high school in Tulsa next year.

An Industry Changes

September 20, 2010 they finally get the Macondo well capped permanently. It's been spitting oil since April and been in the news almost constantly since the tragic explosion. Meanwhile, they tried a couple other operations to stop the flow, but finally built a steel cone to put down over the well head abating the flow. By the time the relief wells drilled from near-by reach the Macondo problem zone and pump cement into the original well bore to seal it seems anti-climactic; considering the limited coverage by the news media. In the end the total discharge is estimated at nearly five million barrels. The industry is changed and the economic climate of the Gulf Coast feels the change. Anything less than three miles offshore is in State commercial waters (Texas up to 9 miles) and beyond that are US Federal waters. "Deep water" operations are defined as water depth exceeding 3000 feet of and may occur in State or Federal waters. The federal government decides to stop issuing any deep water operation drilling permits, which means all the deep water rigs (that cost approximately three hundred to five hundred thousand US$ a day to rent) are on hold after finishing the wells they are on. That decision also impacts all the shallow water operations too, as authorities are overly cautious about issuing permits—causing most Gulf of Mexico offshore drilling activity to cease.

Because of the stoppage estimates are that some 50,000 offshore workers are out of jobs —people with families, and not only in the oil industry but commercial and sport fishing are impacted too.

Companies are arguing with drilling contractors about the liability of drilling contracts worth millions. BP is in serious financial stress. In spite of selling off assets for billions of dollars over the summer they still need billions of dollars to cover cleanup costs and anticipated (by Wall Street) legal costs. The philosophy of keeping the balance sheet under control has enabled companies to afford these buying opportunities while the price is right. As said: "Keep your powder dry."

The cleanup effort involves a massive response utilizing skimmer boats and floating booms to protect the shoreline beaches and wetlands from the spreading oil. Understanding the magnitude of this effort from the outside is impossible, as BP coordinates the effort along with US Government involvement and numerous third party contractors. The cleanup team sprays the giant oil slick with a dispersant that seems to do some good.

It turns out months later most of the oil is gone, although many miles of coastline in a five state area received oil—the most reported in Louisiana. It turns out that after many studies, the Gulf Coast seafood testing shows no dangerous levels of toxins and fishing is back to normal. A group of companies are leading an initiative to build a rapid spill response/offshore clean up system to handle any future spills.

The Macondo incident happens just a year or two after the US oil and gas industry has significantly expanded horizontal drilling for onshore unconventional plays. This play ramped up to develop the extensive U.S. shale gas resources and has expanded to oil prone tight rock targets. Long term these plays may create some US energy independence. Luckily this gives companies an onshore focus to avoid the concerns and risks of offshore play operations.

Our Lives Go On

When major tragedies strike we have a tendency to wonder what the future will look like and how what we're seeing now will affect it. John F. Kennedy's assassination, the bombing of the World Trade Center and other things are burned in our memories, but life goes on.

For us—I commute between Tulsa and Houston, spend time with my family when I can and work long hours while I'm in Texas. We enjoy sweet moments—holidays like Thanksgiving and Christmas together and miss one another while we're apart.

My son and some friends help us take a U-Haul with some furniture to our recently purchased west Houston patio home in September. On New Year's Eve, I have to help a brother out; I fly to San Francisco to help Bill put on the show he's directing; the KollegeTV New Year's Show—it's live comedy and music, a multi-media event to welcome in the New Year. Actually "KollegeTV" is a web TV brand he is building including playlists of short videos of different topics and characters to promote sales of shows and feature length movies as well as books. My wife just puts up with all this travel and tries patiently to do her thing, which is researching her family history and writing a book about it. She has gathered fabulous stories that weave her family into American history from the first settlers through the Revolutionary War, and the first days of Texas. The digital access to historical records these days has created an endless stream of data for her research.

The Industry

The new horizontal drilling industry is under fire, too. The new technology that opened up the tight shale gas play also brings in some environmental push-back against high pressure down hole hydraulic fracturing of the tight rocks—e.g. "fracking." Is this a risk to the water table and people at the surface? The oil and gas producing zones are typically 5,000 to 15,000 feet below the surface—relative to the water table, which typically occurs in the first 1,000 feet—which is cased off and cemented for protection before drilling deeper for the hydrocarbon zones. This fracking technology has been applied in industry for many years and there are no documented cases of fracking causing contamination of the shallow fresh water zones. In recent years the innovation to apply multiple fracks in a horizontal well has opened many rock formation targets that in the past were too tight to be economically attractive. Suddenly people are concerned about the safety of fracking and the government is looking into it.

Horizontal multi-stage frack technology was ramped up to everyday application in the growth of the shale gas play making producing reservoirs out of what was previously thought of as sealing shale rocks—notably in the Barnett of the Fort Worth Basin of Texas, where the concept originally took off in the modern play form. Other new play targets include the Woodford shale in Texas and Oklahoma and the Marcellus shale of Pennsylvania. Horizontal drill and frack has been applied to tight oil zones now as well, which is having a profound reduction on the amount of oil imported to the USA. Both the North Dakota Bakken Formation and the Texas Eagle Ford shale are significant new oil plays and each is expected to produce at a rate over one million barrels a day in the near future.

An inaccurate film documentary is making the rounds with claims of people getting sick near well fracking operations and shows water flowing from a kitchen sink and catching fire. These claims—from what I hear from technical experts and in my experience during my years in industry—are not likely related to fracking. Not that the general public will believe the actual facts. It's much more compelling to believe a famous filmmaker than some oil industry suit. Eventually we will sort things out with data but as an industry worker, it is tough to take at the moment.

Our industry is working to get the message out that the oil industry is responsible environmentally and prudently manages safety in this high risk business. We are not a "dirty industry." The world demands energy and the petroleum industry provides not only engine fuel but the basis for untold plastic related products, jobs and commerce for many people of the world. Yes there are occasional accidents but they are rare relative to the volume of activity. Most people do not understand that oil company profits are tied to huge capital investment and risk. The return on investment varies in this cyclic business; service costs vary and the commodity price received for oil and natural gas produced swings wildly through the years.

The Road

For me the travel has been interesting along with visiting various cultures of the world but the opportunities to learn so much about technology over the years and about business itself has been a great reward. Early on in my career I traveled alone. In recent years it has been a pleasure to share many places with my wife and her cultural curiosity. We are a team; my wife's coordination of various trips and a couple international moves have been significant. We are lucky to have a bright son to share things with too. He has seen many things in his young life, and it will be interesting to see how these experiences, especially international travels, follow him into adulthood. We also appreciate that through my son's friends and school connections we have had a chance to meet many people we otherwise would have missed out on.

Impressions

Looking back I have some crystal clear memories, such as the first time I heard the morning call to prayer echo over the rooftops in Turkey, the sunrise over the South China Sea and seeing children in a central African mud hut village run away because they never saw white people before. Together with my family we had the good fortune to experience many things; riding in the din of Cairo traffic to the toot of the taxi horns, walking among the brilliant chalk rock knobs of the White Desert, hearing the roar of a lion in the Serengeti plains of Tanzania and the echo of Scottish bagpipes off the cathedral walls.

The oil business has taken me to many different, fascinating places. I enjoy working in the various cultures and learning a little—and for me very little—of the various languages I encountered. It is important to maintain respect for the host culture I was in, from Asian to Arab to Latin American to Russian or European. I've seen places of extreme poverty where I met bright people that barely make enough to survive but still have a positive spirit. When new hydrocarbon reserves are discovered in these areas, it brings investment and growth, which is a good thing for that country or region.—I know that money may not trickle down to the local economy. However, job opportunities follow from the investment to drill and produce a newly discovered field. I do know that if my job helps in any way at all as part of a team that creates growth opportunity for the host region, I feel good about that.

For many Europeans life begins after work. For many Americans work is life. I have those American bones, but I'm happy to still take time to play golf when I can. Golf for me is a wonderful way to combine a game with a walk outside in some of the most beautiful places on earth.

The Future

The oil and gas road can be long and twisted, especially in the upstream exploration and development business as it may be years from the initial discovery to first production and cash flow. In spite of a growing demand for alternative fuels, global oil and gas demand will be with us for many years—if anything it will continue to grow. The geoscience craft to decide where to drill for hydrocarbons involves data, science, art, salesmanship and some luck—but I love it.

Onward

Whatever the future, you face a choice to carry on into the day or night with full vigor, to embrace all that you can, or to let life slip by. The mobile society we live in these days is dynamic and can be stressful if you let it. The changes to our world economies and technologies since I began writing this book are significant. Through all my adventures and misadventures, successes and failures, I have one constant thought to share: may the roads you travel cause you to look breathlessly.

Alaska, Cook Inlet view from the plane.

Port O Spain, Trinidad